GREAT AMERICANS

GREAT AMERICANS

Stories of Resilience and Joy in Everyday Life

Michael Vitez
Winner of the Pulitzer Prize

FOREWORD

By Karl Stark
The brain is perfectly wired to get information and meaning through stories. It's why the Bible is so full of parables. It's why HBO is so successful. And it's why Michael Vitez, in three decades at *The Philadelphia Inquirer*, has connected with and inspired so many readers. He is a master storyteller.

Flip through these pages and you will see how Mike possesses an uncanny ability to capture emotion and convey it to a reader.

The words are linguistically simple yet emotionally profound.

Consider my addled brain as a case study. Every day I get 400 emails and pore through scads of stories and social media posts from competitors and colleagues, and nearly all of it I forget. Yet I remember Mike Vitez stories from over a decade ago. I remember the woman with a football-sized tumor in her gut who couldn't get anyone to help her because she lacked health insurance. Mike's story got her treated and likely saved her life.

Mike's stories tend to be like that. They cover the rebound, the recovery, the emotional bond that grows and eases the original hurt. Or they just head straight for felicity and joy. The emotional payoff either way is huge. That's why people remember his pieces. They are little ledges of hope in a gray world.

I was Mike's editor toward the end of his legendary run at *The Inquirer.* Anyone who works with him knows how hard he labors to get it right. His editing process begins almost at the moment of creation, and it often continues into the night. The tweaks sometimes go on until the last minutes before deadline.

He is wracked by questions like these: Is it accurate? Is it fair? How will it impact the subjects? And how will the reader take it all in?

One thing you can learn from Mike is how important it is be in the moment with the people you are writing about. That's when the actions so key to storytelling are revealed.

Recreate if you must, but if you're there, those flashes of lightning will stick in the mind.

So sit back and enjoy. You're in for a treat. It is rare that a book, so full of wisdom, conveys it so easily.

Karl Stark, as assistant managing editor for business and health news at The Philadelphia Inquirer, *edited several stories in this collection when they first appeared in the newspaper.*

INTRODUCTION

As I write this, I am leaving the newspaper business after 36 years. I've written two books, *Rocky Stories* and *The Road Back*, books that I love, but the essence of my life's work has been my stories in *The Philadelphia Inquirer*, thousands of them, written over 30 years. I see my life work as a quilt, a collection of smaller pieces sewn together over decades.

We live in a world overrun with noise, news, channels, websites, tweets and talking heads, an assault of information. Stories are the tonic, the antidote. At their best they bring people together, inspire, affirm. I have found joy and purpose listening to, and sharing the stories of everyday Americans and their resilience, strength, and spirit. The beauty of these people is that they are all around us, and their stories celebrate the very best in us. Our goodness is vast.

Mostly, I have worked from instinct, never really trying to define or classify my stories. Often, they are about the smallest moments. My compass point has long been a quote from William Faulkner, accepting his Nobel Prize in 1950: "It is the writer's privilege to help man endure by lifting his heart." In my own small way as a daily journalist I've tried to do just that.

Many *Inquirer* readers have loved these stories. In this book I have collected many of my favorites, which I am now sharing with people who know my work – and people who may now only be discovering it. I've included a mix of short, medium and long pieces. I'm also offering some of my rules and tools of writing and reporting that I've learned in a lifetime devoted to the craft. I've added a postscript after many of the stories, focusing on a writing point or providing context or an update. I also am telling a little of my own story, reflecting on why I became a storyteller and why I see the world the way I do. (For more on the reporting and writing in each story, go to www.michaelvitez. com/great-americans)

I've been lucky enough to spend a lifetime developing a passion and a craft, and coming to a discovery – the power of stories to improve lives, and, most important, to lift the human spirit. People have allowed me into their lives at the most amazing moments. They have trusted me, and the stories that follow are my way of repaying that trust. They are the world as I saw it, and as I would like you to see it.

—Michael Vitez
March 2016

TABLE OF CONTENTS

Sarah Gray reacts to research made possible
by retinas donated from Thomas

1

A MOTHER'S MISSION

Thomas Gray's life lasted only six days

But in death he has a lasting impact on medical research

March 30, 2015
When she found out early in her pregnancy that one of her identical twins would die at birth, Sarah Gray began a five-year journey that culminated last week in Philadelphia.

She had to carry the sick baby to term in order to protect his healthy twin. And she also looked into organ and tissue donation.

"Instead of thinking of our son as a victim," she said, "I started thinking of him as a contributor to research, to science."

On March 23, 2010, Thomas and Callum Gray were born at Fairfax Hospital in Virginia. Callum, perfect, was five pounds, 10 ounces. Thomas, four pounds, was born without part of his brain. His mother nursed him, diapered him, cradled him.

He died after six days – five years ago on Sunday. Within hours of Thomas' death, his eyes and liver were recovered and sent – along with umbilical-cord blood from him and his brother – to researchers.

But that wasn't the end of it for Sarah Gray.

She often wondered – what became of his eyes, his blood, his liver?

The Grays had received a thank-you letter from the Washington regional transplant organization, telling them their son's corneas had been sent to the Schepens Eye Research Institute in Boston, and his liver and the cord blood to Duke University in North Carolina.

Two years later, on a business trip to Boston, Sarah Gray called the eye institute, which is affiliated with Harvard Medical School.

"I donated my son's eyes to your lab," she said on the phone. "Can I come by for a tour?"

The receptionist said she had never had such a request. "I'm not sure who to transfer you to," she said, "but don't hang up!"

The next day, Gray met James Zieske, the institute's senior scientist, who told her "infant eyes are worth their weight in gold," because, being so young, they have great regenerative properties. Thomas' corneas had been used in a study that could one day help cure corneal blindness.

Thirteen more studies had cited that study. Gray felt a new emotion: pride.

Before leaving, she bought a Harvard T-shirt for Callum, and decided she was going to go with the whole family to North Carolina, where Thomas' liver and the cord blood had been sent.

Zieske also wrote her: "Your visit helped to remind me that all the eyes we receive are an incredibly generous gift from someone who loved and cared about the person who provided the eyes. I thank you for reminding me of this."

A few months later in 2012, the Grays went to the Duke Center for Human Genetics in Durham, N.C., where even though the twins were identical, scientists found epigenetic differences in their cord blood, research that could one day help prevent Thomas' fatal defect, anencephaly.

Sarah Gray bought Callum a Duke T-shirt.

The couple then drove down to the road to visit Cytonet, a biotech company that had used their baby's liver in a trial to determine the best temperature to freeze liver tissue.

Already in the nonprofit public relations field, Sarah Gray became director of marketing for the American Association of Tissue Banks.

Her mantra has become donate, donate, donate, and not just for transplant, but also for research. Even if nobody asks you — doctors are often uncomfortable when a child is dying — bring it up yourself, she says.

At a conference last summer, by coincidence, Gray learned that the Old Dominion Eye Bank in North Chesterfield, Va., had shipped Thomas' retinas to Philadelphia.

She couldn't believe she'd never known this. She immediately wrote to the researcher at the University of Pennsylvania who used the donation in her efforts to cure retinoblastoma, the most common form of eye cancer in children.

Two days later, Gray got a reply from Arupa Ganguly, who runs the lab and is a genetics professor at the Hospital of the University of Pennsylvania.

"It is almost impossible to obtain normal retina from a child," Ganguly wrote. "The sample from Thomas is extremely precious for us."

Ganguly sent Callum a Penn T-shirt.

They arranged to meet last Monday.

First, Sarah, Ross, and Callum Gray went to the National Disease Research Interchange in Center City, which Sarah Gray calls "the Match.com of science." The interchange connects hospitals that supply organs and tissue with researchers who request it.

"This seems to have brought you a lot of peace and joy," Bill Leinweber, the interchange's president and CEO, told Sarah. "You've been such a strong advocate for research and such an eloquent spokesperson for the value of research."

After a visit there, the Gray family went to Penn to meet Ganguly and tour her lab.

Sarah Gray saw the marbled composition book in which the receipt of retinas was logged on March 30, 2010, the 360th specimen to be received. They became "RES 360," short for Research 360.

"Is this the log book?" she asked. "Oh, my gosh."

Gray ran her index finger over the cursive of Jennifer Yutz, the lab manager who recorded the entry.

"Ross, look at this! RES 360!"

Her husband took a look. Callum, 5, hugged an inflatable Godzilla as tall as he is, a gift from Ganguly, bouncing it on the lab floor.

"Wow," Sarah Gray continued. "Can I Xerox this?"

"We have a copy for you," Ganguly said.

Penn also gave the Grays a copy of the Fed Ex packing slip confirming arrival, which Sarah Gray said she would "treasure like a war medal."

Thomas' retina tissue is so rare, so precious, Ganguly and her team are still saving some of it for future research. Ganguly's staff led Sarah Gray into the hallway, where a refrigerator, innocuous and ordinary, stood across from student lockers. Yutz unlocked it.

Inside were hundreds of 1.5 milliliter tubes – smaller than cigarette filters.

Yutz pointed to two.

"There it is," Yutz said.

"Oh my gosh!" Gray said. She couldn't touch them. The tubes were frozen at minus-80 degrees centigrade (minus-112 Fahrenheit).

"It's the RNA isolated from the retina tissue," Yutz said.

Call it what you will, that was a piece of Thomas Gray, her son.

Ross Gray has long supported his wife's journey.

"It helped her get over the loss," he said. "It was part of the healing process, seeing that there's still research going on five years after. His life was worthwhile. He's brought a lot of good to the world."

"The way I see it," Sarah Gray said, "our son got into Harvard, Duke, and Penn. He has a job. He is relevant to the world. I only hope my life can be as relevant."

POSTSCRIPT

This story went viral, getting 100,000 Facebook shares and one million hits on the newspaper's website, *Philly.com*. Readers loved how Sarah Gray turned something so painful into something so positive. Sarah herself was overwhelmed by the response. She was approached by a publisher and got a book contract, "A Life Everlasting." Radio Lab did a story that reached countless more people.

Many readers emailed Sarah Gray directly. One woman suffering from a chronic disease told her that she had wanted to donate her body to a study at Harvard after she died, but her family wasn't supportive. Now the woman said she's just going to tell her family: "I'm going to Harvard when I die."

I love how the T-shirts give the story structure, rhythm and bounce, building a momentum that makes the last quote so powerful. I can't say I set out to do this. It came to me as I wrote, more intuitively than consciously. The story just came out that way.

Photo by PETER TOBIA

Mr. Floyd relaxes with his bike after a
morning's work delivering papers

2

HE JUST KEEPS ROLLING ALONG

Floyd Culver can't be stopped

Not even a broken hip at 91 keeps him from his job

June 23, 1999

By 3 a.m., Floyd Culver is riding his bike, the one he bought in 1954, through the silent streets of Philadelphia.

The rain is pouring. He's wearing a yellow slicker. The balloon tires hum as they spit up water. He is carrying 84 morning newspapers in the basket on the front of his bike, and he has covered them with a brown tarp.

He glides his bike to a stop by the steps of a rowhouse on Bainbridge Street. He dismounts, grabs a paper in one hand, and reaches into the basket for his cane with the other.

He hobbles up three steps. Two quick folds, a firm shove through the mail slot, and then he hobbles back down, one hand on the railing, the other on his cane. He steadies the bicycle seat as though it were a horse, swings a leg over again, drops the cane in the basket, and pushes off the bottom step.

Just 300 stops to go.

Culver, 91, has been delivering newspapers in Center City and South Philadelphia seven days a week since 1947. His territory - where he is beloved - stretches from Pine Street south to Washington Avenue, from Broad Street west to 23d Street.

Mr. Floyd, as he is universally and respectfully known, is a slim man, 129 pounds, almost nothing to him. He was a Navy cook in World War II, and he has never forgotten how to make himself a good breakfast: eggs, grits, bacon, coffee, which he prepares and devours every morning about 2.

Mr. Floyd can't walk two steps without a cane. He's bent, with arthritic knees. In September, he missed a curb cut at the corner of Carpenter and Bouvier Streets, fell and broke his left hip. Surgeons replaced it with an artificial one. By Thanksgiving, he was back on his battered old black bike.

As he pushes off each step, he stands on his pedals, pushes down as hard as he can, and picks up speed slowly, like a long freight train leaving the station. "I don't have the strength in my legs I used to," he says.

Beyond delivering papers, Mr. Floyd's daily goal is to stay alive, to serve others. This job keeps him fit, in contact with scores of people who love and admire him, and gives him purpose. "As soon as I sit down," he says, "I know my health will fail."

Despite his frail, bent body and his heavy load, Mr. Floyd executes movements that are almost balletic. He maneuvers between planters, around street signs, and ducks under wet branches with quickness and precision. He can dismount to his left or his right. He does this hundreds of times a morning, lifting his leg with the grace and economy of a hurdler, just high enough to clear the seat.

He reaches and spins and twists, knowing just how much effort is needed to slip a paper under a door or stash one behind a screen. Every paper is lovingly delivered.

He carries an old transistor radio in his shirt pocket, which he pins closed to keep the radio from falling out.

As he rides, he reaches under his slicker, and, suddenly, the morning silence is broken with: "It's 4:46 and 65 degrees on Independence Mall..." A few blocks later, he reaches back under his slicker, and the news gives way to Frank Sinatra, crooning through the dark and drizzle, This love of mine goes on and on.

Just like Mr. Floyd.

Near 20th and Bainbridge, he drops a paper into the back of a Chevy 4-by-4. "If I put that paper on his step, they'll take it."

By 5:30 a.m., Mr. Floyd's basket is empty. He returns to home base, a storefront at 18th and Bainbridge. There, he reloads with 140 copies of the Daily News - 90 pounds of paper - and he is off again.

Mr. Floyd's basket, custom-built by Via Bicycle at Ninth and Bainbridge, is so large that he rode home last year carrying an air conditioner.

Mr. Floyd has two bikes. "That's his fleet," says Curtis Anthony, owner of Via Bicycle. The black one, which weighs 85 pounds without cargo, is his primary one.

"He's broken them. He's worn them out. He rides a million miles," Anthony says. "When he comes in with a broken bike, we drop everything else to fix it. We know he needs the bike. The man is an inspiration."

From the handlebars of Mr. Floyd's bike hangs an old cloth apron. Its pockets carry all the things he needs - wrenches and other tools to fix a flat, rubber bands, plastic bags, a knife to open bundles.

He has woven old inner tubes in and out of the sides of his basket so he can lean it against walls and cars without scratching anything. Mr. Floyd wears an apron himself as he rides, and in it carries his change, keys and his cell phone, given to him by his daughter, Brenda Taylor, whom he calls "my standby."

In the winter, Mr. Floyd wears two gloves, but the rest of the year he wears only one to keep his right hand free and nimble. "You can't handle the papers with the gloves too good," he explains.

Near 20th and Pemberton, he drops a paper in a rowhouse mailbox and hits the doorbell. He is around the corner when a woman in a nightgown opens her door. "Thank you, sweetheart," she calls.

On Catharine Street, Doris Bell, 59, greets him at the door and pays him. "He delivered the paper to us since I was a schoolgirl," she said.

On Fitzwater, Helen Hampton, 91, opens her third-floor window and yells down, "Good morning, Mr. Floyd." She says, "It's wonderful he can ride that bicycle and carry those papers. That Sunday paper, I can hardly lift it."

Mr. Floyd's mother pulled him out of sixth grade to work in an Alabama grocery store for 25 cents a day. He never saw the money, which helped raise his three sisters and himself. He has never stopped working: a farm boy, a short-order cook, a seaman, and for 52 years, a newspaper deliveryman.

He has been married three times - twice before the war and once since - and said every marriage ended when he came home and found his wife with another man.

He has no more interest in marriage and now lives with his cat, Air Muff.

Mr. Floyd does have an assistant, Norman Chalmers, 63, who had polio as a child and needs two canes to walk. Mr. Chalmers sits on a chair and sells single copies to passersby from the storefront at 18th and Bainbridge on weekday mornings while Mr. Floyd does his route.

On Sundays, when the papers are much bigger and Mr. Floyd can carry fewer at a time, Chalmers rides his own bike to prearranged corners and resupplies Mr. Floyd with a fresh load of papers.

When he is finished with his door-to-door deliveries, Mr. Floyd rides over to Graduate Hospital on South Street. He pedals through the double doors at the main entrance and parks behind the reception desk.

He grabs his cane and walks over to a closet, which he unlocks. He pulls out a grocery cart and loads it with papers.

"How you feeling today, Mr. Floyd?" asks April Jordan Davison, the receptionist. "Pretty good," he says. "Everybody knows Mr. Floyd around here," she says. "He's an inspiration."

Mr. Floyd takes the elevator to the sixth floor, and pushes the grocery cart down every hall on every floor.

"Papers," he snaps. "*Inquirer. Daily News.*"

"Can I have a paper?" comes a weak voice from Room 514. He wheels his cart in. An old woman hurriedly counts out change from a Styrofoam cup.

"Take your time. Take your time," he says. "You've got nothing else in the hospital but time."

The woman smiles at him.

In the hallway, Luis Nieves, a nursing assistant, approaches.

"I'll take a paper," Nieves says.

"You ain't man enough," Mr. Floyd replies.

Nieves laughs. "OK, I'll pay," he says.

On the fourth floor, Roberta Myers, from environmental services, sees him and begins singing: *Is that my lover coming down the street, looking for me? I know it is.*

She buys a paper from Mr. Floyd, as she's been doing for 25 years.

Mr. Floyd thinks people today don't care enough about others. He often says, "Nobody cares anymore about the little man." But his own life offers the best rebuttal.

The hospital threw him a surprise party on his 90th birthday. Scores came. He wept.

Around 10 a.m., after working seven hours straight, Mr. Floyd takes a coffee break. He washes his hands for a good 30 seconds, rubbing off all the ink. He sits in a main hallway, across from the elevators. He puts on his reading glasses, opens a paper to his horoscope, and reads his future as he sips coffee with five sugars and inhales two chocolate doughnuts.

A very sick patient in a bed is wheeled past.

"You look at these people in here," he says. "You got to stop and think, you're blessed to be walking around, to have free time. You got to treasure it.

"A lot of people do not treasure the life that they live."

By 11 a.m., he is back at 18th and Bainbridge. He is finished for the day and does an accounting. He has sold roughly 200 copies of the *Daily News* and 100 of *The Inquirer.* He gets 12 cents for every *Inquirer,* 14 cents for every *Daily News.* He has earned about $40.

He hops on his bike one more time for the short ride home a few blocks away.

He will sleep all afternoon, eat some dinner, listen to the Phillies on the radio. He played catcher for the Birmingham Black Barons in the 1920s. He will not come outside again until early morning, when it's time to deliver his papers.

POSTSCRIPT

I was up at 2 a.m., brought my bike into his neighborhood, and rode with him. The hardest part was keeping up with him and taking notes at the same time. And keeping my notebook dry in the rain.

My favorite quote in the story was from the owner of Via bikes, who drops everything to repair Mr. Floyd's bike. It shows how Mr. Floyd is respected in the community. It tells you something about the shop owner – that he recognizes how important the work is to Mr. Floyd as well as how important Mr. Floyd is to the community.

My goal here was to take the reader for a ride, to follow Mr. Floyd on his route, to share the epic life of a modest man.

At 93, Mr. Floyd was hit by a car, and his knee required surgery. But soon as possible, he was back on the bike. At 94, his bones too brittle to ride the bike, he rode around in an electric wheelchair delivering newspapers at Graduate Hospital. When the hospital shut down a year later, he finally was forced to retire. He died at age 100.

In so many of these stories, you will see I use first names: Crystal. Jordan. Bill. Charlie. These are intimate, informal stories, and the first name feels right. In this case, because he was known as Mr. Floyd, that felt like the proper way to refer to him in the story. Normally, the newspaper stylebook requires us to use last names, without an honorific. I understand a newspaper needs a consistent style. But there's also room for flexibility, and I am grateful that, in this and a few other stories, I was able to go with my gut and my ear.

Floyd Culver – "Mr. Floyd" – on his morning rounds

Dan Harrell congratulates Mike Koller at
the end of a Penn basketball game

3

A CUSTODIAN IN EVERY SENSE

Buffing the hardwood, hitting the books

At 56, the man who cleans the Palestra gets an Ivy degree

March 19, 2000

When Dan Harrell applied to the University of Pennsylvania at age 46, he was asked to take a composition class to prove he was Ivy League material. The first assignment: write about a favorite place.

The young woman on his left chose Paris in the spring; the one on his right, the slopes of Aspen.

"I've never been out of Southwest Philly," Harrell recalled, "and I'm thinking I'm in trouble."

He decided his favorite place was the john.

"Do you know there are 50 different names for it?" he said. "It's a great place to check out the horses for the next race. Your boss can't find you there. I wrote four pages, and I got an A."

On May 22, after 10 years as a part-time student, Harrell will receive his bachelor's degree. He will graduate surrounded by people who revere him as a Penn institution – not only because of his academic achievement at age 56, but because of the love he lavishes on a fabled floor and the students who play on it.

Harrell is custodian of the Palestra.

Once a day, sometimes twice, he mops the hardwood in one of the most celebrated arenas in college hoops. He has spent, in sum, an eternity on one knee, scraping gum. And when he does his job right, the floor sings to him with the squeak of sneakers.

With a toilet brush in one hand, cleanser in the other, he scours the locker rooms. Not once in his eight years there, he brags, "has there been a case of athlete's foot."

Dan Harrell also is a custodian in the larger sense of the word. He looks out for the athletes, scribbles notes of support, gives them rides and good-luck charms, asks about their grand-mothers, advises them on classes to take – and, through his pursuit of a dream, inspires them.

"I think he's the greatest Penn success story," said Cynthia Johnson Crowley, who played basketball at Penn in 1952 and has since been a fixture at the Palestra. "There isn't anything he won't do to make your life better. And in return, it all comes back."

Fran Dunphy, the men's coach, calls him "kind of a hero of mine."

On graduation day, Harrell will dye his six-foot-wide dust mop red and blue, Penn's colors. He will tape photographs of his mother, father, and brother Frankie, all of them gone now, to the back of the mop, and march with it down Locust Walk to collect his diploma.

"The mop," he said, "represents where I'm from."

* * *

At 4:55 a.m. on a March Tuesday, the day of the big Penn-Princeton doubleheader, Dan Harrell parked his 1980 Caprice Classic with the rusted roof right at the Palestra's back door, the best spot in the lot.

Inside, everything was dark. The only sound was Big Daddy Graham talking sports on all-night radio.

"I leave it on for the spirits," Harrell said.

The Palestra opened in 1927; some believe that ghosts of former players and fans reside there. "I've seen them plenty of times," he insisted. "Their faces are misty, and they remain in view only long enough so you know they're there."

Harrell, 6-foot-1 and a husky 240 pounds, went about collecting his supplies. He carried a boom box to the scorer's table at mid-court and popped in a CD of Irish tenors. The same lullabies his mother sang when he was a toddler filled the arena. Championship banners hung from the rafters. Dawn filtered through the skylights. The spirits retreated to the shadows.

Harrell grabbed his dust mop and started sweeping.

He lives just three blocks from the row house where he grew up, near 67th and Elmwood.

His six daughters are sweet on him, but joke that he does not take his work home with him.

"He's never picked up a towel, taken out the trash, cut the lawn, or even picked up the remote," said his third-eldest, Debbie Cianci. "He has the remote handed to him."

"But," added his wife, Regina, "the Palestra sparkles."

After graduating from West Catholic High School in 1961, Harrell went to the mail room at General Electric. "In those days, maybe only one kid in 10 went to college," he said.

He worked at GE 20 years, moving up to marketing. But in 1981, everyone in his office was laid off. He dug ditches for a plumber, processed support payments for Family Court, and tended bar.

"I was down, drinking too much," he said. "I had to get a goal."

In the late '80s, he found work at the Wharton School – in housekeeping – and soon moved to the Palestra. To Harrell, who had been going to Big Five games there since he was a kid, it felt like home.

He learned that, as a university employee, he could enroll for free in the College of General Studies, providing he qualified.

Penn also would pay part of his daughters' tuition. That is how he put Melissa and Jackie, his fourth and fifth, through Penn State.

"I owe this place a lot," he said.

After he graduates, Harrell wants to keep working at Penn. His youngest daughter is a high school junior; the tuition benefit could be a big help. He might continue as the Palestra custodian, but, he said, "I think I have a lot more to offer."

He talks about working in Penn community relations, in neighborhoods he has known since childhood. He talks, as well, about sports facilities management.

"I think a natural for him is to be in teaching or counseling or mentoring," Dunphy said. "He's got a doctorate in life."

Curtis Brown, the equipment manager, said that his close friend "eventually wants to be athletic director. I think he'd like to start in operations and work his way up.

"Nothing wrong with dreaming."

* * *

By 10 a.m., Harrell's forehead was pasted with sweat, and his gray Pennsylvania Athletics XXL T-shirt soaked. He put on another CD, 13 versions of "Danny Boy."

He waxed poetic: "When you get the floors clean, and you come in here, it's like it was the first time when you'd walk into Connie Mack Stadium and see that sea of green grass – a beauty-ful thing."

The floors done, he headed for the locker rooms with a handful of envelopes.

Inside each was a jade shamrock key ring, bought the night before in South Philly, and a handwritten note. He tucked them in the lockers of the seniors on the men's and women's teams, for whom this would be the last home game.

Harrell has a locker, too, filled with books and papers – the sign of a man with a 3.19 GPA.

Most days, he finishes at the Palestra by 1:30, then showers and goes to class or the library. He writes his papers in Catholic-school longhand and hands off to his daughters to type them.

On game days, he is back at 4:30, and rarely leaves before midnight.

In the last decade, he has studied Russian history and the American West, anthropology and even Swahili, though he dropped that. To fulfill the language requirement, he studied sign language – useful for a man who is deaf in one ear.

Some of his favorite courses have been with anthropology professor Melvyn Hammarberg, who inspired him to major in American Civilization. Harrell thrives in the classroom, Hammarberg said, and brings his life experience with him.

For a class on the American Indian, he wrote a paper on the Lenapi's version of football. For a class on modern American cultural values, he observed the dynamics of the Penn women's volleyball team. For another, he studied how West Philadelphia real estate agents adapted to a changing population.

"One of the things I got from going to Penn," Harrell said, "was a better understanding of what happened to my own city. It was white flight based on fear and ignorance. Nobody really knew each other."

This semester, he is doing an independent-study project – on boxball. Of all the street games he played growing up, boxball was his passion. His project, he said, will celebrate the freedom children once had to create their own games and rules.

Since 1961, he has tried to preserve that culture, and his neighborhood, by coaching football at parish schools.

Two weeks ago, he became the first inductee to a new hall of fame established by graduates of St. Barnabas School, his alma mater.

He wore a blue suit and tie. His wife, who works at a shoe store, bought him Italian loafers – his first shoes without laces.

The same night, Penn was playing Yale at the Palestra. Before the induction, he dropped in to check the floor. In suit, tie and fancy loafers, he bent and scraped some gum.

"If you are a good person, you're in with Dan," said Julie Soriero, the former Penn women's coach. "If you are a little shady, you're out. He likes to be around good people. And in return, he's a good person to all those he cares about."

Matt Langel, a senior guard, found the proof of that in his locker that Tuesday afternoon.

When he walked out on the floor for a warmup, the first thing he did was thank Dan for the shamrock and the note and hug him.

Next in line was senior forward Frank Brown. "Dan is such an example of perseverance," Brown said. "He's like another coach to us."

* * *

At 5:30, the women's game began. Harrell was too busy working to catch much of it. Yet at the end, he was posted by the locker room, slapping five to the women as they ran in.

Soon the Palestra was mobbed for the men's game.

In the front row was Karim Sadak, a senior who took Group Dynamics 240 at Wharton with Harrell.

"You walking with me at graduation, right?" Harrell yelled.

"Absolutely," Sadak replied.

With Harrell out of earshot, he confided: "I learned as much from him as I did from the professor in that class. He showed me how to interact with people, to treat people with respect…. He made the classroom a nicer place."

With a minute left, and Penn ahead by 70-48, Harrell worked his way up to the Penn bench, where Michael Koller was getting ready to go in.

Koller, a senior, had played on the junior varsity this season. Because this was the last game, Dunphy let him dress with the varsity and, with Penn so far ahead, let him play the last minute.

With 34 seconds left, Koller drove to the basket and was fouled. He went to the free-throw line with a chance to score his first-ever varsity points.

The crowd roared for him.

He missed the first foul shot.

He hit the second.

Harrell stabbed the air with such glee that his feet left the ground.

When a timeout was called, Koller came to the bench. Harrell kissed him on the cheek.

"Hold on," Koller screamed. "This is what did it!"

Koller rolled down the waistband of his shorts.

Pinned to the inside was a shamrock from Dan Harrell.

POSTSCRIPT

This is my favorite ending of all time. Had I not been with Dan in the morning, I never would have appreciated the significance of what Mike Koller did at night. Nothing could describe Dan's impact on these students – his love for them and their love in return – better than that scene. This is showing, not telling. This is putting in the time. This is loving your story. This is telling it to your keyboard first. These are all rules you will read about later. I can't begin to express the joy I felt as a reporter when I witnessed this moment. Honestly, I feel small moments like this are almost spiritual, the most beautiful expressions of our humanity. What makes my life meaningful is capturing these moments and sharing them with you.

I like to call this kind of story a narrative profile. It is a profile of Dan, but told within a narrative about the biggest day of the year for him. I was going to start the story with him arriving at 5 a.m. My editor, Kathy Hacker, suggested I start with the anecdote about his first assignment in composition class, which, in my original draft, came much later. She thought it would be the most surprising, allow me better frame the story, and lead in gracefully to the narrative. She was so right.

I also wrote one more paragraph at the end, that Dan went off to a stairwell and wept. Kathy thought it too much, and urged me to cut it. She was right again. I love baseball, and I think a pitching analogy is apt here. Once in a while, I can pitch a complete game. But usually I can go seven or eight strong innings, and need to hand off to a closer – an editor who cares as deeply as I do, whose touch will be light but essential. I write with even more confidence knowing I have a superb editor to bring me home. And I have been so fortunate to work with a number of great editors over the years, including Tom Frail, Dotty Brown, and Karl Stark among many others whose deft hands have contributed greatly to this book.

Dan continued working at the Palestra for another decade, and recently retired.

Jack Lawlor and Mark Harris enjoy a laugh
at Abington Memorial Hospital

4

A REMARKABLE FRIENDSHIP

'A welcome stranger' in hospital cafeteria

A cook forms a bond with the husband of a dying patient

December 23, 2012

Mark Harris works the grill in the cafeteria at Abington Memorial Hospital.

Jack Lawlor's wife was dying. He was at the hospital day after day, hoping she'd get better, and every day he'd go into the cafeteria for a steak sandwich.

Mark knows all the regulars, the doctors and nurses. He noticed Jack after a few days in line and concluded that he was visiting a sick relative. Mark tried to be cheerful to him in line, and do what he could – give him extra steak on his sandwich.

Jack was not too lost in grief to notice how hard Mark was working at the grill, hustling, juggling many orders at once, always being cheerful to him – and very generous with the steak.

Mark is a black man, raised in Philadelphia in a series of foster homes, now 42. Jack is a white man, 80, from Hatboro, many years ago the retail advertising manager for *The Philadelphia Inquirer*.

One day, after lunch, Jack was waiting outside the cafeteria for the elevator back to intensive care. Mark walked by, stopped, and asked Jack why he was at Abington.

Jack told him his wife had suffered a second stroke and was declining.

"I could feel his pain," said Mark, "because my own foster mother had just died. She raised me till I was 10. She was the easiest woman in the world to please."

Though the city had moved Mark to a different foster family and expected them to sever contact, he stayed close to her until her last breath.

"He was telling me about her, and tears are coming down," said Jack. "I tell him about my wife, and I'm crying."

Mark rode up the elevator with Jack, sat with him for a while in the ICU.

Next thing, Mark was going up every day, taking balloons, candy, a kind word. "Mark used to bring me a little dish of ice cream, whatever I needed," said Jack. "He's crying along with us all the time. Just a welcome stranger in our lives.

"I was down getting coffee," Jack said. "I told him it looked like it was going to be soon, and sure enough, he was up there, along with a religious person, in the room, and a doctor. They said she would be passing in another minute. There's Mark with us, holding hands, in his white outfit from the grill. He's up there with us until she passed away.

"The hospice people, they were very nice," said Jack. "They said you'd get followup calls, and I did get one or two followup calls from hospice, asking how I was doing. The person who called me every day was Mark. He started calling me Pops. 'Are you OK, Pops?' 'Yeah, I'm OK.' 'Are you sure?' The person who called me regularly for at least a week or more was Mark."

Jack would come back to Abington, to the cafeteria, every few weeks, right around Mark's break time, and have a cup of coffee with him, meet his hospital friends, learn all about his life, give him advice.

About two years after his wife died, Jack was in the hospital himself. It was sudden. He couldn't alert Mark.

"Next morning came," said Jack, "and I heard Mark out in the hallway. He has a lot of spies, and somebody told him I was there. I'm getting a transfusion. He's saying something to the nurse at the desk."

"Who are you looking for?" she asks Mark.

"I'm looking for my Pops."

"No, I don't think he's here," the nurse replies. There were no older black men on that floor.

"Well, let me go look."

"You can't go looking into patients' rooms."

Mark finds Jack.

"Hey, Pops! How about a steak sandwich?"

A year later, Jack was visiting Mark in the Abington cafeteria and saw Dick Jones, who was then the hospital CEO. Mark was still behind the grill, not yet on break.

Jack introduced himself to the CEO.

"What brings you here?" the CEO asked.

"I have a friend here," Jack replied. "He's the greatest spokesman for your organization."

A year ago, when Mark's sister died, Jack went to the funeral. It was at a big Baptist church in West Philly, near 57th and Arch. Jack estimates there were 500 people there, and he was the only white person. Mark was following the casket in a procession up to the altar. He stopped, walked over to Jack, gave him a hug.

Their friendship has been going strong for six years. Mark writes poetry, shares it with Jack, who says, "It's unreal. It's beautiful."

Jack mainly listens to Mark, gives him advice, tries to persuade him to quit smoking.

"We're like father and son," says Mark.

Jack already had a son named Mark.

Now he has two.

Postscript

I had spent a year at Abington Memorial Hospital writing narratives about big issues in health care, starting each one at the bedside. Two years later, I heard about this story from Linda Millevoi, who directs media relations. Jack's wife had already died. Mark's supervisor nominated him for an award.

It would have been better if I could have been present when this all took place. But I wasn't. So I did my best to recreate the action. I interviewed Mark and Jack by phone. They could sense my enthusiasm and responded with great quotes and details. I drilled down deep asking about certain moments. I wanted to see them clearly in my own mind, so I could recreate them for readers. As you report a story, you must also be thinking about how you are going to write it. This will influence what questions you ask, what details you get.

Every quote was something Mark or Jack told me they had said or had been said to them. I wanted to keep the story simple and spare.

After the story appeared, a clothing store owner in Center City Philadelphia invited Mark to his store and gave him his first suit. Mark and Jack are still close.

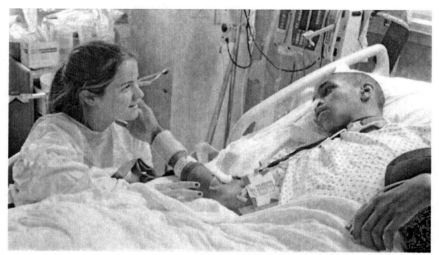

Alison Colatriano visits Jordan Burnham in the hospital

5

A TRAGEDY AND A MIRACLE

A glimpse into a world of teen depression
Jordan Burnham refocuses his life after a 9-story plunge

January 20, 2008

On the evening of Sept. 28, at an apartment complex in King of Prussia, a tragedy and a miracle occurred 2.5 seconds apart.

The tragedy took place when Jordan Burnham, 18, a senior just nominated to the homecoming court at Upper Merion High School, jumped out his ninth-floor window.

The miracle happened 90 feet below, when he hit the ground at 50 mph – and survived.

Jordan has no recollection of going out the window. Even though he was suffering from depression, neither he nor anyone close to him ever expected him to do something so impulsive, so lethal.

"I had everything to live for," he says now.

Today, 114 days later, Jordan's body remains badly broken. With the help of three therapists, he stood on his right leg last week for 60 seconds. He still cannot stand on his left leg, encased in scaffolding.

Doctors can't promise he'll walk, but won't rule it out. He has surprised them every step of his recovery, beginning with his survival. His parents hope the miracle continues.

One million American high school students, like Jordan, attempt suicide every year, according to federal studies, and about 150,000 are treated at hospitals. In 2004, more than 2,000 teens between 15 and 19 killed themselves. Nearly all suffered from depression or some mental illness.

Jordan's story provides a rare glimpse into one family's struggle with teen depression. He was being treated, his parents were tuned in, yet the disease so twisted his mind that he felt going out a ninth-floor window was his only option.

Still, his story also affirms how resilient one life, and one family, can be.

* * *

The day before he went out the window, a Thursday, Jordan learned of his selection to the homecoming court, and told his father to rent himself a white tuxedo.

A year earlier, when Jordan was the only junior on the court, they had done a skit together, a dance-off at the homecoming pep rally. It brought the house down.

This year, Jordan wanted to do a reprise. He told his father, Earl Burnham, the popular director of athletics and activities at Upper Merion High, not to worry about the cost of the tux – Jordan would pay.

In most apparent ways, Jordan Burnham had a life that couldn't get much better. He was a varsity golfer and baseball pitcher. He was sports anchor on the school's morning news show, and called the play-by-play for high school football and basketball games on local cable TV.

He earned good money last summer caddying. He has a car, an iPod, and an Xbox in his bedroom. He has the numbers of 150 friends in his cell phone.

Jordan is African American in a school that is 92 percent white. He and his three best friends, all white, are so tight they call themselves the Entourage, after the HBO show. Many class-mates were sure he'd be voted homecoming king.

The day before his leap, Jordan had a golf match near his mother's school, and asked her to watch. A first-grade teacher at Knapp Elementary in Lansdale, she arrived with four holes to go.

When Jordan saw his mother, he walked over and "gave me a kiss on the cheek," Georgette Burnham said. He was so excited." 'Did Dad tell you about homecoming?'" she recalled him asking. "I said, 'Yes, that's very exciting. You better get back over there.' "

That evening, more good news: Jordan learned he'd be the one golfer from his school in the Suburban One League tournament.

The next morning, Friday, the day Jordan would jump, his father was getting ready to drive him from school to Indian Valley Country Club in Telford to practice for the Monday tournament. Jordan had never played the course.

As Earl went into his son's trunk, to transfer the golf clubs to his own car, he saw a blue Wilson duffel bag. It was open. Inside were 13 twelve-ounce cans of Natural Light beer, a half-gallon and a fifth of Smirnoff Raspberry Vodka, and a half-gallon of Captain Morgan Spiced Rum.

Earl was crestfallen – and angry.

Not again, he thought.

* * *

Earl did not confront Jordan right away. He just drove him to the club, simmering in silence, and tried to think of the best way to handle this.

Jordan's depression complicated the situation.

Tara, Jordan's sister, first spotted his depression, though she didn't realize it. When he was a ninth grader, she came home from Penn State one weekend and sensed an immense sadness in Jordan.

"I remember just crying when I left for school, telling him how sorry I felt that I couldn't make him feel better," Tara, 23, recalled. "I didn't know what was wrong."

The depression finally burst into view in the summer of 2006, a few months before Jordan's 17th birthday, when he flipped out after failing his driver's test for the third time. He argued with the instructor, ranted at his father, and just started walking home from Norristown.

His mother, who went to get him, made an appointment with Jean Phillips, a licensed clinical social worker and counselor in Wayne.

She diagnosed depression.

Earl at first didn't understand. What did Jordan have to be depressed about? But his parents soon came to understand that there had been warning signs: His grades had fallen; he couldn't concentrate; they had even tested him for a sleep disorder.

As the Burnhams learned, "many with depression struggle to look and feel happy," said Jeffrey Staab, a University of Pennsylvania psychiatrist who treated Jordan after he jumped. "They don't want others to know what is happening, and they believe that if they just try harder to look and feel happy, they can break out of the depression."

People who haven't been clinically depressed, Staab said, can't imagine the profound changes it causes.

Jordan talked with Phillips, his therapist, weekly. A psychiatrist prescribed an antidepressant, and he seemed better – for a while.

Six months later, in December 2006, Jordan called his close friend Allison Colatriano, an Upper Merion junior, and told her he had gone out with someone else.

Jordan felt so guilty, so bad about himself, that he had lined up on his bed all the pills he could find in the family medicine cabinets and locked his bedroom door.

Frightened, Allison called Jordan's parents on the house phone. When Earl wedged open the bedroom door with a credit card, Jordan hadn't taken any pills. Earl and Georgette said experts had told them this was a cry for help, not necessarily a suicide attempt.

Jordan went to Brooke Glen Behavioral Hospital in Fort Washington for a week. Few students at Upper Merion knew. He didn't want people to think he was crazy.

Back at school, he seemed to have a new appreciation for life. Allison said his spirits were higher.

Then came three episodes with alcohol.

Last spring, police stopped a car and arrested Jordan and the driver for underage drinking. Jordan worked the summer with a Little League in a first-offenders program.

In August, he hosted a party when his parents went to Pittsburgh overnight to visit Earl's sick mother. Jordan didn't plan the party, but word travels fast when parents go away. Even police heard.

As athletic director, Earl knew the party could cost him his job. But his bigger concern was his son. Earl and Georgette worried Jordan would be despondent over the predicament he had created for his father, and because he had violated their trust.

In accordance with school policy, Jordan and others were suspended from sports for two weeks. But he seemed to weather that crisis fine.

Then, on Sept. 28, Earl found the beer and vodka in the trunk.

* * *

Earl dropped Jordan at golf, and went to see his wife.

"I was devastated," Georgette recalled. "We were at such a good point, and bam!"

She struggled to understand whether this and the previous episodes with alcohol were normal teenage behavior or something more serious. Neither Georgette nor Earl drinks, and Tara said she never drank in high school.

After Earl left, Georgette talked with a fellow teacher who knew of Jordan's problems. "We prayed together," said Georgette. "I felt so distraught. So heavyhearted."

Earl then called Tara, who worked in Atlanta.

Tara wanted to think, and said she'd call back. "I didn't want my dad and mom to make too big a deal of it," she said, "because Jordan had seemed to be doing well."

She was in a meeting when her father called again that afternoon. She didn't answer. She thought she still had time to give her advice: Dispose of the alcohol, and don't say a thing.

Earl that day also called Jordan's therapist, Phillips.

She told him he should confront Jordan, and that there should be consequences. This was also Earl's inclination. Too much alcohol was found, likely intended for many students. Earl felt he couldn't leave the matter alone. Phillips also scheduled an appointment for Jordan on Monday.

On the golf course that Friday afternoon, Jordan felt good about his round. He shot an 87, and thought he could improve on three holes and drop to an 82 in competition.

Driving home with his dad, Jordan didn't suspect his parents were on to him. He called Allison to check in. She was leaving field hockey practice; they'd talk that night.

Around 6 p.m., when Jordan entered the apartment, his mother was sitting on the living-room couch. Jordan could tell that she was sad, but didn't know why.

"What's wrong with you?" he asked her.

"I'm just tired," she told him. "Really tired."

Then Earl walked in with the duffel bag full of alcohol.

"This is where I could see Jordan's whole demeanor change," his mother recalled.

"Whose is this?" Earl asked.

"It's mine," Jordan replied.

Earl had hoped Jordan would say the alcohol belonged to others, but wasn't surprised when Jordan shouldered responsibility.

Earl told his son that he would be grounded. They'd get into the specifics later.

Jordan didn't get angry or protest. "I'm just no good," he told them.

"I didn't say that," Earl insisted.

They talked it through for a few minutes. They hugged.

Earl did tell his son, "I need you to call the crisis team," a county hotline. Considering everything going on with Jordan, Earl believed the call would be a good idea.

Jordan appeared to be handling the incident well, so about 6:30, Earl decided to walk to the high school – 10 minutes away – and get Jordan's car. He'd be right back.

Georgette was still on the couch.

"Jordan came over to me," his mother recalled, "and I just looked at him."

"Why?" she asked him.

"I'm just a mess-up, Mom," he replied. "Just a mess-up."

"I said, 'No, Jordan. You're not a mess-up.' "

Jordan went into his bedroom, shut the door.

"It's not uncommon for him, when he's upset, to go into his room," she said.

Georgette sat wondering what was the right thing to do.

* * *

Around 6:30, Allison, home from practice, had finished dinner when Jordan called.

In an interview, Allison recounted the conversation – none of which Jordan remembers.

"Are you alone?" he asked.

"Yeah. Why?" she replied.

"You know that I care about you, right?"

"Yeah."

"OK, because I'm going to be leaving."

"What?"

"I'm going away."

She noticed right away he sounded strange. At first she thought that he was moving, that his parents had taken a new job. Then he said, "It's time for me to go," and added he had "to write some letters first."

Suddenly she understood. He sounded as he had a year before, as if he were about to do something drastic.

"Why are you doing this?" she asked him.

"I've been letting a lot of people down. Like my mom."

Jordan told Allison that his father had found alcohol in his car.

"Well, that's not the end of the world," Allison told him.

She tried to make him feel better, but it wasn't working.

"I'm going to call your mom," she told him. "I'll call you right back. You'll answer, right?"

He said he would.

Allison reached his mother on the house phone.

She told Mrs. Burnham that she was very worried about Jordan, to check on him.

Allison called Jordan right back, and he did pick up.

They had just started their new conversation when, through the phone, Allison heard knocking.

She heard Jordan say, "No, Mom."

Then she didn't hear anything. The line went dead.

She got scared. She tried calling his cell phone again.

No answer.

Then she sent him text messages repeatedly, according to the police report:

6:49 – "I need you."
6:54 – "Please pick up."
7:04 – "Jordan don't leave me, don't go please."
7:05 – "Please I need you, everyone needs you."
7:12 – "You mean the world to me."

After Allison's call, Georgette knocked on Jordan's door. "He wouldn't let me in," she recalled, "and I'm sort of angry at him at this point."

"Open the door," she tried again. "We can talk."

She began to panic: Jordan might have grabbed pills again. Georgette called Earl, but he had left his cell phone at home.

She hurled herself at the door so hard she was bruised the next day. It didn't budge.

She called Phillips, the therapist, who quickly called Jordan and got his voice mail. At 7:10 p.m., according to police, Phillips left a message on Jordan's phone: "Nothing is so bad it can't be fixed. Call me."

Georgette was again on the phone with Phillips, who had called back, when she heard sirens.

Georgette's first reaction was, "Not another fire drill. Not now."

Then, more sirens. Lots of sirens.

"That's when I saw all these people on the ground. I saw Earl. I'll always remember the shirt he had on – blue and white striped – and saw him running over to underneath where Jordan's window is. I knew, but I didn't want to know. I was crying into the phone."

Driving up, Earl also thought it was a fire drill. Until he saw the maintenance man, holding a phone, who yelled, "I'm trying to call you. It's Jordan."

Earl ran across the yard. Police and EMTs were at the scene.

One officer asked Earl if he knew what had happened. Had the boy been beaten up and ditched there?

Earl looked up and saw the open window.

"He came from up there."

* * *

A woman who lives on the fifth floor was in the courtyard playing with her young son and other children when, according to the police report, "she heard a loud thud and turned around to see Burnham on the ground."

The 911 call came in at 6:56.

According to the police report, the first officer found Jordan "lying still and on his back." His left leg "was wrapped almost completely around his right leg," and Jordan had "deforming fractures to his left wrist and left arm" and "was bleeding from his face, mouth and head."

"Burnham did respond to me when I spoke to him and was able to tell me his name. I asked Burnham if he fell from the window, and he mumbled, 'No.' I sat with Burnham and kept him from moving so he wouldn't further injure himself."

An ambulance raced Jordan to a field for helicopter transport.

Earl accompanied police upstairs. They discovered Jordan had barricaded the door with his desk chair. The window – two feet by three, big enough for an agile teen to climb out – was open. The screen was on the bed.

Police told Earl and Georgette to start driving toward Philadelphia. Dispatch would call to tell them where Jordan was being taken.

Within moments the Burnhams, both 50, college sweethearts at Slippery Rock, found themselves stuck in Friday evening Schuylkill Expressway traffic.

They didn't know if their son was alive or dead. In haste, they had brought only Earl's cell phone, and the battery was dying. They hoped it lasted until police called.

* * *

At the Hospital of the University of Pennsylvania, the chaplain greeted them, and prayed with them, as they awaited news.

They called their daughter.

"I collapsed…. I blamed myself," Tara recalled. "What if I had called my dad and said, 'Don't talk to Jordan about the alcohol?' "

"None of us ever thought, no matter how bad he got, he would ever do something like this," Tara said. "I was an R.A. in college, and I dealt with depression and even one suicide attempt on campus. I didn't feel I saw the signs for him to be close to the edge."

Finally, Earl said, a doctor emerged to tell him and his wife that there was a 60 percent chance Jordan would die. The doctor said he had never seen anyone survive a fall of more than five floors.

Earl went outside to get some air, and prayed:

"God, I know I've asked you for a lot of things. But this is one time I'm going to ask you: I need a miracle. I will rededicate myself. God, if you can save my son's life...I'm giving this over to you, God. I'm letting go. Whatever your will is, I accept."

A friend and former principal of Earl's heard the news and called him at the hospital at 9:30 p.m. Earl told her not to come right away.

"Come at 1:30 a.m.," he said.

She asked why. Earl remembered telling her: "He'll probably be dead by then, and I'll need you here."

* * *

At the Marquis, the Burnhams' nine-story apartment building, scores of students had gathered.

Like so many others, Andre Wessels got a call from a friend on his cell phone:

"Did you hear Jordan jumped?"

"Are you drunk?" Andre responded. "Are you high?"

As Wessels explained later, "Nobody expected this from him, of all people."

Kevin Reifsnyder, a member of Jordan's Entourage, recounted, "We were all obviously shocked because he was the happiest kid."

School officials wisely that night opened the school cafeteria for students to gather. "I've never seen grown boys cry so much," said senior Theresa Esposito.

On Monday, "not one person, not a few people, the whole school was crying," said senior Tom Filandino.

They wore ribbons. Raised money. Gave blood. They decorated Jordan's locker and his parking space.

Allison started a Facebook site, "Stay Strong Jordan B," where students poured out their grief and good wishes, checked on news, posted pictures and videos.

Friends visited him in the intensive care unit.

"The first time it was a miracle because we saw him blink," said Ryan Donovan, of the Entourage.

A senior who visited several times said she suffered from depression and an eating disorder and was thinking about suicide herself – until Jordan jumped.

"It just made me realize you only have one life, and you could throw it away so quickly," she said. "When you're thinking about it, it doesn't seem so extreme. But when you see something like this, you understand."

* * *

Depression is anything but rational. It is tied to chemical imbalances in the brain.

"If something happens that makes most people sad, we'll feel sad, but we'll bounce back," explained Staab, the psychiatrist. "If we get happy about something, we don't walk around for days and days giddy. We're happy for a while, and then we go back down. That's really a regulatory system [of brain chemicals] that allows us to respond, and then settle back down to our usual self."

With depression, the "regulatory system goes awry. It doesn't settle us back down. It drifts," Staab said, leaving people irritable, anxious and moody. They sleep or can't sleep, overeat or don't eat. They magnify negatives, disregard positives. They feel as if they have no value.

Teenagers, Staab said, with their maturing brains, are even more vulnerable to magnifying negatives.

* * *

In the emergency room, staff did a quick assessment:

Jordan had landed on his left side, breaking his pelvis. His left leg was shattered above and below the knee. His left wrist, skull and jaw were fractured.

Extensive internal bleeding was the most urgent priority. Jordan would bleed to death within hours.

He was rushed to interventional radiology, where doctors, injecting a dye, pinpointed the worst area of bleeding – in the violently broken pelvis. Using catheters and wires to snake their way through his arteries, doctors stopped that bleeding from within in about two hours.

For days doctors weren't sure they could save him. They cut open his abdomen to ease the swelling of his major organs, a result of shock, bleeding and resuscitation.

His kidneys failed, and he went on dialysis. He needed a ventilator to breathe.

Jordan had survived the fall because he landed on earth instead of asphalt, and because he didn't land on his head or neck. He was also young and fit and got immediate medical attention – at the scene, then at a superb trauma center, where teams of specialists were waiting.

"The fact that he fell nine stories certainly puts his survival as sort of an exceptional event," said trauma surgeon Patrick Reilly, who worked on Jordan. "Someone who falls nine stories, the majority of those patients should die, many before they ever reach medical attention."

"I think he has an angel," said Allison. "My MomMom passed away the night before he did this. Sometimes I think it's her that saved him."

From the first day, Earl and Georgette, lifelong Baptists, started a prayer chain. They'd call Earl's Aunt Minnie and Georgette's sister. Prayers would spread from Florida to Canada.

"We would tell them specifically his kidneys are failing. He's on dialysis, and they'd pray for his kidneys and they'd come back," said Georgette. "Then we'd say his white blood count is low, and the counts would come up. It's mind-boggling how God has saved him and now he's healing him." Earl and Georgette spent the first five days at the hospital, getting a hotel room next door. They didn't want to leave; they didn't know if they'd ever see Jordan again.

When they finally went home for a night, Earl and Georgette went into Jordan's room. "I smelled his clothes and sat on his bed so I'd have some sense of Jordan," Earl said. He put his son's wallet in his back pocket, and has kept it there, to have something of his son close by.

* * *

After three weeks of constant crises in the ICU, doctors were able to reduce Jordan's sedatives, and he slowly woke up.

Jordan couldn't speak because of his tracheotomy, a breathing tube in his throat for his many surgeries. But he could mouth words. Late in October, he asked his mother what had happened to him.

The Burnhams had been told not to tell Jordan that he had jumped. Doctors wanted to know what he could understand, what he remembered, whether he had suffered a brain injury.

Georgette told her son he was in the hospital, that he had fallen.

"Did somebody push me?"

Jordan asked, mouthing the words.

"No. No one threw you," she replied. "What do you remember?"

He was upset. He couldn't remember. "Did I jump?"

"I'm not sure, Jordan," she told him. "I wasn't there. Do you remember going golfing with Dad at Indian Valley?"

"I remember that," he told her, mouthing the words.

"What about after?" she asked.

"That's all I remember," he said.

His parents wanted so badly to find out why he had done it, but didn't want to upset him.

Tara visited at Halloween.

"That was a horrible moment to me," Tara recalled. "My parents said don't give him a straight-up answer.... He looked at me with that look in his eyes, 'You're my sister – we always tell each other everything,' and he mouthed to me, 'Do you know what happened to me?'"

She would not tell him the whole truth. She did tell him that he had fallen from his bedroom window.

"Why am I alive?" he mouthed the words.

A tear ran down her cheek. She said one word: "God."

* * *

In November, Jordan grew more alert, stable. And it became all too clear just how badly he was broken.

He was able to eat, but had little appetite because of medications and trauma. He remained on intravenous nutrition. He was on heavy pain medication and was often groggy or asleep. With the hole in his throat, he still couldn't talk.

He had suffered nerve damage to both legs and his left arm, and several times described his pain as 8 on a scale of 10, even with drugs.

The injury causing him the greatest pain was around the base of his spine and his rear end, on which he had landed. Surgeons removed so much dead muscle and tissue, and cut so close to the spine, they feared Jordan may never sit again.

Earl's and Georgette's spirits soared or plunged daily, hourly, with every improvement or setback.

When the plastic surgeon put four titanium plates into Jordan's broken jaw – all from the inside and leaving no scars – Earl wept, and had to fight back the urge to kiss the surgeon.

"I just stood there and cried," Earl said. "He hugged me."

But when Jordan endured a shock test to assess nerve damage in his left arm and legs, and writhed helplessly, Earl looked like a defensive lineman about to sack the neurologist.

Georgette wished desperately, constantly, that she could take Jordan's place, bear his pain. Earl became Atlas, keeping Jordan's spirits up, always searching for and trumpeting the positive.

Even for families, visiting hours in HUP's sixth-floor trauma unit are 11 a.m. to 8 p.m. Georgette was there the whole time, on leave from her teaching job.

Earl was there as much as possible, but kept working. His family needed his salary and benefits, and the school, which has given him tremendous latitude, needed an athletic director.

The parents massaged Jordan's feet, or fetched him milkshakes, hoping he'd eat. When Jordan slept, Georgette did crosswords, and Earl, on his BlackBerry or laptop, arranged for buses or referees.

Every night, when the Burnhams pulled into their apartment building's parking lot, they looked up nine floors and re-lived everything.

Some nights Georgette tried to tell herself, it's not that high. Her husband corrected her: *Yes, it is.*

Earl and Jordan had moved into the Marquis six years ago when Earl took the Upper Merion job. Georgette stayed in their Pittsburgh house until she found a job here.

An apartment so near school was perfect. And when a top-floor unit became vacant, Earl fell in love with the view.

Now they spend as little time there as possible.

"Sleep, eat, and get out of here," Georgette said.

* * *

Mouthing some words and spelling others by pointing to letters on a piece of paper, Jordan gave his first interview in mid-November.

His room was filled with get-well cards and posters. He had seen the Facebook comments of his friends.

His parents, so focused on his condition, and still fearful of upsetting him, had not yet really asked Jordan about his feelings, about what had happened, and they hung now on every word.

"I guess I never realized how much people care," he spelled out. "It gives me the motivation to wake up every day with a smile on my face."

"That's great stuff," his father said.

Jordan saw his father cry, and started to cry himself.

"I love you," he mouthed.

"I love you, too, son," Earl replied. He clasped his son's good right hand.

"I want to be strong like you one day," the son mouthed.

"You are," said the father.

"No, I'm not. You are," the son repeated.

"I'm not that strong," Earl continued. "I just believe that through God I get my strength. That's why I believe you're going to get well. Because of your faith in God, you're going to recover."

"I find it very difficult to now complain about anything," Jordan spelled out, "when I am blessed to be even breathing."

His mom kissed him.

He then spelled out his feelings about his parents.

"They impress me more than anything I could ever do. Amazing. Sometimes I feel like I have it easy compared to what they go through every day emotionally."

On Thanksgiving weekend, Jordan got a smaller tracheotomy, and discovered that by putting his finger over the hole, he could speak.

When his father walked in, he surprised him.

"Hey, Dad. What's up?"

Earl Burnham began sobbing. He made so much noise, nurses came running.

Jordan grew concerned.

"What's wrong, Dad?"

"What's wrong?" Earl repeated. "It's been 56 days since I heard your voice. It's Jordan. I got Jordan back."

With his new voice, Jordan was eager to talk. In an interview, he recalled practicing for the golf tournament on the day he jumped.

"It's weird," he said. "I remember the first tee. Dogleg left. Second shot was over the water. Pin was on the left side. Putt was uphill, right to left. But I can't remember anything else that happened that day.

"The reason I go back to that day is I wonder, 'Did I have a reason to commit suicide?' "

This was the first time, his parents said, he had mentioned suicide.

"Was there any motivation? Was I depressed? And nothing comes to mind," he said. "It's mind-boggling to wake up in the hospital – connected to an IV and with all these tubes – and not even know how or why you got here. I don't have the slightest clue."

"Nine stories," he said. "It's amazing that I'm still alive."

A week later, on Dec. 2, Allison told Jordan her account of what had happened that night.

"He was shocked to hear that he had called me and was on the phone with me while it happened," Allison recalled. "He apologized a couple times. Then I asked him if he was happy to be here."

"I'm extremely happy to be here," he told her.

* * *

Jordan's jump was impulsive, but wasn't done in isolation.

"A suicide attempt is not *Something bad happened, I'm going to commit suicide*," said Guy Diamond, who runs the Center for Family Intervention Science at Children's Hospital of Philadelphia.

"It's *Things aren't going well, I'm under a lot of pressure, I've disappointed my parents, I can't fit in,* and what often happens there's a foundation that's fragile…and some incident will be the straw."

Diamond urges parents of children with depression to have a frank discussion about suicide.

"Some parents fear that this will put ideas in their head," he said. "We find that not to be the case. And in fact, if adolescents are not thinking about it, they find their parents' concerns silly but protective…. If they are thinking about it, then adolescents find the conversations a relief…. *I can finally talk with someone about this.*"

From the day Jordan jumped, Earl and Georgette wondered whether the antidepressant he was taking was to blame.

Many experts, including Staab, Jordan's HUP psychiatrist, do not believe so.

In 2004, the Food and Drug Administration caused an uproar when it warned that antidepressants might create suicidal thoughts in teens. As a result, some teens stopped taking their drugs, and suicides increased.

Last year, the FDA modified its warning. The risk, it said, was only in the first few weeks of treatment.

Jordan had been taking his medication for more than a year.

Staab said that Jordan's antidepressant clearly had failed – he attempted suicide – but that he did not believe it encouraged the suicidal behavior.

* * *

On Dec. 7, Jordan was feeling better than in the 10 weeks since his fall. Transferring him into a wheelchair took three people and caused wincing pain. Once in, Jordan felt good sitting. His parents wheeled him around the hospital, a Steelers jersey over his gown.

As usual, he also wore around his neck a Philadelphia Marathon credential that his father, a race volunteer, had given him for inspiration. "What you're going through is just like a marathon," Earl had told him.

He went to get a haircut, to play the piano in the lounge with his right hand. He had taken lessons for five years.

He went to the gift shop and bought a stuffed dog to give to Allison.

His mother decorated his door for Christmas with candy canes, a red bow and Bible passages.

Later, back in bed, after Jordan had eaten three bowls of cereal, Allison visited.

She sat by him, held his hand. He smiled; she giggled. Jordan then pulled the pup out of a plastic bag.

For a moment, he was Jordan Burnham, a high school senior, and he was giving a girl a present.

* * *

Later that evening, Jordan felt like talking. He explained how he had tried to ignore his depression and hide it.

"My parents were asking me how my day was, and they would always try to get deeper in the conversation, but I just wouldn't let it happen."

At school, "I was the funny guy, always upbeat, always positive, even when I didn't feel like it on the inside," he said.

Alcohol, he believed, didn't figure into his depression.

"I probably drink less than the typical high school student. At my school there's usually about two parties at the most a month. Most of those times at those parties I was the designated driver."

And between parties, he routinely stored leftover alcohol in his trunk.

"When I did drink, it was the equivalent of four or five beers or three to four shots. That never got me wasted or out of control. Just something to get me loosened up. If I was feeling down, I wouldn't drink. That would be dangerous."

He felt lots of pressure.

"I would have trouble in school about grades," he said, "and I was constantly stressing about that."

Doctors call this and other common teen pressures "stressors" and "risk factors" that can trigger depression.

Jordan loves his school, and felt he fit in. But he said being in a mostly white school contributed to his stress, primarily when it came to dating. He did not think this had been a factor the day he jumped.

"A lot of parents aren't racists, but they don't like interracial dating," said Jordan. "I found this out the hard way."

The father of one senior girl refused to allow Jordan to date his daughter. There was nothing Jordan could do to change his mind, and it devastated him.

"That definitely added to my depression," he said.

At his lowest moments, Jordan said, he just felt worthless. "You feel like it's you against the world."

He knew people loved him, cared about him, but at the same time he was unable to believe it.

Depression overruled his rational mind.

"I had a lot of emotions that dealt with me not living any-more," he said. "I'm not saying I wanted to commit suicide, not saying I wanted anything completely bad to happen, just saying what if I wasn't here anymore."

Jordan said he now remembered his parents confronting him about the alcohol on the evening he jumped. And how bad he felt.

"That's something I remember," he said. "When I get in trou-ble with my parents, I get a real down, depressed feeling of letting them down, of embarrassing myself. I get just ashamed, really....

"Especially with my mom. I just felt like every time I got in trouble, I just broke her heart. That's the last thing I want. And ev-ery time I got in trouble, I lost more of their trust. It made me sad."

Surviving has changed him profoundly, he said. "I don't know why, but I'm smiling more. I'm happy more.

"Mainly I feel grateful," he added. "I have an appreciation for life. I'm able to express my feelings more."

He wants to go back to his bedroom, to look out his window, and say to himself, "I'm still here."

* * *

On Christmas, Jordan gave his parents a present: a certificate, "A Promise to You."

Jordan had dictated the words to Tara, who crafted the doc-ument on a computer.

"This promise is for Earl and Georgette Burnham," it began. "No matter what the circumstances, good or bad, their loving son will never try to leave them again."

"With Love Always."

Jordan Burnham.

Earl started bawling again, but this time the nurses didn't come running.

The next day, Jordan got his best present: a discharge.

After 89 days at HUP, he rode in an ambulance to Bryn Mawr Rehab Hospital in Malvern.

Jordan was ready for more aggressive therapy. Getting to rehab was the brass ring. A major step on the climb back. Now, though, Jordan and his parents would have to adapt to life at a new place and pace, set new goals.

At Bryn Mawr, Jordan saw himself in a full-length mirror.

"Sometimes I don't recognize myself, I'm so skinny," he said.

His appetite is improving. Last Monday, he ate half a Wawa hoagie for lunch – for him, a veritable feast.

While doctors still won't let Jordan stand on his left leg, on Friday they cleared him to start lifting up to 25 pounds with it. He can also start strengthening his left arm, in the hope of using a walker.

Jordan is upbeat, indicating his resilience, Staab said. This will help him through difficult days ahead.

He will continue with his new antidepressant and counseling. One goal, said Staab, will be to revisit the suicide attempt, identify any warning signs that led to it, and develop strategies to follow if he sees such signs again.

"Depression doesn't have to get the best of you," Jordan says. "No matter how small the possibilities of making it out may seem, there's always a way."

Jordan's short-term goal is to get well enough to ask Allison to a February high school dance, even if he can't get out of the wheelchair.

A year from now, he hopes to be in college, studying to become a sports broadcaster, and telling his story to people who need to hear it.

POSTSCRIPT

A few weeks after this story appeared, I heard from a reader. Her son had been suicidal. He had been locked in his room with a gun, threatening to kill himself. The distraught mother, desperate, slid a copy of my story about Jordan under the door. A half-hour later, the son opened the door, weeping, relieved to learn he was not alone, that Jordan felt just as he did.

After the story appeared, Jordan's phone began to ring. Many mental health organizations wanted him to speak. He was young, handsome, articulate, and a minority. He had a message to share of hope, recovery, second chances. The more he spoke about his experience, the more word spread and the more he was invited to speak. He testified before Congress. And soon, he was traveling the country, appearing in high schools and universities, a spokesman with several mental health organizations.

In the summer of 2014, Jordan spoke at the United Nations, seated next to the Secretary General. Jordan went to community college briefly, but soon dedicated himself full time to traveling the country and speaking at high schools, colleges and military bases about depression and suicide. He continues that today. He still lives with his parents, though after a few years in the same apartment, they moved into a house. In April of 2016, Jordan got engaged to be married.

I set out with no agenda other than to tell a good story. But I soon realized the story gave meaning to his tragedy. It launched him down a new and worthwhile a path. It showed me in a dramatic way the power of stories to change lives on many levels.

The power of this story clearly comes from its intimacy, from the level of detail and honesty. The challenge always is to find the balance – use that access and detail to give an honest account, to create a driving narrative, but not to exploit.

I'm going to go into more detail on the origins of this story:

A former colleague, whose daughter went to Upper Merion, called me to tell me about Jordan's fall. She thought it would be my kind of story. I would guess half of the stories I've written over the years came from readers or colleagues.

I called Earl's office and left a voicemail. I looked up the home number and left a message on that machine, too.

I didn't want to intrude in a time of grief, to pile on to their misery or to exploit their tragedy, but I truly believed that if I could tell the story, whatever it was, I could do so in a way that would dignify the experience and serve a constructive purpose. I had no idea what that would be, but I believed it. All I knew at the outset was the amazing fact that he survived a fall of nine floors.

I also told Earl he didn't have to make a decision right away. I was leaving for China in a couple of days, and would be gone for nearly three weeks. I would love to tell the story when I got back.

There was no reply. As soon as I returned from China, I left another voicemail.

Earl called back. Jordan was out of his coma, but Earl had no idea if Jordan would ever be himself again, mentally or physically.

Earl's wife and Jordan's therapist didn't want a story. They felt it could harm Jordan. But Earl overruled them. He went with his gut. "It might be good for Jordan to have something to do during recovery, and chances are nothing would come of it or at the most a story on page 14, and we could stop at any point," he told me recently. "I felt the therapeutic outcome was worth the risk.

"Once we were able to meet," he added, "the low-key approach and style of your personality was a welcome calming effect during that time."

I was nervous as I interviewed Jordan at first, afraid of causing him harm by having him relive a painful memory. The doctors had cautioned Jordan's parents from discussing his fall with him. But I just followed my instincts. I asked simple questions, never pushed, never felt I was taking him some place he didn't want to go. Earl and Georgette hung on his every word. I believe they were more grateful for these interviews than for anything else I did.

I also have discovered, as so many other journalists have, that the subjects of stories often get as much out of the process of being interviewed as they do in reading the final story. The opportunity to talk about their story can be cathartic. And when I write stories in real time, as I did this one, the main characters are grateful to have a passenger along for the ride. (In the tradition of journalism, I am always careful not to alter the course of events – to be a passenger, not the driver.)

I asked Earl to get the police reports, and they were an invaluable resource. I also interviewed as many of Jordan's friends and doctors as I could get. I wanted to know all about Jordan and why he jumped and how he survived. I wanted to give readers the big picture.

I wanted to keep the narrative moving, but enrich it with context that would give the story more scope, more value. I wanted to educate readers about depression and suicide.

Photo by EARL BURNHAM

Jordan Burnham speaks at the United Nations for
the International Youth Day Campaign

MAGAZINE, JANUARY 10, 1954

Ann Sopp as a young woman at Inglis House, with
her photo in unidentified magazine.

6

AN INCURABLE SPIRIT

Ann Sopp found joy, creativity and love
As she fought muscular dystrophy in 64 years at Inglis House

July 3, 2001
On May 20, 1937, Ann Sopp arrived in Philadelphia at Inglis House, then known as Home for Incurables. She was 6. Doctors had told her mother not to get too attached: Her daughter wouldn't live very long.

Sixty-four years later, still at Inglis House, the most incurable thing about Ms. Sopp was her spirit.

"I decided to make this my home and have learned to love it here," she said recently. She lived inside her "stone castle" in West Philadelphia longer than anyone.

Until Sunday night, when Ann Sopp, 70, died of pneumonia at the Hospital of the University of Pennsylvania.

Her parents immigrated from Ukraine and the former Czechoslovakia. Her father was a coal miner in Wilkes-Barre. Her parents sent her to Inglis House to make the best of what was expected to be a very short life.

When Ms. Sopp moved in, she spoke not a word of English. She had never seen a wheelchair. She had never realized she was crippled – her eight siblings just carried her around.

The only person at Inglis House who could interpret for her was a Polish resident with such severe deformities that Ms. Sopp was terrified to go near her. "I was petrified. I cried and cried," she recalled.

By the time Ms. Sopp was 8, her muscular dystrophy was so severe she could no longer take a step, and she was confined to a wheelchair. In her last years, she could barely use her hands. On good days, she would still prop her left elbow on an open drawer and apply her own lipstick. She had not been able to hug anyone or hold a baby in more than 40 years.

To sit up straight, to face the world and to live in it, she wore a steel brace across and down her back. This bruised and hurt her mercilessly. She never complained.

Ms. Sopp's room for the last 30 years was an oasis, with plants, rocking chair, faux fireplace, and stuffed animals on her bed. She had a series of parakeets, one of which, Misty, called her "baby girl." Chopin played on the radio. Parquet covered the institutional tile floor. Her own paintings hung on the walls.

"When dolls got too heavy for me to hold, I picked up paint-brushes," she said two weeks ago, reflecting on her childhood. One painting is of a ballet dancer, which she dreamed of being. "I did this with eye makeup. I was too weak to hold anything else," she said.

"I've done my most creative stuff when I was hurting the most. Then you're not frivolous."

Inglis House, at 2600 Belmont Ave., is home to about 300 people, many with multiple sclerosis, spinal-cord injuries, cerebral palsy. Many times, Ms. Sopp said, she could have moved out. She refused marriage proposals; she never wanted to burden any one person with her extensive care.

Inglis House offered her a great education and an opportunity to work. In her 20s, she worked four jobs at once – involving editing, writing, and calling check-cashing outlets all over the city from her room and alerting them to forgeries. Ms. Sopp made so many friends that her Christmas card list last year exceeded 250 – priests who brought over pizza, old nurses she trained, even a murderer who once worked there.

Friends urged her to write a book. "I'd have to leave the country," she joked.

Two quick anecdotes from her youth:

"Once, at 17, I was going to a dance, and somebody gave me a lovely gown, and I was all ready to go. And the administrator said, 'She can't go. She's not well enough.' And I was as well as you are. And the party left without me. She just hated me, because I was always happy. She had no other way to get even with me."

Also: "There was a chef all the children loved. One day, during lunch, the FBI came and arrested him. He was on its 10 most-wanted list. He had cut up a woman. We were probably eating her! He had a limp, and they traced him because he had to buy special shoes."

In 1948, Ms. Sopp met Lois Roberts, an aide who was a year older. Roberts, who lives in Mount Holly, Burlington County, visited Wednesday evenings and Saturdays. She did Ms. Sopp's laundry. She laid Ms. Sopp's parquet floor and vacationed with her in the mountains and at the shore.

She also took Ms. Sopp shopping. Ms. Sopp called herself a clothes horse.

As a child, Ms. Sopp said the house mothers insisted she had to look her best, had to work twice as hard to convince people that she was educable, employable. "If I raced through the lobby with a curler in my hair," she recalled, "I'd get in huge trouble. We were taught to live in a fishbowl, as if people were always looking at us."

Twenty-one years ago, Ms. Sopp found true love. He is known to everyone else at Inglis House as George Newmeyer. But she called him Yuri. "He doesn't look like a George," she said.

Newmeyer, 57, is from South Philly. When he was 17, his spinal cord was severed in a car accident. He was in the front seat alongside the driver, who was killed. A third boy who jumped into the back just before the crash walked away.

"Oh, Yuri," Ms. Sopp would say, "why didn't you jump into the backseat?"

"Because then I'd never have met you," he would reply.

Newmeyer came to Inglis House around 1980.

"He's my rock, my soul mate," Ms. Sopp said.

"She's my lifeline," he said.

Newmeyer spends his days on a gurney with wheels, on his stomach. He can no longer sit, but he can use his arms and neck. He is the Inglis House postmaster. He has a fleet of mail couriers, who go from room to room in wheelchairs.

When they fail to show, Newmeyer delivers the mail himself, carrying it on his back – even boxes of fruit from Florida. "I tell him not to overdo it," Ms. Sopp said, "but he's so macho."

Every afternoon about 4, Ms. Sopp would go to the mail room and meet Newmeyer. They knew virtually every inch of Inglis House and traveled the halls together in search of a little privacy, a place to hold hands.

Ms. Sopp motored along in her battery-powered wheelchair. Newmeyer, on his gurney, would grab the back and catch a tow – a caravan of love.

"She was my hope," Newmeyer said yesterday, before a small memorial service outside Ms. Sopp's room. "She was my light in the darkness."

Ms. Sopp, survived by four sisters and two brothers, will be buried next to her mother in a cemetery near Wilkes-Barre, overlooking a valley and a church she loved, with bells that chime.

POSTSCRIPT

Ron Speer, my first editor, used to say good reporters are lucky, and by that of course he meant hard work and sound instincts put good reporters in a position to get lucky. And this story may be a dark but accurate example.

I had been writing about aging issues for the paper, and when I heard about Ann, I went to do a feature on her. I couldn't believe what an amazing life she had lived. I visited her twice, spending much of each day with her. A few days later, as I was writing the story (I had gotten interrupted for a few days working on a news story) I heard that she had gone to the hospital and died. Because I had spent time with her, I was able to write this amazing obituary.

I include this story in the book because it contains one of my favorite scenes. The image of this frail woman motoring down the hallway, Yuri trailing on his gurney – their caravan of love – was one of the most beautiful things I have ever seen. Talk about light in the darkness! Just remembering it now, my heart fills.

I hadn't yet assigned a photographer, believing I had time. I'm sad we journalists never captured this scene on film.

In 2014, over a decade later, I decided to check on Yuri. He had finally stopped delivering the mail. He'd had a stroke, and he could no longer pull himself on the stretcher, could no longer get around, and could not even feed himself. His loneliness and depression had gotten worse.

On his dresser was a picture of himself and his beloved Ann at a party. He still thought about her every day. Most who knew her had died, retired or moved on to other jobs. Everyone at Inglis House now knew him only as George. I couldn't help thinking, imagining Ann's voice, saying, "Yuri, why didn't you get into the back seat?" But if he had, they never would have found one another.

My mother in Fort Tryon Park, New York City, around age 20

Thomas Vitez, my father, in one of his proudest moments

MY JOURNEY AS A STORYTELLER

The inspiration of my parents' lives

I think the simple truth is I am a storyteller because of my parents. I grew up part of their amazing story.

In 1933, when my mother, a German Jew, was 7, Hitler came to power. "The skating rink where I used to go in winter," she recalled, "had a sign posted: 'Juden Verboten.' The SS marched endlessly in the streets and my classmates called me Jude and beat me up on the way home from school."

One night in 1937, without warning, her parents dropped her at her grandparents' house and moved to Belgium to start a new life. They figured it would be easier without their daughter, and once settled they would send for her.

"I do not understand how they could have left me behind, knowing that they could never come back," my mother wrote a few years ago in a 25-page memoir. "It all came to an abrupt end when my grandfather and I took the train to the Dutch border. He did not want to take me. Life in Germany under the Nazis was dangerous enough without taking added risks. I could hear my grandparents argue about it, but they had no choice. They had gotten word from my father to take me to the German side of the border at a particular time. My grandfather must have gone right back to Krefeld and I walked across the border to meet my parents on the other side. I cannot visualize it anymore. It all must have been so frightening that I suppressed it." She was 11.

My mother was living in Belgium when the Germans invaded May 10, 1940. She was initially happy when she heard the bombing because she had a big test and knew school would be canceled. She had no idea what those bombs really meant. She quickly found out.

They fled to France, but her father was apprehended because he was a German, and sent to an internment camp in France. My mother and her mother hid in basements for days, and then just went back to their Antwerp home, hoping somehow my grandfather would make contact.

"I lived in constant fear," she said. "German soldiers were quartered in many houses on the street and the British bombed us nightly."

They did get word that summer that her father was in a detention camp in Perpignan. It is her understanding that someone paid women to sleep with the guards, who then let her father go. They met him in December 1940 in Lyons.

They had to leave Europe. The only place they could get a visa to was Ecuador, and Ecuador would take only Catholics. So in Lyons, in the first months of 1941, my mother stood in breadlines every morning and went to a convent in the afternoon to become a Catholic.

"I kept telling those sweet nuns day after day that I did not believe any of it and did not want to be baptized," my mother wrote. "With infinite patience and faith, they kept telling me that I was just a child and that they and my parents knew what was good for me."

They set sail from Marseilles on May 15, but the ship went straight to Casablanca, where my mother and her parents waited, just as in the famous movie with Humphrey Bogart and Ingrid Bergman. The passengers were taken by train to a village in the desert, where they bunked in straw in old military barracks, and soon my mother got malaria. Still very sick, she and her parents took another train to Tangiers, and finally on August 4, 1941, they set sail on the Cuidad de Sevilla. My mother and her parents had no money, and my mother just assumes that relatives who had escaped to Toronto somehow paid for the passage.

They arrived in New York on August 21, 1941. My mother and her parents only had transit visas – their destination was Ecuador – so they were taken to Ellis Island, the federal immigration processing station in New York harbor. They were among the last immigrants to pass through.

My mother spent five weeks on Ellis Island, battling bouts of malaria but doing her best to conceal it. Meanwhile, Jewish charities were working hard to get the transit visas converted into visitors' visas, which would allow my mother and her parents to come ashore and give them time to work on getting permanent status.

At the end of September, their dream came true. A ferry took them to Manhattan to begin their new lives. My mother was 15. Eventually she and her parents settled in Washington Heights.

In 1984, after Ellis Island was reopened by the National Park Service, I went there with my wife and parents. The ranger dutifully asked if anyone on our tour had relatives who had gone through Ellis Island. "I came through here," my mother said meekly.

I tear up now as I think about it. The ranger and all the people on the tour stopped and suddenly treated my mother like royalty, and everyone felt so lucky to have history brought to life by this woman who shared a little of her story.

* * *

My father grew up in a comfortable Budapest home. My father's uncle, Uncle Laci, a chemist, had immigrated to America in 1933 and immediately urged his sister back in Budapest to sign up for the American quota. Each country in those days was rationed a certain number of entrants into America each year, and the Hungarian quota was fewer than 100.

In 1936, my Hungarian grandparents couldn't imagine that Nazism and Hitler were a threat to their marvelous, cultured Budapest life. My father and his parents were Jewish but saw themselves as Hungarians first and thought Hungary's leaders would always protect them. But my grandparents listened to Uncle Laci and put their name on the list.

Even in 1940, when their name at last came up on the quota list, their decision to go was still considered risky and bold by their peers. "My parents' courageous act saved our lives," my father wrote in his memoir, "and when we left on the Italian ocean liner Roma," it was one of the last ships to pass through the Straits of Gibraltar before Italy declared war on the Allies and the British sealed off the Mediterranean.

Into New York harbor they sailed on May 16, 1940, welcomed by Uncle Laci and his wife, Aunt Zsuzsi. (I have always loved all these wonderful Hungarian and German nicknames of my relatives: Bözsi, Zsuzsi, Laci, Mutti, Muschi, Aggi, Josca and so many more.) They settled temporarily into New Jersey, and my dad's cousin, Peter, Laci's son, taught my dad a poem to recite to his teacher on the first day of school. Peter assured my dad the teacher would love it. My dad recited: "Roses are red, violets are blue, teachers stink and so do you." His teacher had a good sense of humor.

They soon settled into Washington Heights in New York City, home to so many European Jewish immigrants. My father went to high school and on evenings and weekends he set tables at Zimmernman's Hungaria on Broadway for $8 a week. His first purchase with his earnings in America was a Royal typewriter on sale at Macy's for $34. Is writing in my blood or what?

He got drafted July 31, 1944, a few weeks after graduating from high school and also only weeks after D-Day. To his great surprise, perhaps because of his flat feet, he was sent not to the infantry but to Army Air Corps basic training in the Texas Panhandle.

"These six weeks of basic training were really a transforming event in my life," he wrote. "A scant four years ago I was a refugee who could not even speak English, and here was a newly minted soldier, in the heart of Texas, surrounded by buddies, noncoms, and officers from all over the USA but mostly from small towns and rural areas. And all those southern belles, with their deep accents and fantastic bodies. But they were not really interested in buck privates like me, here today and gone tomorrow, so mostly I learned to drink beer and eat steak."

My father spent two years in the Army. He was trained as a radio operator and assigned to the 4th Emergency Rescue Squadron on Guam. He spent the last months of the war flying in B-17s, looking for downed pilots in the South Pacific. Aside from his children, there wasn't anything he was more proud of than his military service. Nothing made him feel more like an American. And literally, as he lay dying from cancer, so many years later, among his last wishes was that the American flag fly at his memorial service.

I tear up as I write this. How this man loved his country!

He came home from war in July 1946, attended City College of New York majoring in accounting, and began dating my mother, whom he had met through a mutual friend, another Jewish refugee. He eventually got a job with the Internal Revenue Service and, after several years as a revenue agent in Buffalo, was transferred to headquarters in Washington, D.C. He saw government service as the highest calling. My parents and their three young sons settled into a new split-level brick home in suburban Virginia and built a beautiful life.

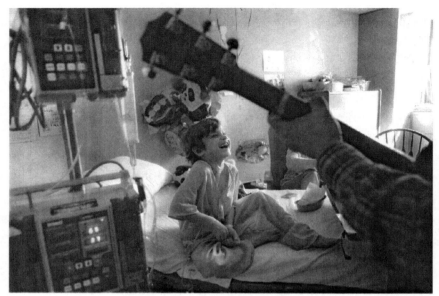

Photo by APRIL SAUL

Connor Nestler laughs as Woody sings to him

7

THE MUSICIANARY

Winning the hearts of children with song

At hospitals, ailing youngsters keep asking for Woody Wolfe

April 23, 2000

Every weekday, Woody Wolfe does something he thought he never could.

Usually by the time the sun is up in the Susquehanna River town of Danville, he's on the road in a 1988 Plymouth Reliant that already has given him 118,000 miles. In the backseat is a worn-out guitar, cracked and epoxied in six places, and a bulging canvas pack that is his "magic bag."

He might be headed for Pittsburgh or Hershey or Philadelphia, but the end of the line is always the same: a hospital where sick children, many gravely so, wait for Woody Wolfe to sing to them.

He calls himself a musicianary. It's a word he made up for the calling that he answered eight years ago, when he quit his job as a cardiac technician and began riding the circuit of pediatric wards across Pennsylvania.

"The last place I want to be is with families in the midst of the most horrible sufferings of their children," he said. "I don't want to be there. Yet God has shown me the most incredible blessings there."

Like in Jake Waltman's room at St. Christopher's Hospital for Children. In the world of chronically ill youngsters, the 7-year-old Feasterville boy is a "frequent flier" – a regular – whose cancer keeps him coming back.

On a Thursday, a Philly day for Woody, Jake lay curled in pain in bed, alternately sleeping and vomiting. Woody peeked in, but when Jake's father and the nurses waved him off, he moved to the next room.

A moment later, John Waltman rushed into the hall, tears in his eyes.

"Please, can you come play for Jake?" he asked. The boy, he said, had "hollered out, 'Woody!' "

Woodrow Wilson Wolfe Jr. is 46 and looks like an old folkie, bald and bearded, with wire-rim glasses and sandals that he wears through the winter. He can play hundreds of songs by heart. "Itsy Bitsy Spider" for a toddler, Carole King's "You've Got a Friend" for a lonely teenager, "The Booger Song" for a child who will laugh at nothing else.

"In a hospital where there are so many people ready to poke you and measure you and examine you, he just comes in and gives," said Gail Hertz, a pediatric resident at the M.S. Hershey Medical Center, where Woody spends Wednesdays.

"The kids go nuts for him. So do the nurses," said Lynn Dempsey, a cardiac ICU nurse at Children's Hospital of Philadelphia, his Friday stop. "I follow him around."

In a simple studio he built in his little white duplex by the river, Woody has recorded five cassettes of songs. He has given away 30,000 copies to children and their families, so his music can be there when he is not.

He charges nothing for what he does. Hospitals give him small stipends – $75 a day, tops – and donations from churches and admirers keep him on the road. When he got a haircut the other morning, his barber wouldn't take his money. "Put it in your gas tank," he said.

Woody might travel with just $10 in his wallet, yet he counts himself a rich man.

"People often live their whole lives hoping to meet their heroes," he said. "I get to meet mine every day."

* * *

Walking down a corridor at Hershey Medical Center the other day, he spotted one of them.

Jonathan Jagozinski, a Luzerne County boy who has battled leukemia for two of his four years, was playing in bed with Power Rangers and Legos.

The boy looked up.

"Woodyyyyyyyy!" he yelled.

Soon he was singing along to "Love Is." Bending his knees when Woody sang "Love is deeper than the oceans." Raising his arms as far as they would go when Woody sang "Love is higher than a mountain." Flexing his muscles when Woody sang "Love is stronger than a freight train." Running to Woody and hugging his hips with all his might when the song ended.

"Through every spinal tap that Jonathan has ever had," said his mother, Jeanne, "he had Woody's music on."

* * *

At age 10, Woody Wolfe wanted to be a minister, but he grew up to be a paramedic, assigned to helicopter medevac at Geisinger Medical Center in Danville, his hometown.

One afternoon in 1981, he got a call from pediatric oncology. A 17-year-old cancer patient, bored with lying in bed, wanted a ride. He took the teen up in the chopper.

Woody mentioned he played guitar, and had ever since the Beatles invaded America. "Maybe I could come by and play," he offered.

Almost as soon as he said it, Woody panicked. He was terrified at the thought of playing to sick children, of even talking to them.

But he was stuck. So he went. The children loved him.

At the time, Woody was thinking about quitting his job and going into seminary. He had a long talk with a minister, a friend who knew about Woody's debut in pediatrics.

"Did you ever think your ministry is right where you're at?" the pastor asked.

"It can't be," Woody argued. "I crumble around critically ill kids."

"That's the point," the pastor replied. "You rely on the greater strength to get through it. That's when you can really get through to parents and kids."

Woody went back to the Geisinger children's ward – every few months at first, then almost daily on his lunch break and after work.

"I'd see these kids who looked pretty miserable and soon enough they're smiling," he said. "And their parents, they were pretty wiped out. But when they saw their kids smiling, they became so rejuvenated. To me, that was just a joy."

There Woody met Little Matt.

Seven years old, he was not only a cancer patient but also a foster child. Woody, his wife, Debbie, and their two sons – one of whom also is named Matt – visited the boy so often that "he really became like ours," Woody said.

Little Matt was 10 when he died.

"The last thing he said to me," Woody said, "was, 'You'll be OK when I'm gone. But I couldn't have done it without you. I love you.' "

Woody paused. "I think that's as close as I've come to really knowing what these parents feel."

A year later, Woody left Geisinger, where he had become a technician. He called his new one-man mission Heart to Hand Ministries.

His wife, a day-care worker, encouraged him – but kept her distance from his work.

She told him, "Fine, if that's what you want to do." But after the pain of Little Matt's death, "I just can't get involved with every child."

Word of Woody's music was spread by families, physicians and staff at Geisinger. Soon he was playing hospitals in Arizona, Florida, South Carolina, and camps for sick children as far away as Montana.

In the last year, he has stayed closer to home, to be consistently available to Pennsylvania children.

On Mondays, he drives to Children's Hospital of Pittsburgh, or occasionally to Baltimore.

On Tuesdays, he plays Geisinger. Wednesdays, Hershey. Thursdays and Fridays, Philadelphia – with a night at a Motel 6 in King of Prussia.

He always drives the back roads, a tape recorder on the seat beside him. When inspired or discouraged by the day's experience, he talks.

Coming over Blue Mountain in Schuylkill County on a recent morning, he watched a hawk catch the wind and soar over his car.

Woody recorded: "The beauty of this hawk comes from it simply being what it was created to be, no more no less. My prayer today is, like that hawk, I might be simply what God created me to be.

"May I catch the wind of His spirit and fly."

* * *

Connor Nestler, 8, lay alone in his bed at St. Christopher's, surrounded by an armada of machines.

When Woody asked whether he wanted a song, Connor refused. Woody doesn't mind if children send him away. They have so little control over their lives, he figures, that if he can give them even the power to say no – well, that's giving them something important.

He left a tape.

A week later, he visited again.

Connor saw him coming and sat up in bed. Woody pulled a chair alongside and, in a voice as easy as an old shoe, started out with "You've Got a Friend in Me," from the movie *Toy Story*.

Two weeks later, Connor had improved enough to move from intensive care to a regular pediatric floor. When a nurse told him Woody was around, Connor posted himself by his door and, at the first sight of him, screamed "Wooodddyyy!"

The boy had a request: "Can you do 'The Booger Song?'"

Always aiming to please, Woody began singing, to the tune of "She'll Be Comin' Round the Mountain":

"There's a booger in the sugar. No there snot."

Connor laughed so hard and loud that parents and children from other rooms gathered at the door.

"That was pretty disgusting, huh?" Woody asked at the end.

"Yeah," Connor replied. "Can you sing it again?"

* * *

Slung over Woody's shoulder with his guitar is the magic bag.

When he digs into it, just about anything could come out.

For families who live more than an hour from the hospital, he reaches deep and fishes out phone cards with 30 minutes of free long-distance calling – a gift from a church that supports him.

He might come up with tapes and batteries, candies and McDonald's coupons, even a picture of himself at age 19, long-haired, in front of a VW bus.

"I know what it's like to lose your hair," he tells youngsters in oncology as he shows the photo. "I'm still waiting for mine to grow back."

He also carries a legal pad with a rap song that he and a patient are writing (they call themselves The Candy Wrappers).

Always with him is a Bible. Woody doesn't sing religious songs or talk about his faith, unless a patient or family asks. The Bible is for himself, to read after hard days.

Also tucked in the magic bag is bereavement literature. Because many of the children Woody meets don't go home.

At St. Christopher's recently, he spent an afternoon with Erica Willits, a 4-year-old with cancer.

While he sang to Erica, said nurse Rhonda Gibson, "her heart rate and blood pressure got better. And I was, like, 'Woody can't leave!' "

Ninety minutes after he did, the girl died.

In the last year, Woody has sung at about 70 funerals and memorial services, and he sang at Erica's, in Fishtown. He performed one of his own compositions, "Because of You," and her family, having heard it so often before, joined in:

> *Because of you, I've learned to live,*
> *Sharing the joy that your life gives.*

Which is why, the next day, Woody Wolfe was on the road again to a hospital, where sick children waited to hear him sing.

Postscript

Woody is still at it. An amazing man and much loved. I admire him for his courage, for his decision to spend his life as he has.

The best stories come from being rooted in the world. I coached youth soccer with a friend in our community. My friend went to Ursinus College, and his college roommate had a very sick daughter. When he went to visit her in the hospital, Woody was singing to her. My friend called me up, and told me he might have a good story. Was he ever right!

Photo by APRIL SAUL

Woody Wolfe making his rounds, about to visit another sick child

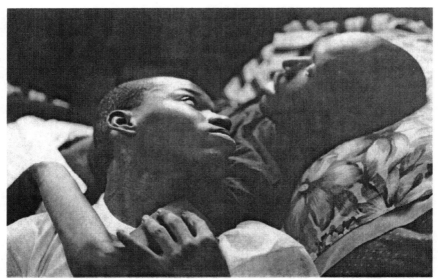

Photo by RON CORTES

A man dying of cancer comforts his son. The
photographers also won Pulitzer Prizes.

8

FROM THE PULITZER SERIES

Families agonizing over when to let go
Medicine can keep a patient alive even if recovery is impossible

November 17, 1996

Patricia Moore read a poem to her husband in the intensive-care unit. She stood beside him wearing a surgical gown, holding the dog-eared book in her latex gloves.

Through her surgical mask came the tender, muffled words of "Knee-deep in June," by James Whitcomb Riley:

> *Orchard's where I'd ruther be –*
> *Needn't fence it in fer me!*

Gene Moore lay before her, unconscious. An IV line entered a vein in his neck and ran through his heart, into the pulmonary artery. It measured blood flow and carried five medicines into his infected body.

A ventilator tube ran like a garden hose down his throat. A feeding tube pushed through his nose and into his stomach.

Bags on his legs inflated and deflated every few minutes to prevent clotting. A catheter drained urine from his bladder. He wore orthotic boots to keep his feet bent so that, should he ever, miraculously, get out of bed, this retired 63-year-old steelworker would be able to stand.

Mrs. Moore stood beside her husband of 44 years, her heart aching with indecision.

Were she and her two sons doing the right thing putting him through this torture? Or should they stop?

Should they tell the doctors to let him die?

* * *

Medicine has gotten so good at keeping people alive that Americans increasingly must decide how and when they will die.

They must choose if death will come in a hospital room with beeping machines and blinking monitors or if it will come at home, with hospice workers blunting the fear and pain that so often accompany the final hours.

And soon, they may have a remarkable choice: Will they kill themselves with their doctor's help?

Americans are demanding options because they are beginning to care as much about the quality of their death as the length of their life.

They want control at the end. They want a humane death, a good death.

Throughout the country, in hospitals and medical schools and courtrooms and statehouses, reformers are pushing hard to improve the way Americans die.

Already, they have won the right for families to turn off ventilators, hold back life-sustaining drugs, and even take out feeding tubes.

Nearly 400,000 Americans every year now seek a tranquil death through hospice. Since 1982, when Medicare began covering hospice care, the cost had grown to $2 billion in 1996.

Only recently had the world heard of Jack Kevorkian. In 1996, two federal appeals courts ruled that patients have a right to assisted suicide. The issue now stands before the U.S. Supreme Court.

With this quest for control have come difficult ethical, social and personal decisions that Americans are only beginning to wrestle with.

The intensive-care unit offers a hope for recovery, but the price can be a miserable death. Deciding when to surrender can be a torture all its own.

Thousands of Americans find themselves in the same position as Mrs. Moore, standing beside a loved one, in intensive care, wondering what's happening, wondering what's the right thing to do.

* * *

For 24 years, Gene Moore had lived in an 18th-century farmhouse in rural Ottsville, Upper Bucks County.

From his back porch, he watched the sun set over endless hills. He grew grapes and made wine, shoed horses, and played classical guitar and poker with his grandsons. Every summer he'd go crabbing with the family in Ocean City, Maryland, and pour on the bay seasoning.

He dreamed of buying an RV and roaming the country with his wife and younger son, Ron, 35, who still lived at home. But then his lungs went bad – pulmonary fibrosis. By January, Gene Moore couldn't breathe. Then came the lung transplant in February at the University of Pennsylvania Medical Center. A step from death, he was reborn.

He regained enough stamina to walk two miles a day on his treadmill and went to a flea market where he showed strangers the scar – shaped like bat wings – that streaked across his chest. "One hundred and twenty staples," he would tell them proudly.

He bought a 1981 Thunderbird, a lifelong dream, and drove it twice before he found himself back in the hospital in late June. His body had rejected the lungs.

On July 7, Gene Moore was wheeled into Penn's medical intensive-care unit – the MICU. He was being kept alive by mechanical ventilator, feeding tube, blood transfusions, blood-pressure medicines, steroids, antibiotics. He was heavily sedated.

Like many Americans, the Moores believed doctors could save almost anyone, cure almost anything. They had experienced one miracle, the transplant, and expected another.

Death was inconceivable.

But so was the agony of the MICU - until they lived it.

* * *

The moment Mrs. Moore walked through the big double doors into the ninth-floor MICU, she entered a world like no other, a world in which she was a complete stranger. Death was so near, the language of doctors so foreign.

The MICU consisted of 12 large rooms, wrapped around a busy nurses' station. Inside each room lay an extremely sick patient surrounded by a confusing array of pumps and monitors incessantly beeping. A solemn-faced visitor often sat at the bedside.

Doctors, nurses went in and out. They were busy, on the move.

Gene Moore landed in 979, a corner room with a large window facing the nurses' station. Because of the risk of infection, everyone had to put on a gown, gloves and mask to enter his room.

Mrs. Moore usually sat in a chair next to her husband's bed, waiting for a good word from a doctor. Something, anything, to sustain her, to give her hope. Perhaps his creatinine level was up, or some other obscure measurement she didn't understand.

Mr. Moore didn't have a living will – a legal document stating his preferences for end-of-life treatment – because he thought, incorrectly, that a will would take the decision-making out of his wife's hands and give it to the doctors.

Mrs. Moore and Ron believed they would be in control.

"We are his living will," she said. But Mrs. Moore didn't understand what was happening, even though the doctors and nurses were very pleasant and answered all her questions.

"I just don't know what to ask," she said.

How could she decide what was best?

"You just don't know how far, how much to let him go through," Mrs. Moore said. "He has been to hell and back. He's had so many blood tests. His arms are so scarred they can't even get a needle in."

So she sat, hour after hour, day after day, beside her husband. He lay there, unresponsive, somewhere between life and death, while she passed the time doing the most ordinary things: reading him poems, planning vacations, mulling recipes for baked lobster Savannah.

She wanted to believe he would return home again, soon. After all, almost 80 percent of the 700 or so patients treated in Penn's MICU each year leave alive, so why not her husband?

* * *

Many reformers believe that doctors and hospitals still focus too much on curing and not enough on caring for people at the end.

The largest clinical study ever of the sick and dying (10,000 patients, five hospitals, eight years) reported last year that more than a third of terminally ill hospital patients died in pain.

Many spent their last hours isolated from their families, their wishes about withdrawing life support ignored by doctors.

Patient-doctor communication in the last days of life was poor, according to the $28 million study, funded by the Robert Wood Johnson Foundation in Princeton.

"We withdraw care when it's too late, when death is certain, when even the janitor knows," said Joan Teno, of the Center to

Improve Care of the Dying at George Washington University, a lead researcher in the study, which ended in 1994.

Advocates for change believe doctors are too optimistic, too sparing in what they tell patients. They say that families would be more willing to accept death earlier if doctors were more honest, more realistic.

Doctors at Penn's MICU say they are aggressive at withdrawing care – making the decision that further efforts would be futile and recommending to the family that the patient be allowed to die as comfortably as possible.

They say the families don't want them to quit.

"Almost invariably families want us to push on when we want to stop," said Dave Gaieski, a resident doctor on the MICU.

"It's only one in 20 that a family comes to us and says stop," said Cheryl Maguire, a MICU nurse for 10 years. "It's much more the case that we see there's no hope, and we keep working until they get to that point, too."

Ronald Collman, one of two attending doctors on the MICU last July and the man ultimately responsible for Gene Moore's care, knew that the odds were against him. But some patients like Moore survived. Collman thought Mr. Moore had a chance, and he knew the family wanted to fight.

Collman said he believed MICU doctors give patients the ending they want.

"I think most of our patients die with dignity," Collman said. "We've confused death with dignity with a romantic death. Death usually is not beautiful. It's ugly. Death with dignity is death that's right for them. I don't mean futile things, but fighting and really giving them a chance.

"Patients are here because their family chose an aggressive fight. To die after an aggressive fight is an honorable thing, appropriate for that person."

* * *

Mrs. Moore made a friend – Mary Lou Stephano, the wife of the comatose cancer patient in the next room.

The Stephanos had met as students on the Penn campus 40 years earlier, in Houston Hall, across the street from the hospital.

Mrs. Stephano also expected her husband, Stephen, 62, to wake up and enjoy life again – at least for another year. Mrs. Stephano looked forward every morning to talking with Mrs. Moore in the lounge. Better than even Mrs. Stephano's children, Pat Moore understood what she was going through.

On Friday afternoon, July 19, doctors requested a meeting with Mrs. Stephano and her family. They scheduled it for Sunday. Mrs. Stephano told Mrs. Moore she thought the meeting was to update the family on how her husband was progressing. She was impressed by how considerate the doctors were.

Nurse Maguire knew that doctors didn't have much hope that Mr. Stephano would recover, and she wanted, gently, to alter Mrs. Stephano's expectations. Maguire told her that after three weeks in the MICU her husband would face a very long recovery.

Sunday morning, a few hours before the meeting, Mrs. Stephano asked the resident a blunt question: "Is he going to wake up?" She expected him to say, "Of course."

The resident took a long time to answer.

"A 15-to-20 percent chance," he told her.

Mrs. Stephano was stunned.

During the hour-long meeting, the news only got worse.

Cynthia Robinson, an attending doctor working with Collman on the MICU in July, called the meeting.

Attending doctors decide when it's time to recommend withdrawal, when to call a family meeting.

Resident doctors say some attendings on the MICU have a reputation for keeping patients going as long as possible, while others recommend withdrawing life support much sooner.

Whenever Robinson or Collman held a family meeting, at least a couple of residents or interns sat in. What they learned was a vital part of their medical education: how to help families let go.

Robinson brought the Stephano family up to date. She was pleasant, thorough and compassionate. But she was also clear: If Mr. Stephano didn't improve within a week, she would suggest withdrawing life support.

"Keep him comfortable," the doctor said, "and let the inevitable happen."

One son and a daughter-in-law sobbed quietly, crumpling tissues into piles on the conference table.

"If he could participate in this discussion here," the doctor asked, "what would he want?"

"We never had a chance to talk about it," Mrs. Stephano said. "But he lived for his mind."

Robinson left the family members to talk among themselves. After some discussion, the family concurred with Robinson.

As they walked back to Mr. Stephano's room, Mrs. Moore could see their faces, their tears, as they passed by.

Now she knew what the meeting was really about.

* * *

Mrs. Moore and Ron always tried to arrive by 9:30 a.m., in time for staff rounds. Not that they understood much, but they might pick up something.

On Wednesday morning, July 24, they found Collman and a bevy of younger doctors clustered outside Mr. Moore's room.

Paul McGovern, the resident in charge of Mr. Moore's day-to-day care, was giving his usual technical talk. The Moores stood off to the side and listened.

"Good bowel sounds...hypernatremic...positive 2 liters over last 24 hours...his wedge went up initially, BP 130/70...white blood count was point 6."

"Oooooh," flinched Collman. "What was his chest film?"

"Worse," said Joe Schellenberg, another doctor. "Significantly worse."

After more discussion, McGovern concluded, "The plan here is pretty much the same, changing his lines over, begin weaning...."

Mrs. Moore looked through the window at her husband and saw blood in his urine bag.

After the medical report, Collman walked over to Ron and his mother, as the residents, interns, medical and pharmacy students stood by quietly. When families are around, they get quiet.

"He's had some backward steps," Collman said, looking into Mrs. Moore's soft, green eyes, which welled with tears behind the mask.

"His white count is down, most likely one of the drugs we're giving him."

She pointed to the bag with the bloody urine.

"Probably from the low platelets," he said reassuringly. "Not something to worry about."

"His X-ray is looking worse," Collman said. "The remarkable thing is his lungs are functioning well. It doesn't make sense; they look so bad, yet are functioning well."

Mr. Moore wasn't improving. And the dangerously low white blood-cell count signaled another crisis, this time for his bone marrow.

Collman knew the odds of recovery were getting slimmer with each passing day in the MICU.

"We should all get together, in the next few days, and talk about what's happening," he said to Mrs. Moore and Ron, "just so we're all on the same page."

Mrs. Moore let go a long sigh. Ron reached out and held his mother, hugged her, then held her hand.

"Doesn't sound good," he said.

"No, it's not good," she agreed.

The Moores slowly, sadly, began to put on their masks, gowns and gloves.

"He's a fighter," Mrs. Moore said quietly. "But I don't think he'd like this. What do you think, Ron?"

"He'd hate this," Ron said. "He'd hate it."

* * *

The next day, 43-year-old Terry Moore, the elder son, visited his father.

Terry is a fundamentalist minister, pastor of Victorious Christian Church in Marlton. He believes in the word of God. He believes that everything possible should be done to sustain a human life.

Taking his hand, Terry spoke to his unconscious father with a preacher's conviction.

"You're doing fine," he said. "Everything is going good. You're doing all right. BP's good, heartbeat is good, Dad. They're giving you some food, too, Dad. So you have every reason to be encouraged. We love you. And Jesus loves you most of all. He's right here by your side. He's got the situation right under control...."

Terry Moore shared none of his mother's reservations.

He told a story about his wife's grandmother in Northeast Philadelphia. She had a stroke. "They were all getting ready to shovel dirt on her," he said. "They were withdrawing things from her, and I said, 'What are you doing? She's not dead yet.'"

The grandmother recovered.

"We believe in God," Terry Moore said. "We believe in prayer. We believe in miracles. So as long as there is life, there is hope."

* * *

By Friday, July 26, Mr. Moore had a new neighbor, two doors down.

Rose Kennedy, 75, had had a stroke getting ready for church that week.

In the MICU, Mrs. Kennedy was put on a ventilator. But the morning following her stroke, her family found her living will in a dining room drawer.

"If to a reasonable degree of medical certainty my condition is hopeless. . ," the living will said, "if I have brain damage that makes me unable to recognize people or communicate . . , I do not want my life prolonged. I do not want mechanical ventilation...."

The family members agonized over what to do.

Collman gathered them in the conference room. He said Mrs. Kennedy wasn't in pain and might recover some function in the next few days as swelling in the brain diminished. He urged them to delay a decision.

"Her paper says no tube and no vent," insisted Betty Pryor, her daughter and the person Mrs. Kennedy had designated as her proxy.

"I agree, that's what the paper says," Collman said. But he thought she might improve.

"She's going to have brain damage. Not enough that she'll be a vegetable. But the difficult question is how much brain damage would be acceptable to her."

"When she filled out this paper, she didn't tell me anything," the daughter said. "That's why she's on the ventilator now."

The daughter was crying. "It's just so hard to make a decision. So many ifs, buts."

"Her condition is not really covered in the will," Collman said.

Betty read aloud the key sentence: "I do not want mechanical respiration, no artificial nourishment."

Collman was quick to respond.

"When somebody says no artificial ventilation, we never had a chance to ask her about four days of artificial ventilation. We see a lot of strokes. From our point of view, that's not an extreme amount of time."

"Betty, let's give her two more days and see," said one of Rose Kennedy's sisters.

"OK," whispered the daughter, crying. "I'm just trying to do what she asked me to do...."

Two days later, when Collman said it was unlikely Mrs. Kennedy would improve, the family chose to remove all life support.

Mrs. Kennedy died peacefully a day later, her family at her bedside, soft jazz playing in the background.

* * *

On Saturday, Mr. Moore was worse than ever. Even though he was sedated, he was so agitated. To his wife it seemed as if he were trying to wake up and talk, to scream.

And his kidneys were starting to fail, a complication of his many medicines.

About 3:30 p.m., Paul McGovern, the resident, talked about Mr. Moore in the doctors' conference room.

"He's losing all his cell lines," McGovern said. "Reds, whites and platelets. He's transfusion-dependent right now."

He elaborated on the medical dilemma that Mr. Moore had become.

The treatments were wreaking their own havoc: One anti-infection drug was damaging his blood cells; another impaired his kidneys; infection-fighting steroids further decimated his immune system. And so on.

"We're doing more harm than good," McGovern said.

"My personal belief is that we probably let these people go on longer than they should."

* * *

Caring for extremely sick people is expensive. The average daily cost at Penn's MICU is $1,575. America has 78,000 intensive-care beds, and the cost of caring for patients in those beds has been estimated at 28 percent of all hospital costs.

Reformers want to make sure that patients get the care they need, but not unnecessary or unwanted treatment.

The key to humane and cost-effective intensive care is to treat those who will benefit, but not squander precious resources and impose futile treatments on those who will not.

But often it is impossible to know who will live and who won't.

Ronald Collman says America wants to offer the most advanced technology and treatments to everyone, yet keep health-care costs down.

How to balance those desires, Collman said, "is a discussion nobody wants to have."

* * *

Later that afternoon, nurse Lorrie Bokelman went into Mr. Moore's room to turn him, a routine procedure.

As she turned him, Mr. Moore stopped breathing and became so agitated that the nurse pulled the curtain shut, leaving Mrs. Moore on the other side. The nurse began to "bag" him, forcing oxygen into his lungs manually.

The curtain, a pretty plaid, fluttered as Mrs. Moore sat in her chair, next to a trash can for old bandages and used gloves, worrying.

She had heard the alarms and beeps, and seen that curtain close so many times, yet it never became easier.

Mrs. Moore folded her face into her hands.

"Is he still kind of out of it?" she asked hopefully.

"Yeah," said Bokelman. "He just tried to hold his breath while we turned him. He looked like a beet for a second."

Bokelman pulled back the curtain.

Mrs. Moore walked to her husband's side; she took his hand, stroked his head, spoke so softly that her words were nearly music.

"How you doing, Love? Just breathe, slow and easy, slow and easy, Babe. It's all right."

* * *

On Sunday, July 28, Mrs. Moore took an RV guide to read. But before she and Ron could gown up, Collman and McGovern called them into the family room.

Mr. Moore's blood pressure was plunging. He appeared more agitated than ever.

Already that morning, doctors had suctioned "coffee grounds" – dried blood – out of his stomach. They also found something alarming on his chest X-ray.

Collman wanted a family meeting.

Mrs. Moore called Terry, then she and Ron collapsed in a corner of the hallway by the waiting rooms, sobbing in each other's arms.

Even though Mrs. Moore had seen so much, had endured so much, 21 days in the MICU, this news devastated her.

Until this point, no doctor had suggested she give up hope.

She still had reservations the following month for their favorite apartment in Ocean City, Maryland.

Collman assigned Mr. Moore a new status: *Do Not Resuscitate: Level B.* This meant that no additional treatment of any kind, no more blood or antibiotics would be given. But life-sustaining care – the ventilator, the blood pressure medicine – would continue.

At least until the family meeting.

Nurse Bokelman injected Moore with a significant dose of an anesthetic to relax him.

When Mrs. Moore gathered herself and walked back into her husband's room, he was resting more easily than he had in a week.

"Ohhhhh, that's better," she said with relief.

When Terry Moore arrived shortly after noon, the family gathered in the family lounge.

"Your dad has been through a series of complications, and with each complication are new complications," Collman said to Terry.

"We gave him a full course of treatment. The bottom line is that he overall has gotten much worse.... The blood counts are worse. He's fevery again. Lungs are worse. And he's had a real deterioration today. The big picture is the situation has progressed to the point where, in my medical opinion, there is no way we're turning this around.

"What worries me today is he seems much more uncomfortable. Lorrie's worked very hard to keep him comfortable.

"What I think we're doing is giving him treatments just to give treatments. They're not helping him. They're not prolonging his life."

Collman continued: "I think we should make absolutely certain he has as much pain medication as possible, even if that means the blood pressure gets lower, because keeping him comfortable is most important.

"I recommend we wean him off all the medications he's on, except for pain and sedation. I think it's likely if we stop the blood-pressure medicine, he won't last very long."

Terry recounted the miraculous recovery of his wife's grandmother.

Terry was polite but direct.

"I don't want your mind-set – whether you're pro-abortion or whatever – to affect your decision," he said to Collman. "Have we maxed out on every technological thing – not just to keep him going – but to bring about a recovery?"

Collman responded softly and looked right in Terry's eyes. Mrs. Moore held her son's hand.

"I believe we have not missed anything that could possibly help him recover. I'm even afraid we have possibly gone too far. We're at the point now, there is no chance of making him better. And I'm afraid we're making him suffer."

Collman asked the family to talk about it and let him know their decision. He shook their hands, thanked them, and left the room.

"Daddy was a fighter, all the way to the end," Mrs. Moore said. "But we have to let him go. Things are overwhelming."

"You make the decision, Mom," said Terry. "I'm satisfied they've done as much as they could do. It's in the hands of God."

Mrs. Moore went to find Mrs. Stephano. She needed someone who understood how she felt.

Doctors had removed all life support from Mr. Stephano two days before and moved him to the step-down unit, down the hall from the MICU, to spend his last days or hours.

Mr. Stephano's room was empty.

He had died the night before.

* * *

By 4 p.m., the hard decision had all been made. Gene Moore was peaceful. His family was resigned to his death. Bokelman inconspicuously reduced the blood pressure medicine. She turned off all the alarms and beeps – no more mechanical distractions.

The family surrounded Gene Moore. They whispered their final farewells. Mrs. Moore rested her head against his chest.

"Love you a whole bunch, Sweetie Pie. I love you so much. Here's Ron, your bowling buddy, holding your bowling hand. Just relax," she said to him softly, almost singing. "Just relax."

By 4:45, he had no blood pressure, but the heart kept fighting. Finally, at 5:15, Gene Moore's heart stopped.

Terry walked out and scribbled on his father's medical chart: "Homeward bound to see Jesus."

* * *

Four days later, on Thursday afternoon, Ron and Terry went to a Quakertown funeral home and returned home with a cardboard box filled with their father's ashes.

Mrs. Moore was surprised at how much the box weighed – four or five pounds.

Just as Gene Moore had wanted, the family gathered in a wooded area of the family's property. In front of a tall pine, on the side of a hill, Mrs. Moore sprinkled the ashes of the man she married at 16. Terry said a prayer.

They opened a bottle of champagne and drank from plastic champagne glasses.

* * *

Six weeks later, Mrs. Moore still couldn't write thank-you notes to those who had sent flowers and cards.

"I just can't get started," she said. "I can't get back to living again."

Every day she relived the MICU.

"I have to conjure up all those awful things in order to say it was the right thing to do," she said. "I have to think of all the bad things to justify why we let him go."

Ron said, in retrospect, that he would have withdrawn care much sooner.

Yet Mrs. Moore said she would do it all over again. She would fight until the doctors gave up hope.

EPILOGUE: Two weeks ago, Mrs. Moore had lunch at Mrs. Stephano's house. They were joined by another woman they met on the MICU, whose mother had died after a long fight. "We all had red noses and went through many tissues," Mrs. Moore said, "but it was very cathartic. It was wonderful."

93

POSTSCRIPT

This story was the most important one of my career, and not just because it was the first in a series that won the Pulitzer Prize. It reflects a discovery and a turning point. I learned an invaluable lesson. Prior to this story, this series, I would write human interest stories, sweet features, which my mother (and many readers) loved. But my father always had the same reaction: Where's the news? Where's the significance? Where's the big picture?

In this story, and in the four that followed in this series, I received the highest praise from both my mother and my father. I was long past living for or needing their approval; that's not my point. But my parents were great test audiences.

I knew I had done something significant; I had married great human interest with an important national issue. This was underscored by reader response, hundreds and hundreds of emails, significant in those early days of email in 1996, as well as passionate phone calls by the hundreds. As one reader wrote of the stories: "They were hard to pick up but harder to put down."

This story had human interest and the qualities my mother loved. But it also included exposition, context, information about important this individual's situation or story illustrated a crucial national issue. Mrs. Moore was just an ordinary American. But her story reflected a national issue – trying to improve how we die in America – and also highlighted one new and critical piece of that struggle: the decision to let somebody die in the intensive care unit. I took short breaks from the narrative flow to provide tight blocks of information about the issue.

So in this series not only did I understand the importance of context and the big picture, but I really developed my ability to use the narrative form. I had conversations with a fabulous editor, Don Drake, about recreating scenes and how to slow down a moment, to draw it out. I grew in so many ways in this series and learned so much. I learned these lessons months before I won any prize.

I remember sitting on the floor in a hallway and writing longhand about scenes I had just observed. I didn't want to wait until I got back to the office, and the waiting room was full and there was no seat. So I sat in a hallway and scribbled. Later, I would revise and check facts. I was in the ICU in July, and the series didn't run until November. Thank God I didn't wait to write.

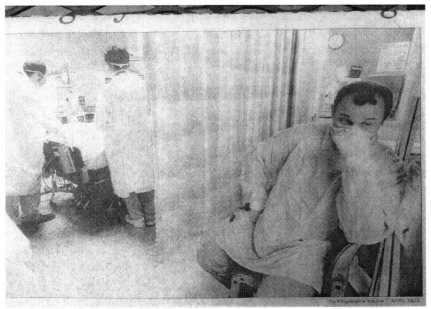

Photo by APRIL SAUL

Ron Moore waits and worries as doctors work on
his father. When was it time to let go?

Photo by APRIL SAUL

Karin Smith, 7, was unable to hold back her tears. This is a
photograph of the original image on microfilm, the best I could find.

9

SCHOOL CLOSIN'

Amid tears, a school shuts its doors

At St. Stephen's, the children learn a sad lesson in life

June 12, 1993

By 8 a.m. yesterday, Sister Nancy Fitzgerald already was working on her second box of tissues. One dress pocket was stuffed with white, the other with yellow.

Standing just inside the schoolyard gate, she greeted the children, all 250 of them, for the last time. Her eyes were rimmed by red half-moons. Her cheeks already smudged with lipstick from parents' kisses. Her heart broken by the sobs of the little ones who buried their faces in her shoulders and hips…"Why, Sister? Why?"

After 103 years at Broad and Butler, St. Stephen School closed yesterday, a victim of cost-saving consolidation by the Archdiocese of Philadelphia. Four other Catholic parish schools in some of the poorest neighborhoods in North Philadelphia – St. Edward, St. Bonaventure, St. Henry and St. Elizabeth – also will be shut down this week or next.

"This is the kind of neighborhood Jesus would be in if he were alive today," said Sister Nancy, principal at St. Stephen for eight years. "The church is leaving a terrible gap, a credibility gap. We're supposed to stand with the neediest...."

"What we created here was unique – like it was an oasis compared to the rest of the neighborhood," she said. "Kids were able to feel really valued, special, challenged. It's certainly not a Camelot – we have our struggles – but the kids are precious."

All week Sister Nancy kept her composure, giving away all the ice cream in the cafeteria, raffling off the office goldfish. When Philadelphia public school officials came to inspect the building – the rumor is the district will buy it – she turned them away.

"That's heartless," she said. "Like picking at the corpse."

St. Stephen's students spent the first hour of school yesterday in their homerooms, getting report cards and health records.

Dot McCarthy, the kindergarten teacher for 16 years, pried the numeral 2 off her classroom door. "And I'm going to take the crucifix," she said, choking up. It was in a laundry basket, next to a dozen other boxes waiting for moving day.

In the back of the room, Annie Ingram, a cafeteria and kindergarten aide for five years, was exchanging phone numbers with twenty-two 6-year-olds.

"I'm going to call them all," she pledged, tears streaming down her cheeks.

Around 9 a.m., the children began to assemble in the main hall, for a procession into St. Stephen's Church and one final prayer service. The church itself will close at the end of this month, one of 15 North Philadelphia parishes that will be merged into six.

"I want us to sing our hearts out," Sister Nancy instructed them. "I want the roof to shake, the windows to rattle!"

And sing the children did. Music teacher Ken Peak, one of the most beloved on the staff, had them singing and swaying, "I just want to thank you, Lord...thank you, Lord...."

The hour-long service was part celebration and part wake, alternately joyous and wrenchingly sad. An entire pew of second graders – Michael Sean, Amber Cain, Cheryia Rosboro, Omar Alvarado, among others – sat sobbing.

Karin Smith, 7, her hair beautifully braided, a crayon box and composition pad on her lap, spilled tears like a driving rain.

"School closin'" was all she could whisper.

Sister Nancy had wanted Cardinal Anthony Bevilacqua to come to the school, just to see what would soon vanish. The first time she wrote him a letter, she received an acknowledgment. The second time, she sent him class pictures and heard nothing.

"The cardinal is supposed to be the shepherd," she said. "He should be here today. You have to face the faces."

Yesterday Sister Nancy handed out honors and attendance awards to the children, and then presented each teacher and staff member with a rose and a fountain pen. As the teachers walked to the altar, the church was filled with thunderous applause and cheering – a sound that will ring in the ears of teachers long after St. Stephen has gone silent.

"It's a very sad day," said seventh-grade teacher Anthony Clemmons. "But there's a certain joy in knowing you've been able to touch the children."

The parents then presented Sister Nancy with a gift. She clutched it like a Bible.

"If you didn't know she was a nun, and if she wasn't white, you'd think she was one of us, fighting for her own brown babies," said Belinda Randolph, the computer teacher and a parent. "She really loves our children."

Finally, Sister Nancy spoke.

"One of the greatest joys of my life has been to work here with you," she said, choking back her tears. "To the students here, I simply say, 'I love you.' I love your goodness, your energy, your laughs and warmth, your jokes and smiles, even the tricks and the hugs. Remember always this special school at Broad and

Butler. Our bonds will not be broken. Our lives and hearts will be one in Jesus."

It was nearing noon now, and the students streamed out into the sunlight of Broad Street, each handed a cross and a plastic "St. Stephen School" cup. They hugged one last time and posed for pictures with their teachers and principal.

The students will be scattered among many Catholic and public schools next year. Sister Nancy will teach sixth grade at St. Columba at 23d and Lehigh.

Gradually, the families drifted home. Sister Nancy and a few teachers remained on the church steps.

Sister Nancy began to speak, then paused and put a tissue to her lips. "The world's broken," she said. "A community like this takes years to build.

"We'll never get it back."

POSTSCRIPT

When news broke that the archdiocese was closing so many schools, the editors assigned me to go to St. Stephen on its last day. The editors intended to run two stories. One would be an overarching news story about how many schools were closing, why they were closing, and where children would be going next year. The second would be some sort of feature story. That second story was to be mine.

When I showed up at the school that morning, I started with no expectations of what I would find or what I would write. I had my eyes and my notebook open. I knew in my gut, though perhaps not in my brain, that I wanted to do a narrative, and therefore I needed to be there for the whole school day. I knew I was writing for the daily paper and deadlines would be tight, so I had better get there early to ease the time pressure.

I saw Sister Nancy out front and was struck immediately by her passion, by her love. As she interacted with the arriving children, I noticed her pockets stuffed with tissues and thought: *This is a terrific detail – tangible evidence of the tears being shed.* I noticed the two different colors of tissues and asked her about it, confirming that she was on her second box.

When the children were in homeroom, I wandered around talking to people. My editor in Norfolk, Ron Speer, had taught me that good reporters are lucky. I happened upon Dot McCarthy as she pried the numeral 2 off her door. She showed me the crucifix in the laundry basket. These details and actions conveyed such images in the mind's eye.

The paragraph about Karin Smith is my favorite. I might have just described her crying with crayons and notebook in her lap. But I thought it important to approach her, get her name, and ask why she was crying. Her comment, "School closin'," and her name gave the paragraph more poignancy and intimacy.

The school day ended at noon, but I waited until only the last few teachers were left on the school steps. I decided I had enough material, and headed back to the office.

I had a rough outline in my head before I typed my first word – I would start with Sister Nancy on the steps and then take readers through the day, simple and effective. I had an idea of the quotes and details I wanted to include. I opened my notebook and found what I needed when I needed it. Even though I had only the afternoon to write, I took my time, and that's actually how you work the fastest – a lesson I learned in a college magazine-writing class taught by Champ Clark, a retired *Time* cover writer. It is a lesson that has proven its worth to me countless times. Don't rush. Do it right the first time. Write with confidence.

Fourteen years later, in 2007, I did a story on Crystal Brown, whose story is next in this book. Crystal's younger two children attended St. Martin De Porres School, and the pastor there, Father Ed, would play a huge role in her life. I got access to the story, and earned the trust of everybody there, in part because Sister Nancy was the principal of the St. Martin De Porres School. She remembered me. She trusted me. And that helped opening doors.

Photo by APRIL SAUL

Crystal Brown carries her son, Chris, down the
steps of St. Martin de Porres Church

10

CRYSTAL'S STORY

She carried the burden of a bitter secret
Until she discovered the power in revealing it

October 1, 2006

The body of Joseph Baxter Sr., 68, lay in an open casket – goatee freshly trimmed, dress shoes shined – as the pastor's eulogy resonated through the crowded funeral home.

"He knew that God had blessed him so that if he never got back what he gave, hallelujah, it didn't matter," the pastor orated.

"He had love in his heart."

Aylisha Brown, 16, sitting in a wheelchair in the front row, turned to her mother.

"Mom, who he talking about?"

"I don't know," Crystal Brown fumed. "Sure ain't my father."

Certainly not the father she knew.

The Rev. Jeremiah Norris continued his tribute, describing how the deceased had donated hot dogs from his small store in North Philadelphia for church picnics, or offered cash from a cigar box every time the pastor stopped in.

Crystal's feet started tapping.

She fought an urge to get up, approach the casket from behind, and knock it over so her father's body would fall onto the floor.

At least the deception would be shattered, and people would wonder what this man had done to Crystal Brown, his own daughter.

But the hot lava of hatred had cooled just enough over the years that Crystal restrained herself. She had her sick children to think about. She had channeled her anger and pain into a maternal mission to fight for them, protect them.

And her long-secret story was beginning to come out anyway.

* * *

Crystal, now 36, first contemplated killing her father when she was 16, watching an episode of *Hardcastle and McCormick*. A bad guy smuggled a gun into the courtroom in a hollowed-out Bible, hoping to shoot Judge Hardcastle.

Of course, Crystal couldn't murder her father. Even though she hated and feared him, she loved him, too. Her first recollections of him are letters from prison. She saved them all. "Chrissy Sweetheart, I do love you and I do miss not seeing you. Have pictures taken so I can see how big you've grown. – With lots of love, Daddy."

When Crystal was 4, in 1974, her father abducted a Center City executive at gunpoint, held him for $250,000 ransom, and let him go 48 hours later.

After he was paroled in 1979, Crystal was so happy to have a daddy. He didn't live with Crystal and her mother; he already had a family. But Crystal would go on Saturdays to clean trucks at his small trucking company.

When she was 8, "he climbed on top of me and molested me in his van," she said. He threatened her and told her not to tell.

Her father declined two requests to be interviewed for this article before he died last winter.

Crystal hated what her father did and would return home scratched and bruised from efforts to get away, but thought, "That's just what daddies do."

This lasted eight years, she said, before she told anyone.

In 1987, when Crystal was a sophomore, her English teacher at Strawberry Mansion High School, Diane Holliday, showed *The Color Purple*, about a 14-year-old abused by her father.

"I am Celie," Crystal suddenly realized. "I'm her."

* * *

The next Saturday, Crystal refused to go to her father's and told her mother why.

Shirley Brown confronted Baxter, who, she said, denied everything. Afterward, Crystal felt her mother no longer believed her.

"I was her child," said Crystal, "and she should have just believed me."

Tears pouring out with the memories, Shirley Brown said that of course she believed her daughter that day, but also that she probably didn't.

Shirley had always thought of Crystal's father as a good man. He had been kind to her when her babies were small, buying food, giving her a job.

On the other hand, Shirley said, "I don't know why it would be unbelievable to me, being as I was molested when I was a child."

She did not take Crystal to a doctor or call police.

The abuse resumed.

No one realized what was happening to Crystal, who had been elected class secretary and wrote poetry for the yearbook.

Evan Brockington, now a chief petty officer in Virginia Beach, Virginia, was crushed when Crystal, 17, rejected his proposal of marriage. He was 20, in the Navy, and asked her to move away with him. He didn't learn about the incest for many years.

"I remember he would come around and give her gifts of money," Brockington said. "It was as if he really loved his daughter, not to do anything to hurt her. That was just a facade."

Crystal's teacher, Holliday, said Crystal had been an excellent student and, at the end of her junior year, won a coveted after-school job at the Federal Reserve Bank of Philadelphia.

But Crystal had other things on her mind and soon quit.

On September 9, 1989, the second week of her senior year, Crystal gave birth to Aylisha.

She said she didn't realize she was pregnant until her sixth month.

Crystal was certain that her own father was Aylisha's father. But on the birth certificate, she listed a neighborhood boy.

"If they didn't believe me at 16," Crystal reasoned, "why would they believe me now?"

Her father demanded she keep the secret, Crystal said, and promised he'd never again get her pregnant.

But four months later, she was pregnant with Chris. She went to an abortion clinic, but changed her mind and decided to keep the baby.

Chris was born 13 months after Aylisha. Again, Crystal listed another boy in the neighborhood as the father.

At least the abuse stopped, she said. Her father had broken his promise, enabling her to break free.

* * *

Crystal poured out her anger at her father into late-night poetry.

Was your nights filled with horror?

Did you ever wonder why you did the things you took such pride in doing?

God, she felt, had abandoned her.

She struggled to care for her two small children while working as a home-health aide and living with her mother, whom she blamed. She worried about Aylisha, who had a thyroid problem and didn't walk until age 3.

When Chris was 5, Crystal gathered the courage to strike back. Spurring her decision was Aylisha's doctor, who urged Crystal to sue for child support.

Crystal went to court alone. Desperation trumped her fear.

She believes the judge had no idea the defendant was her father. "She thought I was trying to get something over on him," Crystal said, "on an older man." When Baxter denied in court that Aylisha and Chris were his children, Crystal hurled a stapler at him.

Family Court Judge Esther R. Sylvester ordered DNA testing.

That night, in Crystal's poetry, a new confidence emerged, maybe even a new image of herself:

...Constantly doing as I was told
Trusting him because he was gold
Now I know that he was not right.
Giving my all to win this fight.

She signed it," Crystal Brown, Survivor."

On May 8, 1996, DNA results confirmed a 99.96 percent probability that Baxter was Chris' father, 99.98 percent for Aylisha.

Baxter signed paternity papers and began paying child support.

Said Crystal: "That was the most important thing I ever did in my life, to prove this man did that to me."

That summer, Crystal said she went to police to file criminal charges but was told that the statute of limitations, then five years for a sex crime, had run out.

That limit is now 12 years, and the District Attorney's Office is trying to eliminate any time limit in light of the clergy sex-abuse scandals.

*　*　*

Crystal has had men in her life, but has never married. She has no close girlfriends. It can be hard for victims of child sexual abuse to build lasting relationships as adults, to trust others.

The father of Crystal's third child, Jasmine, now 11, had to fight Crystal for visitation rights. "I had to take her to court just to be in my daughter's life," he said.

Crystal has little contact with the father of her fourth child, Brandon, 7. She said he would not be a good influence.

She had run-ins with staff at her children's former school, where she hovered constantly, first worrying about Aylisha, then her other children.

Ultimately, the principal said Crystal was too disruptive and, citing a list of infractions, banned her from the building unless she was escorted.

Crystal will never apologize for her behavior as a mother – it is what she's most proud of. Her children are polite, respectful. Aylisha was just elected president of the Widener Memorial School for the physically challenged, which she and Chris attend.

But there are consequences. The children rarely do anything or go anywhere, other than school, without their mother.

Crystal's brother Bill, for instance, long ago gave up inviting Aylisha for sleepovers with his children. Crystal would never let her go, worrying who might drop by.

"If my father could do that to me," she said, "anybody is capable of anything. I'm not taking any chances with my kids."

Most of all, Crystal tried to protect Chris and Aylisha from their father. She didn't even want them to know who he was.

"I smothered them with love so they would never ask."

Then, in 2001, he showed up, uninvited, at Aylisha's sixth-grade graduation.

"Who is this man, Mama?" they kept asking.

"He's your dad," she said, not revealing he was her dad, too.

She felt bad about lying, but would have felt worse telling the truth.

*   *   *

In 2002, Crystal landed a job she loved – driving a SEPTA bus. She always wanted to drive a truck like her father. This was the next best thing.

She would earn $17 an hour, and even started a 401(k). But within months, Aylisha and Chris began falling down.

Crystal had long suspected something wasn't right. Aylisha had had trouble learning to walk, and Chris had been walking on tiptoe since grade school.

This, though, was different.

"Their legs just gave out on them," said Sonya, Crystal's sister. "We knew there was something major wrong going on."

At first, Crystal couldn't face it. She told them to stop being so clumsy, to tie their shoes. But soon the children needed a doctor's note to ride the school elevator.

Aylisha was three days shy of 13 when a doctor asked her to sit on the floor and get up without using her hands.

She couldn't.

Crystal was blown away.

Three weeks later, Crystal learned the children had muscular dystrophy. She remembers this as the worst day of her life.

In her heart, Crystal knew that the incest was to blame.

Later, Gihan Tennekoon, chief of neurology at Children's Hospital of Philadelphia, confirmed it.

Both children had inherited two rare recessive genes – one from their mother and one from their father.

Their form of muscular dystrophy, called limb girdle, attacks the hip and shoulder muscles and can progress to the heart and lungs.

As this sank in, Crystal said, her mission became clear. "I don't want them to be sad," she said. "I will do everything in my power to make them have a better day."

Crystal took them to malls, to parks, to parties, lugging them and their wheelchairs in and out of her 1990 Toyota station wagon. Once she carried Chris up the steep steps of an Air Force jet – in two-inch heels – so he could speed down the runway at a Make-A-Wish Foundation event.

Crystal began missing more and more work. In 2005, SEPTA fired her.

* * *

When she was little, Crystal's father had told her that whatever she did, she should do it the biggest and best she could.

By last fall, she decided to take a dramatic step.

Determined to get a van with a wheelchair lift, she revealed her story in a four-page letter.

"How you going to ask for help," she later explained, "if you don't tell the truth?"

Starting "To Whom It May Concern," she wrote: "There was a time in my life where I had no belief in the Lord. You see I am an INCEST SURVIVOR.... If you could see through my eyes all the pain I have felt you too would have had doubt.... If you can help us, God will bless you 10 times over."

She handed copies to strangers in parks, to dog walkers. She sent one to Oprah Winfrey, another to Allen Iverson. His came back because it had the wrong address.

She also addressed a copy with a glitter pen to "Father Hallinan," and dropped it off at St. Martin de Porres Catholic

Church at 23d Street and Lehigh Avenue, where Jasmine and Brandon, her two youngest, had just started school.

The Rev. Ed Hallinan had never met Crystal. But her letter moved him.

On a windy, cold November morning, he watched as Crystal ascended the rectory steps to meet him, shouldering Aylisha and Chris, one by one, in a fireman's carry.

He loved "the spark in her," he recalled. "She's gritty. She's aggressive. She wasn't going to get locked into that house and have these kids be victims their entire life."

Father Ed turned to his cadre of benefactors who help raise $400,000 a year for the parish.

"I'm in," said one, although the van, customized for two wheelchairs, would cost $53,000.

On Dec. 21, Crystal carried Chris and Aylisha from the station wagon one last time.

In the rectory, they met the benefactor and his family. He was 48, well-known, and asked that his name not be published.

Crystal, tears pouring down her cheeks like rain, hugged him long and tight, as if glue were between them and she wanted to make sure they never came unstuck.

"Thank you," she said.

"Congratulations," he said.

"Thank you so much," she repeated.

He handed Crystal the keys.

"God bless you all," said Crystal. "No more lifting."

The benefactor turned to his children, and hers.

"This is the power of a mother's love," he said. "Remember that. The power of a mother's love. Everything is possible."

* * *

Sharing her story had led to a miracle – the van. Suddenly, she was speaking about the unspeakable.

She talked about it with her mother, and apologized.

"I blamed my mom for a long time," said Crystal. "And it hurt her. But it wasn't her fault. It was his fault."

Crystal insists she wouldn't be the mother she is were it not for her mother's example.

She finally told Chris and Aylisha the whole truth.

Aylisha said she kind of knew.

The children said they were comfortable with *The Inquirer's* publishing their story. They know it's important to their mother. But they prefer to focus on picking out prom shoes or watching pro wrestling.

Who can blame them?

"Life is a real painful thing," said Crystal. "But if they have a mom that loves them...to have this come out is not going to hurt them."

Besides, she said, "how else they going to have some kind of way to talk about their feelings? Eventually it's going to come out to everybody, even though everybody already knows and just doesn't talk about it."

Aylisha revealed a bit of herself in June in a poem.

Do you wish to feel
the way I feel
I doubt it.
'Cause...I can't have love or hold it
I can't talk the way I want...
I can't even show emotion when I need to...
I wish I had an Island all my own to live on...

* * *

One Friday last February, Crystal's father, wheezing and coughing, called.

"Will you ever forgive me?" he asked.

"I already did," she said, and slammed down the phone.

Three days later, he was dead.

A tear rolled down Crystal's cheek. She didn't know why.

"I've dreamed of this day since I was 16," she said.

Emotions swirled within her: She felt cheated. He had asked for forgiveness, yet he had never told her he was sorry. She felt a loss for her children. She had never let them know their father. Now they ever could. She felt panic about losing his child support of $390, paid faithfully each month.

That evening, Crystal called a relative of her father's with whom she was on good terms.

He asked Crystal a question that shocked her.

How did she want Chris' and Aylisha's names listed in the funeral program:

As kids or grandkids?

"You put them down any way you want," Crystal finally replied. "Either way is the truth."

Aylisha and Chris didn't want to go to the viewing and funeral, but Crystal made them.

As Aylisha was getting dressed, she decided to put a dress shoe on one foot, but leave a sneaker on the other.

"This shows how confused I am," Aylisha told her mother. In sympathy and in agreement, Crystal also put on shoes that did not match.

They arrived an hour early. The funeral home was empty, but for the open casket.

Stacked on a table were the programs. Crystal, Chris and Aylisha were all listed as his children – a declaration in print of what had long been whispered.

Crystal pushed her son in his wheelchair toward his dead father, a man he barely knew.

She said to Chris but really to herself, "We can do this."

"Oh, my, he looks the same," she said, arriving at the casket.

They paused in silence, each looking at their father.

"You cool?" Crystal asked.

"Yeah," Chris said. "I'm cool."

Neither shed a tear.

"Say goodbye," said Crystal. "Or hello. Whichever."

In a record of the moment she had so long wished for, Crystal snapped a picture of her father's body, and of Chris in front of the casket. "Just so they can say, 'Mommy took me.'"

She pushed Chris back around. "We can go to [T.G.I.] Friday's now," she joked.

"You ready, Aylisha?" Crystal asked.

"No," she said.

Crystal wheeled Aylisha to the body, but Aylisha would not look.

Crystal took a long look at the once-powerful man and shook her head.

"I don't feel it anymore," she said. "Not no more. I feel safe."

* * *

Any closure that Crystal felt at the funeral quickly vanished.

She'd had this fantasy that her father would one day buy them a house with bathroom doors and showers wide enough for wheelchairs.

The Philadelphia Housing Authority had installed a stair glide in her rowhouse, but she dreamed of a house designed for the disabled. Lifting the children into the tub was exhausting.

He left them nothing.

"My kids have to suffer every single day because of what he did to me," she said. "I hate him. If I could dig him up and kill him again, I would do it."

Crystal became relentless in pursuit of a house. She has called City Councilman Darrell L. Clarke's office, among others, three or four times a day for months.

"I do not have any other constituents like her," said Clarke's administrative assistant, Norma Morales. "The councilman would like to help, but we have to follow the guidelines."

And more and more, she told her story.

At an April "Speak Out" rally in Center City led by Women Organized Against Rape, executive director Carole Johnson handed Crystal a microphone.

"I'm not sure I'm ready," Crystal said.

"You're ready," Johnson said.

Crystal spoke from the stage, introducing Chris and Aylisha. People clapped. A few cried. They hugged Crystal and her children.

"For other victims, that is what they want to hear, that she got through it," said Johnson.

Telling her story was also a way of getting back at her father. And she wasn't above using it to raise money – anything that would help her get a house for the kids.

In July, she and her children drove to her father's old store. Crystal sat on a milk crate, wearing a white T-shirt on which she had written her story in black marker. The last line asked for help to get a house for her kids.

Many passersby knew Crystal's father and were shocked. Others were not.

Many had stories of their own, about how they were molested or nearly so by their fathers or relatives. One man said he was a foster parent to a girl raped by her father, now in jail; their baby was given up for adoption.

One woman told Crystal that after her uncle tried to molest her, her mother gave her a bus ticket and told her to leave town. Another woman, sexually abused by her father, said that what Crystal was doing was pointless and destructive. She should work to heal her family.

Though Crystal got no money that day and in the end never asked for any, she didn't feel the time had been a waste.

On the contrary, she had told her story, and others had shared their own. To Crystal, that was worth plenty.

POSTSCRIPT

Three weeks after my story on Crystal ran in the paper, she got a call from a staffer to Barack Obama, who was just about to declare his candidacy for president, and who had come to town to campaign for local Democrats. Crystal had never heard of him, but was interested in anyone who was interested in her kids. She talked with the future president briefly about her story. She told him she was trying to raise money to buy a handicapped-accessible house for her kids. Obama, she said, told her if she collected just $2 from everyone she met, she'd soon have enough. "Two dollars can change a life," he told her.

Crystal never got her dream house, where her kids could move about easily, and she could finally do less lifting, but she never stopped doing for her kids and for others. In early 2015, eight years after my story appeared, Crystal founded a nonprofit to perform random acts of kindness for other people. She got IRS 501c(3) tax-exempt status. She named her charity Two Dollars Can Change a Life. She and the charity are going strong! Her first event was to provide showers for the homeless, now an annual affair. And Crystal is still driving around in that van.

Crystal posing with the future president, Chris, Aylisha and Brandon

Photo by MIKE PEREZ

In the freezing waterfall in Kentucky, Bill
Bucher feels the spirit of his son

11

THE WATERFALL

A journey to keep a son's spirit alive

Traveling to Appalachia, helping students help others

March 10, 2002

For months, Bill Bucher had been dreaming about the waterfall, about hiking up to it, standing under it, posing for a photograph—just as his son Eric had done.

The hike on Wednesday was harder than he ever expected. Whoever was in the lead lost the trail, and they had to forge a path over boulders and streams.

And now, Bill, like the other 35 La Salle University students here on spring break, could hear the thundering waterfall.

Bill is 47 and graying, with a generous girth, but there was no doubt in his mind, or anyone else's, that he would make it.

This odyssey for Bill Bucher began 10 months ago, on the Ohio Turnpike, about 1 a.m., when his son Eric died.

The Buchers, from Northeast Philadelphia, were headed to Chicago, to the college graduation of their oldest son, one of five children. Bill, a splicer for Verizon, was driving the minivan. Eric, his third child, a sophomore at La Salle, was in the front passenger seat.

A deer darted across the highway. The minivan hit the animal, and its backside flew through the windshield, crushing

Eric. His mother cradled him until the ambulance came. He never regained consciousness and died the next day.

One of Eric's favorite things in life was to go to Appalachia on spring break with his La Salle friends to build houses for the poor. The trip always included the traditional hike to the waterfall. Last week, as a junior, Eric would have led the trip.

This time, Bill decided to come in his son's place. "I wanted to do it," he said, "because Eric did it."

Eric's death launched Bill on a spiritual journey, and he wanted to treat the trip as a retreat. But mostly he wanted to be around Eric's friends, to revel in Eric's spirit, to honor his son.

"Eric's death has really changed him," said Louise Bucher, Bill's wife. "We're both looking for things to do to continue Eric's life. I haven't found what I want to do yet. But he has. He wants to go and continue doing things that Eric would have wanted to do."

Bill completed two years at Drexel 25 years ago. Last fall he returned to La Salle, taking night classes in religion and philosophy. Part of the reason Bill loves La Salle is that Eric changed so much there.

"He grew into a confident, giving person," Bill said. "You could see it almost in front of your eyes, from a meek-mannered, not-quite-sure-of-himself guy into a self-confident young man. He knew who he was." Eric had talked about becoming a pediatric surgeon, and he volunteered as a tutor with children in the North Philadelphia neighborhoods around La Salle.

His sophomore year, he wrote a humor column for the college paper called "A dyslexic walks into a bra." After his trip to Harlan County, Kentucky, he wrote in it: "I learned so many things, that we weren't building houses, rather we were building homes…. I learned it's possible to be poor and rich at the same time. And I came back completely at peace, with the feeling that I made a difference."

Last fall, Bill decided to make the trip. As the days got closer, he grew nervous. Was he kidding? He was going to spend seven days with 35 undergraduates, sleeping side-by-side in a room no larger than a classroom, sharing two bathrooms. Was he ready? Would they want him?

The Sunday before they left, the group met at the La Salle chapel. They stood in a circle and tossed around a bundle of orange yarn, creating a giant web. As each person threw the bundle, he or she had to express a hope or a fear about the trip.

Bill said: "I'm going down, really, to be with you guys. I just want to meet kids that go to Appalachia instead of Cancún. Don't feel weird coming up to me or talking to me…and don't call me Mr. Bucher. I'm Bill."

From the start, he was one of the gang. He reminded the others of his son. "We can see where Eric got his sense of humor," said Trish Gauss, 21, a senior. He was unfazed by their humor and language.

The students left at 6 a.m. last Sunday and drove the 600 miles in four rented vans, eight to a van. Bill drove. When Andrea Carpenter, 20, a junior, shouted from the back that they should name their van "The Sleepless Bitch," Bill embraced the idea. "That's a great name!" he said. The college kids were a little shocked at first, but he affectionately referred to the van by its name.

Their Spartan living quarters were in a converted funeral parlor behind an old church. Bill was such a good sport they elected him mayor. Everybody got a title: dog catcher, town hottie, jester.

All week, Bill did his share of cooking and cleaning, even the bathrooms. One evening, he emerged from a bathroom carrying three containers. "OK, ladies, what scent would you like: After the Rain, Powder Fresh Potpourri, or Tangerine Ginger?" The kids laughed.

Bill made nightly trips with the students to Walmart, the best entertainment in an alcohol-free county. He tried on straw hats and bought bunny slippers for $2. He was as wide-eyed as any other student about the poverty – shacks and outhouses and abandoned cars. Philadelphia has poverty that is no doubt as bad or worse – but different.

For 10 years, La Salle has run trips over spring break to Harlan County with COAP, Christian Outreach with Appalachian

People. The students split up each day into groups working on houses in different stages of completion.

Bill painted and hauled trash and mopped floors and hammered nails. He quickly learned the local lingo. As they cleaned trash from a ditch, Bill said to La Salle senior Rita Marino, as if he'd lived in southeastern Kentucky all his life, "Watch out you don't slip into that crick."

For Bill, the highlight was the Wednesday hike.

They ate peanut butter sandwiches and drove an hour north of Harlan to the Bad Branch of the Poor Fork of the Cumberland River, where they would hike a mile and a half to the waterfall.

Many of the students knew this hike was special for Bill. "It's so great he's here, and I'm sure he's loving it," said Grant Lodes, 22, a senior. "At the same time, this must be a constant reminder."

When they got off the trail, Bill refused any help. He wanted to do this on his own. But to scale a wall of rock, everybody needed help, so three of the strongest guys hoisted Bill up.

After an hour of hiking, there it was: Bad Branch Falls. It was a majestic sight. Many of the students had been here with Eric, but none had seen it like this, looking almost polar, with ice everywhere. Gushing water plummeted 60 feet over a sheer rock face, crashing onto flat, ice-covered rocks near where the students stood.

Several had intended to walk out and immerse themselves in the waterfall. The ice gave everyone pause except Bill. He climbed over and took the last few steps into the freezing waterfall – to wild cheers.

Standing there in his shirt and jeans and boots, Bill opened his arms, as if to embrace the heavens, closed his eyes, and traveled to another place in his mind. All of the others felt privileged to be there. Bill said he felt Eric's spirit. He knew his son was with him, watching, laughing, thinking, "That's pretty cool, Dad."

He stayed in as long as he could endure, maybe 30 seconds.

Soaked, Bill came out, sat on a rock, and stared up at the waterfall bathed in sunlight. The others left him alone for a while.

Oh, how he missed his son. After a few minutes, Bill got up and encouraged the others to soak themselves, too: 28 did. Bill had inspired almost all of them. He lit a cigar. "I talk to Eric when I smoke my cigars," he said. "I believe he's here right now, getting a kick out of this whole thing."

On the way back to Harlan, Bill put a tape on in the van. It was a tape of four songs Eric had recorded at La Salle during a karaoke night a few months before he died. It started with Billy Joel's "It's Still Rock and Roll to Me." Eric crooned and wisecracked through it. The final song was "Puff (the Magic Dragon)." Before it began, Eric said, "This is dedicated to my Mommy. I love you, Mommy." The van fell silent. Tears welled in the eyes of several of the girls. Bill's, too.

A few miles down the road, Bill was back to his mischievous self. Harlan is coal country, and they passed piles of coal along the road. Bill, riding shotgun, told the driver to pull over. He jumped out, ran over to the piles of coal and grabbed a handful, maybe eight lumps.

"We need souvenirs!" he shouted.

They drove home all day yesterday, getting back to Philadelphia late last night. Instead of going to his house, Bill got permission from his wife to party at La Salle all night with the students from the trip.

"I'll crash somewhere," he said.

POSTSCRIPT

When I heard about the story, I decided I had to go. I had to be there, so I could put the readers there. Let me here say a word about Mike Perez, and photographers in general. I long believed that the most talented staff at the newspaper was our photo staff. As you can see from the photos in this book, their work is magnificent. I learned long ago the value of photos. They add another critical dimension to storytelling. They let the reader see.

In this particular case, Mike Perez was sick as a dog. I remember him – sorry, Mikey – puking on the streets of Harlan County. But he was there with me every step. He made the hike. To get this photo, he had to walk out into the waterfall himself, get soaked himself in freezing water, risk his life on the icy rocks. And what an amazing photo! I am grateful to the photographers in this book and to all the others I have worked with over the years.

A day or two after the story appeared, I got this email from one of the students on the trip:

"As we drove back, Bill took the last driving shift into Philly, and we stopped and picked up some papers when we hit town. As we continued on, I read the story aloud. I had to stop and dry my eyes a few times. There were sobs coming from everyone in the van. After the part about Puff the Magic Dragon, Bill had to pull over to the side of the road."

My brothers and I reading the Sunday paper,
circa 1972. I'm in the middle.

MY JOURNEY AS A STORYTELLER

An idyllic childhood that led to newspapers

My first real contact with a newspaper was a paper route. In junior high school, I delivered *The Washington Star,* the afternoon paper. I loved seeing people, seeing the neighborhood every day, making my rounds on my Schwinn. I thought it was important work: People counted on me.

I loved getting up before dawn on Sunday mornings, getting out into the stillness and silence when the rest of my world was asleep. I was terrified only of the horrible alarm clock, and amazingly my own body clock would wake me minutes before it went off at 5 a.m. The world is filled with wonders!

When I felt like king of the world, master of the universe, I would ride my bike two and a half miles to the Ravensworth Shopping Center and withdraw $5 of my newspaper earnings from the Northern Virginia Bank and buy a steak and cheese and a Coke at Pizza Bazzano. Years later in Philly, of course, I would call the very same thing a cheesesteak and soda. And to be honest, no cheesesteak I have eaten in Philly, the cheesesteak capital of the world, ever tasted as good as one at Pizza Bazzano, perhaps because I was never so innocent or carefree. I would roam North Springfield as if it were the entire world and the entire world were my dominion.

I do not ever remember making a decision to be a newspaper reporter. I just always was.

I edited my high school paper and then my college paper. What attracted me to the school papers were a couple of things.

First, I think I inherited some of my mother's feelings of being an outsider. I lived in a largely Christian world with no religious identity of my own. I was a first-generation child of Jews who had become Unitarians, and everyone around me seemed to be the Christian son or daughter of a crew-cutted Pentagon colonel or captain. Newspaper staffs have always been filled with outsiders, with colorful characters, oddballs and eccentrics – people who are open-minded and accepting and caring and crusading and often brilliant. I felt at home in a newsroom.

Second, I loved the access that being a reporter gave me. I didn't yet appreciate the craft of a storyteller, or the felicity I would find in celebrating the lives of ordinary people. But working for the newspaper gave me a ticket to meet anyone, explore any subject, go anywhere. I loved it.

I read every Hardy Boys book – my idea of great storytelling back in fourth grade – but I was never a big reader or a strong writer. I was a B student in English.

Somehow in my youth I found the work of Ernie Pyle, a World War II columnist who wrote about common soldiers and sailors, Marines and airmen. He chronicled their daily lives with dignity and simplicity. He put his readers on the beaches and in the foxholes, and he died in combat, in service to his profession and his country.

Another writer I loved as a young journalist was Joseph Mitchell of *The New Yorker* magazine. His works are in a fabulous collection titled *Up in the Old Hotel.* He is unsurpassed in writing profiles of the colorful characters he found on the streets of New York in the 1940s. I love his style and sensibility, his reverence for and appreciation of these people who lived so far from traditional news headlines.

My father thought writing was an essential skill but hardly a career. He thought my working for a newspaper in high school and college was a phase, a fad, a cute diversion, a tolerable extracurricular. When I graduated from college, he pushed me to give up that foolishness and pursue an M.B.A.

He had nothing against it, really. He just saw no future in it.

I must say also I remember him, God bless him, coming up to me after I had won the Pulitzer Prize, and telling me, with love and sincerity and honesty and surrender, that he finally had come to accept that I had probably made the right choice in turning down admission to the University of Virginia's business school.

I laugh now. It has been a wonderful and fulfilling and satisfying career, but as the newspaper business collapsed in the 21st century, hammered by technological change and a difficult economy – as pensions were frozen and pay raises vanished – I can picture him saying, "Miklos, you should have listened!"

Charlie Birnbaum plays Brahms in his Atlantic City home

12

A LIFE IN TUNE

His hands still touch the face of God

Once a prodigy, he has found peace as a piano tuner

November 14, 2004

Usually in the afternoon, in the stale stillness of his mother's living room, Charles Birnbaum sits at the grand piano and plays Brahms.

A prodigy who soloed at 13 with the Philadelphia Orchestra and competed at 15 against André Watts for an appearance with the New York Philharmonic, Birnbaum was destined for greatness. And in his own way, he achieved it – not in a concert hall, but in this weary old house on Oriental Avenue where he performs, brilliantly, for the lengthening shadows.

The three-story building is a block from the ocean and three blocks from The Showboat, one of the casinos where Birnbaum, 57, works as a piano tuner. Trash and broken glass litter the yard. Vandals paint graffiti on the windows and doors.

His mother, Dora, survived the Holocaust and, helped by his tireless care, the torment of depression and frailties of old age. But she did not survive the neighborhood. A widow of 86, she was beaten to death in her parlor by a crack-crazed thug on Nov. 17, 1998, after her son left from his twice-daily visit. All the killer got was a broken VCR.

Birnbaum himself took up the bloody carpets, washed the spattered walls, and painted over the black smudges where police had dusted for prints. Remaking it into a truly living room eased his grief. He bought not one but two Yamaha grands discarded by casinos, rebuilt them, and moved them in.

His daughters will not set foot in the house, and his wife, with whom he lives in Hammonton, rarely does. But nowhere is Birnbaum more at peace. The virtuoso who has shied away from the stage for 30 years comes nearly every day to play, seeking to "touch the face of God" through the music that was his parents' gift to him.

After a passage of transcendent beauty, he looks at their photos on the pale pink walls. He knows they are pleased.

* * *

Tuning a piano isn't as challenging as playing one on the world stage. But in a casino, it comes close.

Charlie Birnbaum has worked at most of the casinos, making his rounds in khakis and an open-collar shirt, his tools in a pouch tied with string. He is a perpetually jovial man, with a soft face, glasses, and short fingers that look better suited to hanging drywall.

Mornings often start at The Showboat, where he tends a white Yamaha in the lobby. Slots ching. The air pulses with pop music. A worker on a ladder guns a power tool.

"It's almost impossible to try and do what I'm doing," Birnbaum says, laughing. "The one thing I cannot tune to is the vacuum cleaner. I'm dead."

Backstage hands listen for the moment when he finishes tuning. They know what's coming – a flash of the artist, test-driving the instrument through a Chopin étude.

"Oh, God, have you heard him play?" asks Jill Passarella, a stage technician at the Taj Mahal. "I'm getting teary-eyed."

Last November, a video crew chronicling Jon Bon Jovi's gig at the Borgata was mesmerized by the monotony of Birnbaum's tuning the band's piano, striking one key again and again, then blown away as he let loose with a torrent of Scarlatti.

That is how he wound up in the DVD *This Left Feels Right: Live*, though he didn't know until a friend glimpsed him in it. One of his son's buddies on the Hammonton High bowling team asked for his autograph.

Passarella has grander plans.

"I'd like to set up an event where Charlie will play for an hour," she says as he works. "We'll charge admission to people who want to come in, who appreciate good music."

He stops tuning.

"I'll have something to say about that," he protests.

She ignores him, thinking him too modest. "We need to get him an outlet."

He tries again. "No. No. I've done that. And I find performing, compared to tuning – I'd rather live the stress-free life."

For those who don't know his story – and hardly anyone does – Charlie Birnbaum's choices in life and art can be confounding. Understanding begins in the forests of Poland, where Abe Birnbaum and Dora Rotstein met, hiding from Nazis.

Dora lived in the village of Slonim, and when soldiers came one day to round up Jews, she grabbed her 4-year-old daughter and ran. The child was shot and died. Her husband was caught and hanged in the town square. No one in her family – not parents, grandparents, uncles, aunts – survived.

Abe Birnbaum also was newly widowed. His wife, a Krakow beauty who competed in pageants, had been arrested, shot and dumped in a pit.

He and Dora met in the woods. In 1944, a week after the Russians liberated Poland, their son Sam was born. Charlie followed in 1947, in a displaced-persons camp in Germany.

Though the Nazis temporarily silenced it, music was in both families' blood. Abe's father had been a cantor, Dora's father a music teacher and her brother a violinist. In the camp, Sam took up the accordion.

The Birnbaums moved to San Francisco in 1952, and Abe opened a jewelry store.

"Someone mentioned to my father, in this country accordion isn't that big a thing," Charlie recalls. "You should have Sam study something else. He did. Sam started studying piano."

Charlie watched him play, and wished he could, too. Soon both boys were taking lessons at the San Francisco Conservatory.

By 12, Sam was so proficient that he was accepted to the Curtis Institute of Music in Philadelphia, where all students are on full scholarship. The family followed him, renting a rundown apartment at 11th and Pine with "granddaddy rats," Charlie says, and "an elevator that if it worked, great. If it didn't, you walked up six flights."

Abe earned just $60 a week in the smoke shop at Lit Bros. But each boy had a piano.

"My parents dedicated their lives to us," says Charlie, who practiced up to four hours a day even as a grade schooler at McCall Elementary. "We didn't go to synagogue. We didn't have associations with Jewish friends. Music, that's all we knew."

At 10, he began studying at Settlement Music School under the great pianist Marian Filar, a Warsaw Ghetto survivor.

"When Charlie came to me," Filar says, "I smelled right away a big talent."

Indeed, within a year, he auditioned for Philadelphia Orchestra conductor Eugene Ormandy, who gave him a $1,000 scholarship in honor of the Academy of Music's 101st anniversary.

By 13, he had performed at Robin Hood Dell and the Academy – at the latter, playing from Mozart's Concerto for Two Pianos in E flat major with a girl named Rena Fruchter. She would one day become actor and musician Dudley Moore's concert partner.

Just blocks from the Birnbaums lived a colossus in the making. When Charlie passed the small house, he could hear André Watts practicing away.

One afternoon, lured by the sound of Saint-Saëns, he knocked on the door.

Watts, a year his senior, opened it and "knew who I was, because our pictures were in the paper," Charlie recounts. "He was a little flustered because he had broken a bass string on his piano."

Charlie recalls Watts' mother's coming home and "the look on her face. Some stranger being in the house. I remember making a quick exit."

He met up with Watts again on Dec. 5, 1962, when both auditioned for Leonard Bernstein and the New York Philharmonic's annual Young People's Concert. Charlie played the first movement of Beethoven's Piano Concerto No. 3 in C minor (Op. 37) and Filar was sure his student had bested Watts. But Watts was chosen instead.

"Some people win. Some don't," Charlie says. "That's just the way it is."

When his brother left Curtis to study at Juilliard in New York, and then the Peabody Conservatory in Baltimore under Leon Fleischer, Charlie spent summers with him, "practicing our hearts out," he recalls.

"We'd sweat like crazy and work like crazy. This was our summers. Intensive study, and very, very lonely."

Charlie was coming to a discomforting realization. In performance, if you are not on top of the mountain, the mountain is on top of you.

"I was seeing the struggles of my brother, who was working at very difficult levels and with a tremendous amount of dedication. At the same time, you see, there are always pianists who are superior. The reality starts to set in, that what we're pursuing, it's not an easy thing."

* * *

In March 1968, in his senior year as a music major at Temple University, Charlie had an epiphany, "like someone turning a switch in my head."

The "truth," as he saw it in instantaneous clarity, was his utter unpreparedness for life.

" 'You don't have the skills to deal with people, to communicate, to just survive,'" he remembers telling himself. "I looked in the mirror, like an executioner. 'You're the biggest failure who ever existed. You have no right to live.' "

At Filar's urging, Dora and Abe took their son to Temple University Hospital. In a bathroom in the psychiatric ward, he found a triple-track razor. When he was done, he says, "I went to the chair. I sat down. That was it."

Surgeons repaired damage so horrific that he required a feeding tube and six weeks of hospitalization. Every day, Sam was by his bed, commuting from Fort Dix, where he was posted with the 19th Army Band.

The psychotic self-loathing that had pulled Charlie into hell loosed its grip. But as it did, the magnitude of what he had done – more to his parents than to himself – began to sink in.

"I'd do anything not to put them through that again. All they experienced. And their shining light…," his voice trails to a whisper. From then on, "the prime directive in my life was, whatever time I had, I would try and make it up to them."

But Dora Birnbaum already was retreating into her own shadows. Even before Charlie tried suicide, she had become depressed – Holocaust survivor's guilt, her family thought. Afterward, being in the city where her son had done such a thing only deepened the pain. Abe transferred to the Lits Atlantic City store, and bought the house on Oriental Avenue.

Temple welcomed Charlie back, extending his scholarship so he could finish his degree. He moved into an apartment with other music students.

For his first 21 years, he says, "I had been like a horse with blinders on." Now he was seeing things – grass, trees, flowers – that he had never noticed before.

And he met a girl.

* * *

Cindy Toomey grew up in a strong Christian household in Harleysville in rural Montgomery County, majored in piano at Kent State University in Ohio, and came to Temple for her master's.

Her life and Charlie's intersected in Chopin's Ballade in G minor (Op. 23).

Passing the practice rooms, she heard it through a closed door, being played as she had not imagined it could be.

"I asked my friend, 'Gosh, who's that?' She looked in and said, 'Oh, that's Charlie Birnbaum,'" Cindy recalls. "She just opens up the door. He was deep in this piece, but he stopped and turned around and introduced himself. I said, 'Go ahead and play it again.' "

As he did, "I had tears coming down. I had never heard a pianist who moved me like that."

For their first date he showed up in a lime-green shirt and maroon jacket "and a tie that didn't match," she says. "That really didn't bother me. He was so filled with *joie de vivre*. I loved that about him."

She noticed, but did not mention, the strange hoarseness in his voice. Only after a few months did he explain.

"I remember telling my mother, crying and sobbing, telling her the story of what had happened to him," Cindy says. "She didn't know what to make of it. 'How safe do you think he is now? Do you think this will happen again?' How do you guarantee that to your parents?

"It was a chance I took, too. But I felt, you take a chance with anybody."

Charlie and Cindy married in 1971 and moved to Hammonton. She taught music in a local school, he taught piano at Temple and what was then Atlantic Community College. And although performing stressed him more than ever, he kept an agent and a frenetic concert schedule that put him on the college circuit much of the time.

"A lot of decisions were made to make his parents proud," Cindy says. "He was their hope for success. And in his mind, success was concertizing."

On his way to the mountaintop was the Leventritt, a premier international piano competition. In 1973, he went to New York in the hope of joining an illustrious roster of winners that have included Van Cliburn and Gary Graffman. He had committed to memory the thousands of notes and nuances of Beethoven's "Appassionata" Sonata.

Somewhere in the complex movements, Charlie got lost, and couldn't find his way back.

He got up and left the stage.

"My memory failed me, and that was that," he says. "I made the judges' job easy that day."

If Charlie Birnbaum's performance career would soon close, the Leventritt was not the clincher. He gave recitals for two more years, until his first child, Rachel, was born. And that "more than anything was the catalyst for seeing more to my life than the constant practice needed to get ready for the next performance," he says.

"To be a world-class performer, you have to sacrifice everything for the love of music."

He adds, "I'm lucky in my life that I had options."

He discovered one of them while sitting in on a tuning class at Temple, taught by renowned piano rebuilder Victor Benvenuto. Charlie could hear something that no beginning student of Benvenuto's ever had.

"Tuning involves listening and adjusting 'beats' that are caused when two different notes are played at the same time," Charlie explains. "The rate of speed that these beats occur are what we listen for. They are very subtle; they practically don't exist for the general listener. That is why Victor was so surprised that I was able to pick out seven beats per second when he played F and A. Over a five-second duration, the total number of beats was 35."

In 1980, with casinos going up in Atlantic City, Charlie was offered a job tuning pianos at Bally's. He was at a crossroads.

He could pursue a Ph.D. and a professorship, which likely would require him to relocate.

Or he could be a tuner, able to stay put and support his family, which eventually grew to two daughters and a son. And every day he could go to Oriental Avenue to care for Dora and Abe.

"Was it the right decision or the wrong decision?" he asks. "It was the only decision."

Atlantic City was an emerging entertainment mecca with a vast fleet of pianos that went out of tune daily, and no dearth of artists to fuss about it. Resorts hired him in 1982 after Frank Sinatra groused during a concert, "Who tuned this piano? Johnnie Ray?" – a pop crooner who was partly deaf.

So Charlie got an emergency call and tuned the piano between shows. Sinatra did not complain again.

In Atlantic City, Benvenuto says, "everybody got to know Charles Birnbaum, the greatest tuner."

* * *

Charlie was visiting his parents the day in 1986 when word came.

Sam had committed suicide.

He was 42, married with two children, and teaching piano in Australia, where he had moved in the early 1970s at the urging of an uncle there.

"He was facing a job loss – that was the trigger," says Charlie, who once hoped Sam would join him in Atlantic City, tuning.

"He pulled me out of that abyss, that black hole. I owed him everything. I only wish he could have learned something from my debacle."

Hearing the news, Charlie went to the cellar and began sweeping the concrete floor.

* * *

Abe would die the next year at age 73, having outlived by more than a decade an aneurysm that destroyed his esophagus. Save for short stays in a nursing home, Charlie kept him where he wanted most to be, the house on Oriental Avenue. It was half of what Charlie calls "my greatest accomplishment."

Gaming's good fortune wasn't smiling on South Inlet. Once a thriving Jewish neighborhood, it had become a haunt of drug dealers and derelicts; two arsons a night wasn't unusual.

Abe, his mind and body failing, would go prospecting each morning among the shells of buildings.

"I'm looking out the porch," Charlie says, "and two blocks down is this guy with a Russian hat, a dolly and a long rope, like out of *Fiddler on the Roof.* He's carrying furniture! I realized, that represented life to him."

When Abe died, Dora was frail, depressed and unable to live alone. But in a nursing home, Charlie figured, "she'd be gone in three months."

A social worker recommended Beatrice Cabarrus – BeeBee – an African American woman from southern Virginia just two years younger than his mother but in good health. She moved in as Dora's caretaker, and Charlie feverishly renovated the first floor so that the two would not have to climb stairs.

"Everything I needed was from the next abandoned or burned-down building," he says. "It was like Beirut."

In 1996, after surgery, Dora nearly died of an infection. After six weeks in the hospital, she went to a nursing home to convalesce, and there she stopped eating.

"The doctor said, 'She wants to die. What do you want to do?'" Charlie recalls. "I talked to my wife. We both said, 'Look, if she's going to die of something, it's not going to be starvation. She survived living in holes in the ground in the forest of Poland, and she's going to die because she didn't have food and it was my decision? No.'"

Doctors inserted a feeding tube, but warned Charlie that she might not live long. He vowed to bring her home in six weeks.

BeeBee would be of little help, as she was showing signs of dementia. So he rented the second floor of the house to a nurse who cared for both women in the evening. By day, between casino jobs, he was there.

Within eight months, Dora not only started eating but "she was able to get around a little bit," he says. "In my opinion, we were doing the impossible."

Every few weeks, she snapped out of her depression and, for a day, was lucid and smiling and clear-eyed.

"It was worth waiting for," he says. "Because that one day, life was worth living again."

On November 17, 1998, Charlie stretched his lunch visit to an extra hour. Soon after he left, Louis Crumpton, 36, broke in and killed Dora and BeeBee.

Four months later, Crumpton was arrested and pleaded guilty. That day in court, Charlie clutched his mother's picture and lambasted the killer for "an evil beyond words."

"I wish you hell on earth," declared Charlie, who had been there once himself.

Two years ago, Crumpton died of AIDS in prison.

* * *

Odds are, Charlie's interludes on Oriental Avenue are numbered.

The empty oceanfront lot across the street was purchased for $14 million by a developer who wants to put up two condo towers and a boutique casino. City planners envision a renaissance for all of South Inlet within five years.

One day, Abe and Dora's property could be worth something. Any money, Charlie says, would be their legacy to their grandchildren, and the loss his alone.

"Just by being here, in a funny way, is keeping my side of the family intact," he says.

The house is, as well, a reminder of life's lessons, many learned the hard way.

"You have to find a way to find joy in life," Charlie says. "I don't care if it means sweeping the sidewalk. What I've learned through my process is that I won't trade my little successes that I have every day for one grand success."

He plays now purely "for the love of it," surrounded by the accumulated music of a lifetime, sheets of it, books of it, stacked on shelves in the living room. But Charlie reaches reflexively for the same small volume of Brahms opuses, what he calls "my little bible."

The pieces, he says, are "all about reflection. You're reflecting on all your life experiences, and sitting in on Mr. Brahms' reflecting on his experiences."

Charlie has been playing from the book 30 years – a measure, perhaps, of how much he has to reflect on, in the quiet of an afternoon on Oriental Avenue.

POSTSCRIPT

Charlie Birnbaum had never told his story publicly. He trusted me to tell it. I found it to be a beautiful, haunting story. I identified with it on a personal level because of my own mother's story, though her experiences were nothing like those of Charlie's mother. And classical music was so much a part of my parents' lives.

I so badly wanted to do justice to Charlie's story. Most important to me was to be sensitive to his attempt on his own life. What I am proudest of in this story is that I never say he cut his own throat. Or attempted suicide. I worked hard to make it perfectly clear to the reader what he had tried to do, but I tried to do it gently, respectfully, with subtlety. And I even used this to my advantage as a writer, creating suspense and curiosity. I simply write:

In a bathroom in the psychiatric ward, he found a triple-track razor.
When he was done, he says, "I went to the chair. I sat down. That was
it."

The reader at this point understands he has attempted suicide. But I
never say whether Charlie cut his wrists or his throat or both. I knew
I would answer the question later in the story. Essential questions like
this *must* be answered. It would be a failure of journalism and of storytelling to leave this vague. So later in the story, I try to do this with
subtlety again:

For their first date he showed up in a lime-green shirt and maroon
jacket "and a tie that didn't match," she says. "That really didn't bother
me. He was so filled with joie de vivre. I loved that about him."
She noticed, but did not mention, the strange hoarseness in his
voice. Only after a few months did he explain.

And that was it. I am confident the reader understood the hoarseness
was caused by the razor blade. I felt strongly I did not want to be any
more direct than that. Charlie in my story was announcing to the
world an immensely painful and private truth. But saying so directly
would have been so unnecessary and unfair. There had been enough
violence in his life already.

Years later, when Filar got dementia, and needed care, Charlie and
another former student took care of him. Filar had saved Charlie's life,
and Charlie repaid the debt, caring for his beloved teacher until the
very end. Even when Charlie came down with a debilitating disease
himself, myasthenia gravis, he would still go twice a week.

A decade after this story appeared, Atlantic City wanted to take
Charlie's house through eminent domain, hoping a casino or resort hotel might be built there. There was no actual project, just wishful thinking. Under such circumstances, the house meant too much to Charlie
to surrender. He decided to fight.

Desperate, and in an incredible longshot, he wrote a big advocacy
law firm in Washington, D.C., asking it to take his case. "When I sent
your article to the Institute for Justice, I really believe that set the stage
for their interest in the case," Charlie told me. Charlie and his lawyers
fought and won.

"Life is like a circle," he says, "and you just don't know where it will
lead you." He continues to play in the lengthening shadows.

Valery Swope at "accepted students" day at Cabrini College

13

SURVIVAL AND SUCCESS

Emerging from a childhood of misery

Abandoned at birth, a young woman gains college admission

July 13, 2015

Valery Swope, 18, answered her phone one afternoon in March. It was Cabrini College, telling her she had been accepted.

"I feel so great. Oh, my Lord. I've got to tell everybody!"

First, she posed for a selfie. "I've got to take a picture of this face!"

Then she got on the phone.

The first six people she called were two caseworkers with the state child welfare agency, two social workers appointed by the court, a child advocate in the public defender's office, and an FBI agent. She lamented that she didn't have her guidance counselor's number.

This posse of public servants is Valery's rudder in life.

Valery's teenage mother gave birth to her in a bathroom, placed her in a plastic bag, and left her in a boarded-up building in the Philadelphia's Frankford section, before dawn Jan. 4, 1997.

The police officer who rescued the newborn would become the first of many individuals – from law-enforcement officers to social workers to educators – who would step in to help and guide a child with few constants in her life.

Valery identifies with Marilyn Monroe – abandoned by her mother, raised for a time by foster parents. Last year, Valery had a Marilyn quote tattooed on her right forearm – *I am good, but not an angel. I do sin, but I'm not the devil. I am just a small girl in a big world.* She even tried being blond for a while.

Valery has lived with relatives, with strangers in foster care, in institutions and group homes – even briefly, disastrously, back with her mother. At age 15, she went missing for months, living under the control of – and exploited by – men whom she later helped send to prison for 22 years.

"I don't think she can say she ever had a childhood," said Yolanda Shepherd, a Department of Human Services worker who sat with Valery when she was hospitalized with migraines last summer.

"I want to shout from the rooftop that Valery made it!" Shepherd added.

Valery graduated June 25 – after a sprint to get her work done – from her fourth high school in four years. She lives with a paid house mother and two other girls in a Germantown row-house, her third residence just this year.

Attending Cabrini, a small Catholic college in Radnor, could be Valery's chance to start anew.

"The experiences she has been through and the depths of her pain are what motion pictures are made from," Megan Hannah, her guidance counselor at Arise Academy Charter High School, wrote in a recommendation to college. "Only this is real. She is real."

Valery said she hoped sharing her story will help other children, and she gave her posse permission to talk about her.

"I want people to read my story and say: 'Wow, she can still do it. Maybe I can do it, too.' "

* * *

Valery wrote her college application essay in the form of a poem.
It begins:

> *It was the New Year, January 4, 1997,*
> *A miracle was about to be born.*
> *You can say she came straight from heaven,*
> *But her mother could beg to differ; she didn't want her.*
> *And on that night,*
> *Like Satan, she tries to take a life.*

Valery was delivered in secret in the bathroom of her grandparents' home on Unity Street and left in the building next
door. Her mother was 18.

> *And down her face, I bet not a tear drops.*
> *All she wished for was for that tiny heart to stop.*

At 2:45 a.m., according to a police report, one of Valery's
uncles heard what he believed was a cat crying. He grabbed a
flashlight, looked in a window. Through a small opening in the
bag he could see a baby's head. He called police.

> *And they smashed through bolted doors trying to find her.*
> *A beautiful life was almost taken, but God protected her.*

Philadelphia police officer Robert Varley found the baby,
wrapped her in his coat, and rushed her to St. Christopher's
Hospital for Children.

Nurses named her Valery, after Officer Varley. He returned
later that morning and put a teddy bear in her crib.

* * *

Police quickly learned the identity of Valery's mother, Shannon Swope.

Shannon had given birth just 11 months earlier. Shannon's stepmother – already raising three grandchildren in that house – had said the next child who had a baby out of wedlock would be "put on the street." Shannon believed her.

Shannon, now 36, said she never intended to harm her baby. She said she thought she could hide the pregnancy, give birth secretly and leave the infant on the front step for her parents to find and adopt. They had adopted other children.

"In my head, back then, I thought it would work," Shannon said recently. "Looking at it now, most likely it probably wouldn't have."

When her brother came home unexpectedly, Shannon said she panicked and stashed the baby next door.

She pleaded guilty to attempted murder, went to jail for a year, and then spent two more years in an alternative program to prison for women. Once released, her father and stepmother, Leroy and Linda Swope, would not let her near Valery, she said.

"I don't think you can get any lower than I was," she said of the years after her release. "I was in the ICU at least six times for trying to kill myself. I lost everything and everyone."

Valery and her sister, Jaylynn, 11 months older, were adopted by Linda and Leroy Swope, their grandparents. It would be the only time Valery felt part of a real family.

When Valery was 8, in January 2005, Leroy Swope died from lung cancer. Six months later, Linda Swope died of an infection after hip replacement. Valery and her sister were placed with a relative for a few years, but by the time Valery was 13, a judge determined that situation was no longer in the girls' best interest.

Jaylynn went to live in a residential facility. Valery went to a foster home. (Valery says she has no relationship with her biological father.)

When she turned 14, Valery says, her foster dad kissed her on the lips and put his hand down her shirt. Convinced no one believed her, she ran away, only to be placed in a succession of foster homes.

A lifetime of hopping from home to home,
Running away was all she could understand.

* * *

In 2012, by then a freshman at Bartram High in Southwest Philadelphia, living in foster care, 15-year-old Valery ran away again, missing 63 days of school.

Mike Goodhue, a special agent with the FBI assigned to crimes against children, met Valery that summer, when she became a key witness in three investigations.

"All of these investigations were successful because of the efforts of Miss Swope," he wrote recently in her college recommendation letter. "Miss Swope had the strength and courage to stand up against the criminals that stole her innocence and she was able to face them in a courtroom setting. As you can imagine, this can be extremely difficult, especially as a child."

* * *

At the beginning of sophomore year, Valery moved into St. Mary's Villa in Ambler, a residential facility for teens. She went to Upper Dublin High, a suburban school, and got B's in English and geometry.

On weekends and holidays, other kids went home. Valery hated being left behind.

She sneaked out, she said, to meet her mother, whom she found on Facebook.

Valery had never even seen a picture of her mother until then, she said.

"At that point," Valery said, "I didn't have anybody, so I was desperate, I guess. And I wanted her. I wanted it to be different."

Valery had heard about being left for dead, but she didn't want to believe it.

"I wanted whatever they were telling me to be a lie," she said. "So when I met her, I gave her the chance."

* * *

By 2014, Shannon Swope had a small, federally subsidized apartment. Jaylynn had just moved in. Valery's social workers and court representatives felt that giving Shannon custody of Valery would be risky but worth trying.

We tried to give them a chance because nowhere else was working," said Shepherd, the DHS worker.

And whenever possible, Shepherd added, it is "still necessary for a child to be connected with a family member. It's what we shoot for. It's what the children want, and they thrive so much more with family."

Shannon Swope says the process to get her daughter back was rigorous. "I went through mental health evaluations, psychological screenings, everything, everything all over again. I went through hell."

In April 2014, a Family Court judge gave Shannon Swope temporary custody of Valery, then 17.

"We were in there [the courtroom] crying," Shepherd recalled. "It was a happy day.

* * *

She thought it was perfect, thought it was worth it,
Hoped it'd be what exactly she had longed [for].
But boy, was she guessing, because she was so wrong.

Happiness didn't last.

Mother and daughters give very different versions of what happened, but the bottom line is that three months after granting Shannon custody of Valery, the judge revoked it. The mother had left. The girls changed the locks. Police got involved.

Mother and daughter have had no contact since last July.

Shannon Swope says she still loves her daughter. Valery says she doesn't believe a word her mother says.

* * *

Last fall, Valery enrolled at Arise Academy Charter in West Oak Lane, created five years ago for students in foster care, community homes, or shelters.

Valery did so well at Arise that in January her guidance counselor brought up the subject of college.

"We're going to do a college essay," Megan Hannah said.

"Be ready," Valery replied.

She wrote her poem in a day, and improved it over the next several weeks.

Valery always wanted to go to college, but acknowledges it likely wouldn't be happening now if not for Arise, which was closed at the end of the school year by the Philadelphia School District. Arise leaders plan to reopen in September, with private funding.

Arise, with about 100 students, provided an environment where Valery felt respected, where school officials recognized many students were dealing with trauma, and deadlines were soft.

School officials intervened when Valery needed clothes, housing, even tokens. But they insisted she get her work done. As graduation approached, Valery often stayed until 7 p.m. and came in on weekends.

* * *

Robert Reese, vice president of enrollment at Cabrini, said officials were impressed by Valery's progress, resilience, and of course her poem. He believes Cabrini has the resources and commitment to help Valery succeed.

Hannah, the guidance counselor, who completed Valery's financial-aid forms and has helped at every step of the application process, said that after generous grants from Cabrini and a few smaller scholarships, Valery will need only to borrow $9,500 in federal loans to cover the $40,000 in tuition and room and board.

"I'm not really thinking about it," Valery said of the debt. "I just want to go to Cabrini."

As Valery walked into a campus event this spring for accepted students, undergraduates in blue Cabrini T-shirts stood in two lines cheering.

Valery high-fived them. She posed for a photo with the mascot, the Cavalier.

It was a glorious Sunday, azaleas and dogwoods about to pop.

All around were accepted students and their families. Valery was accompanied by Hannah.

Valery wants to major in criminology. She'd like to be an FBI agent or to work in the justice system helping sexually abused children. As Cabrini professors explained the courses and opportunities, Hannah whispered to Valery, explained what semesters are, that everyone starts with introductory classes.

At lunch, Valery visited booths for various campus groups, talked with students from the dance club, swim team, and literary magazine. Students at Pura Vida (Pure Life) told her she didn't need to be Hispanic or speak Spanish to join, just to "have pride in who you are."

Valery signed up.

* * *

Valery lost touch with Officer Varley, but never stopped thinking about him.

This spring, on the advice of Goodhue, the FBI agent, she called the 17th Precinct and found him.

They arranged to meet.

In a mall parking lot, she ran to him, hugging him with all her strength.

"Helloooooo," she sang out, still in his embrace.

He was carrying a bag.

"This is for you."

Inside were a teddy bear and a heart necklace.

They walked into the Cheesecake Factory for dinner. The officer introduced his wife, Sue.

He told Valery what he remembered of the first hours of her life, what he saw when he looked in a window of the abandoned building.

"I saw a plastic bag tied in a knot and the bag was moving."

He took an ax to the door frame, then kicked in the steel door. At last, with building debris and dust falling all around, he got to the wriggling bag and ripped it open. Her umbilical cord was still attached.

"Your body temperature was in the 70s when I got you," he told Valery. "They didn't know if you were going to make it."

Both were choking up.

"You brought tears to my eyes, from point one all the way till now," he said.

Varley, 51, was retiring after 25 years on the force. Seeing Valery again, accepted into college, was the perfect ending to his career, he said.

"If you make the wrong moves now," he added, "guess who's coming for you."

The Varleys drove her home.

Valery slept that night with her bear.

* * *

On June 24, Valery passed her last high school class.

The next night, in white cap and gown, Valery entered a small auditorium at William Way Community Center. She put her hand to her mouth, as 60 people stood and cheered.

Among them were:

Officer Varley with another gift, a small sterling silver replica of his badge on a silver chain that he said she'd asked for.

Mike Goodhue and two other FBI agents.

Shemaria McKnight, a supervisor with Carson Valley Child Services, holding flowers.

A child advocate from the public defender's office.

Valery's sister, Jaylynn, who hopes to finish high school one day and go to college herself; and Valery's old boyfriend and his mother, who remain close to her.

Just before graduation, Roberta Trombetta, the acting CEO at Arise, asked Valery to speak.

For one nervous minute, she talked about "trying to stay persistent and positive." She gave "a big thanks to everyone who helped us along the way," especially Hannah and school leader Meredith Lowe. She congratulated her classmates.

Later, the nerves were gone and the joy set in.

"I'm done. I'm done. I'm really done! And I did it. I did it. I made it to this day," she said after the ceremony.

She is working as a counselor at a summer camp in the city. Next month, she will start college.

The first thing she'll do is hang a Marilyn Monroe poster on her dormitory wall. Then she'll try to figure out the rest.

POSTSCRIPT

I had written about Valery's charter high school years earlier, and had asked the principal to be on the lookout for a story about one student that would convey the challenges her students faced and the ways her school helped. When I read Valery's poem, I knew I had to tell her story.

I followed Valery for months, making sure she graduated before I published the story. I had to be mindful of the impact on her mother after all these years, and to be extremely careful how I handled the darkest moments of her past. My favorite moment in the story: when Valery reunites with the cop who saved her.

Valery received an avalanche of support from readers, one of whom took her shopping to outfit her dorm room.

But the narratives in this book are true stories, not fairy tales. Even with all the help and support, Valery didn't do well academically at Cabrini. She left after the fall semester. She still has her struggles, but her posse hasn't given up on her.

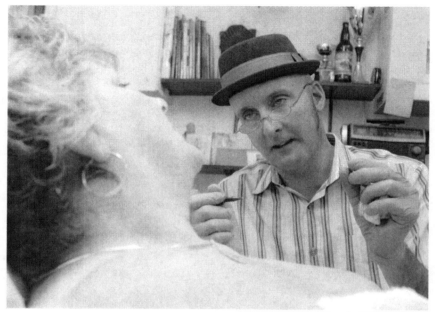

Photo by CHARLES FOX

Vinnie Myers works on a patient

14

THE NIPPLE MAN

A godsend for breast cancer survivors

Vinnie Myers, tattoo artist, practices a restorative art

October 22, 2012
FINKSBURG, Maryland

Penny Kurek, 53, sat in the chair. Her breasts were exposed. She stared at them in the mirror.

"I've been cut on so much," she said. "I just want to feel like a woman again."

Her voice was weary. But there was also relief. "I'm happy. This is the final step. I'm ready to move on with my life."

Breast cancer nearly did her in. So many complications. For eight years she stuffed a washcloth in her bra. But now the odyssey was almost over. She looked in the mirror at her reconstructed breasts, with scars going across them from double mastectomies. They had a nice, feminine shape, but no nipples. The nipples, as in most mastectomies, had been removed.

Penny had never been to a tattoo parlor, like nearly all of the 2,000 women here before her. But she wasn't as nervous as she had expected.

"Stand up for me, Darlin'," Vinnie Myers said.

He studied her breasts.

"There is some asymmetry, obviously," said Vinnie. "So we're not going to be able to get them exact."

"I know," she said. "But like my doctor told me, 'They're not twins, they're sisters.'"

"That's right," laughed Vinnie, who is tall, trim, and always works in a porkpie hat, because he doesn't want women staring at his shaved head.

Vinnie took a peach-colored Sharpie and drew concentric circles where the areola, the dark area around the nipple, and the nipple itself ought to be. First on her right breast, then her left.

"This is the main thing that you do?" Penny asked him.

"Yep. Just nipples. No more Tasmanian devils for me."

Vinnie, 50, started out in Army boot camp tattooing serpents on soldiers. In the last decade, in a wonderfully American evolution, he has become almost a folk hero in the breast cancer world, saluted and admired by doctors and patients alike.

He has perfected the three-dimensional nipple tattoo, restoring a final mark of femininity to at least three women a day, who have come from as far as Saudi Arabia and Brazil to Vinnie's Tattoo Parlor in a strip shopping center 30 miles west of Baltimore.

"His results are just so superior to what else we've seen, and I've seen nipples from all over the world," said Marisa Weiss, founder of *BreastCancer.org* and a radiation oncologist at Lankenau Hospital in the Philadelphia suburbs. Many area hospitals are now using tattoo artists.

"Women have been through so much," Weiss says, "and then they make a big commitment to reconstruction, and if the nipple doesn't look good, it screws up the whole thing. It's hard to get a perfect result from reconstruction. But if you get a great nipple in the middle, it distracts the eye, which is very forgiving. It doesn't see the scars or imperfections, or little bulges; the eye goes to the nipple, and nipples rule. Definitely."

This is certainly what Penny, secretary to a Maryland state court judge and mother of three, was hoping for. When Vinnie finished outlining circles with his marker, she faced the mirror again.

"Better than what I have now," she said.

"I can just give you the Sharpie," he quipped. "You can draw them every morning."

"Takes me too long to do my hair and stuff," she said. "I don't have time for that."

Penny sat back in the artist's chair. Vinnie put a blue drape over her. He leaned her back, as a dentist would.

"Let's go, Darlin'," he said.

* * *

Vinnie stumbled into this meaningful life quite by accident. He joined the Army at 18, and his roommate in boot camp was a heavily tatted grunt from Long Island. The roommate saw Vinnie sketching all the time, sketching, sketching. He saw that Vinnie was a terrific artist and persuaded him to get into tattoos. So Vinnie experimented on some "not so bright MPs" and developed his art.

His was a conventional tattoo existence – fighting the stereo-type, the public's disdain – until 2001.

Vinnie got a call from a Baltimore plastic surgeon who was doing nipple tattoos during breast reconstruction. But he wasn't very good, and he asked Vinnie if he'd give it a try on some of his patients.

Vinnie did. He started learning all he could, and he conclud-ed that techniques used by mainstream medicine were primitive.

"The industry standard has always been draw a circle where the nipple should be and color it in," Vinnie said. "When I first started doing it, I said to myself: ''Why should I do a tattoo of a nipple and make it look like a pepperoni, when I can make it look like a nipple?'"

Here are the facts:

About 290,000 women will get diagnosed with breast cancer this year. About 50,000 will get reconstructive surgery, and 90 percent of those get some sort of areola. But it can be unsatisfy-ing, with no image of a nipple. Furthermore, says Vinnie, sur-geons often use vegetable-based dyes that fade quickly.

Vinnie developed a better-looking nipple, and the world be-gan to notice.

In 2008, *Vogue* magazine wrote one paragraph about Vinnie. A pa-tient at the Johns Hopkins Breast Center read it and asked staff there whether they knew Vinnie, since he was local, and whether they would recommend she go see him. The answer in both cases was no.

But the patient went to see Vinnie anyway, got the tattoos, and returned to Hopkins to show Lillie Shockney. She is the administrative director of the Hopkins center, a renowned figure in breast cancer circles, and a survivor who has had double mastectomy and reconstruction.

Shockney visited Vinnie and got the tattoos herself.

When she had finished crying, she asked Vinnie: "How busy do you want to be doing this? You have no idea."

* * *

Penny lay back in the chair, her chest exposed.

"I've been in this position way too many times," she said. "But this is a good thing. You're not going to cut on me, right?

"No, Darlin'," he said.

Vinnie's workplace feels clinical. He wears purple latex gloves, like any health professional, although clients often suggest he wear pink ones, something he's considered.

He leaves the room while his patients undress and dress, just another way to keep the feeling professional.

He has an assistant, Richie French, home from two tours in Afghanistan, who is tattooed from head to toe but wears an Oxford shirt and tie. He is like a dentist's assistant, preparing the space, wiping down the instruments, putting fresh plastic over the wires of the tattoo guns, setting up a row of little cups, the size of toothpaste caps, in which Vinnie will squirt all his colors. Vinnie starts with a basic mix, but he tints each one differently, even finding use in Penny's case for a dab of turquoise.

"You're really fair with a slightly yellow tint to your skin," he told Penny. "So I have to account for that. I'm going to go somewhere between a mauve and a suntan brown. I think that will work for you."

Penny, from Bel Air, Maryland, liked the sound of that, suntan brown. A day at the beach. She relaxed.

Vinnie rubbed a diaper cream like a petroleum jelly on the work space, then began to paint his canvas.

He alternated between two tattoo guns. One is a shader, the other a liner. The guns sounded like an electric shaver.

Because of nerve damage from their mastectomies, many women don't feel significant pain. Some surely do, but the range of discomfort varies from one woman to another, from one breast to another.

Vinnie said with certainty that if these nipple tattoos felt like other tattoos, "none of these women would be sitting here."

Penny felt the tattoo gun for sure. "Kind of feels like a needle when they numb you," she said, and later described it as "bee stings." But she was easy, a model client, the pain insignificant compared with all the pain she had experienced before, and as Vinnie worked, he and Penny continued a relaxed conversation.

"My husband encouraged me to come," she said of the man she met at 14 and married at 18. "He is the only one who will see me. He wanted me to feel more like myself."

Vinnie first tattooed in the lines of the two circles, then started shading the areola, making his way to the nipple itself. He also took special care to do what are called Montgomery Glands, the little raised dots in the areola.

Creating a three-dimensional image, the appearance of a raised nipple, is all about using light, shadow, and color to create illusion. This is what distinguishes a gifted artist.

Doing one breast on a woman is actually harder than doing both, and can take longer. When Vinnie's doing two breasts, for a client who has had a double mastectomy, he can use the same color on each and knows they will look alike. But with a single breast, he has to match his tattoo with the color, texture, and shading of the existing nipple, and that can be tricky.

"You should teach other artists," Penny suggests.

"I'd like to," he says. But right now he can't. He recently signed a contract with the prestigious Center for Restorative Breast Surgery in New Orleans to do tattooing there one week every month. He has no time, and he has also stopped regular trips to Lankenau.

Vinnie charges $400 per client, what he feels is a fair price. He says that because of the Women's Health and Cancer Rights Act of 1998, insurers will cover them, though often not without a fight.

"We found over the years," he said, "first they needed a diagnosis code, than a CPT code, then a prescription, and over time we've learned what these things were, so now we tell the ladies. And they submit these things with their receipt."

* * *

About two years ago, Weiss, the Lankenau physician, led a bus trip of 10 women to meet Vinnie. She'd heard about him from Shockney.

Rather than go to his parlor west of the city, the women met Vinnie on a yacht in Baltimore's Inner Harbor. One by one, they went into a state room with him, showed their breasts, and he did evaluations and set appointments.

"We went nipple shopping. Really, we did," said Nancy Schmidt, one of the 10. "We looked at all of his pictures, and all of the women were showing their breasts and saying, 'What do you think?' It was like having a private consultation with a doctor, except he was a tattoo artist."

Afterward, they all went to lunch.

Vinnie dresses nicely, in slacks and a long-sleeved collared shirt. When he's working, he has no visible tattoos. He promised his wife years ago that he'd keep them off his neck and forearms, hidden from view in any professional setting.

But his back and chest are covered with body art, and these 10 women from Philadelphia wanted to see it.

They told him to take off his shirt.

"Now?" he said meekly. "In the middle of this restaurant?"

"Yes," they insisted. They had all taken their shirts off in front of him. He was embarrassed but stood and unbuttoned in front of all of Baltimore.

"It gave me a really good perspective of what it's like for them," he said.

Schmidt, a nurse from Rosemont, was the first of the Philadelphians to get tattoos from Vinnie.

"I love them," she said. "He picked the perfect color, the perfect size. I feel I could undress in a female locker room, and I don't think women would notice."

* * *

After an hour in the chair, Penny was finished.

He had her sit up, and look at herself in the mirror.

"Wow. That is amazing. It's been almost two years since I had a nipple. It's really incredible. It really makes the scar look less there."

There were days she thought she would die from cancer, never have breasts again, and never feel like a woman again. And here she was staring at what looked like healthy normal breasts, with fabulous nipples.

"It's incredible," she repeated.

"I'm going to go to Victoria's Secret and get a pretty bra."

"It's got to be see-through," said Vinnie.

Lost in her thoughts, she was not really listening to him.

"I feel complete again," she said. "Now I can feel like I'm done."

"You are," said Vinnie.

He left the room, so she could take her time, enjoy the moment, and get dressed.

POSTSCRIPT

The serendipity of life is just wonderful, where and how people find meaning and purpose. Vinnie's business has grown and grown, and now his daughter is working with and learning from her father.

Kevin McCloskey and Bridget McGeehan
in front of their home

15

ON HIS OWN TWO LEGS

This wounded veteran is standing tall
Rebuilding his life after an explosion in Afghanistan

July 7, 2014

Kevin McCloskey, 27, is getting married in May to a girl he first kissed under the Wildwood boardwalk in fifth grade. At least that's what he says. She swears it was the summer after sixth grade, maybe seventh.

"Every time he tells the story," says Bridget McGeehan, 27, "it gets earlier and earlier."

Kevin and Bridget, who grew up blocks apart in Mayfair, own a house now in Elkins Park. They have two dogs, a mastiff, Murdock, who pees at the slightest excitement, and a tougher little terrier named Dean, as in Martin.

Kevin bartends two nights a week on Frankford Avenue. He pivots behind the bar with a dexterity you only get on the job.

Two or three days a week, Kevin golfs. On a good day, he scores in the low 90s, although he did wrap a 6-iron around a tree this spring on not such a good day.

Six years ago last month, Kevin was blown up in Afghanistan. When he saw out of his left eye that he had no legs – his right eye had shrapnel in it, and is now blind – he told his guys to let him die on the mountain: "I don't want to go home like this. Just let it go."

He has come home. Perhaps the most extraordinary thing about his life is that it can be so ordinary – celebrating his birthday last week in North Wildwood, watching the World Cup at the Piazza in Northern Liberties, drinking beer after bar-league golf outings.

According to a 2013 Veterans Affairs report, an estimated 22 American veterans were committing suicide every day. Tens of thousands of Iraq and Afghanistan war veterans struggle with addiction or post-traumatic stress disorder. The VA has been widely criticized for its handling of these and other problems.

"We hear about all those veterans who have issues," said Pat Dugan, a municipal court judge who also runs Philadelphia's veterans court. "They become the headlines. We're not hearing about guys like Kevin. They go and serve and come home and become citizens. Kevin is the best example. He's a bartender. He stands on his feet working."

Dugan asked Kevin to speak at the Korean War Memorial at Penn's Landing on Memorial Day.

"This city has brought me back," Kevin said that day. "My family, my friends forced me to walk, to work. I wouldn't have made it without them."

* * *

After graduation from North Catholic High School in 2005, Kevin worked a year restocking fruit at Capriotti Brothers on Frankford Avenue before joining the Army. He wasn't driven by patriotism, at least he didn't realize it at the time. He wanted to prove to himself and his family that he could get his act together. He thought he'd get a great experience, come home, and get a union job like his father and brother.

After four months in country, on June 8, 2008, he was driving in a convoy of humvees. Kevin doesn't remember the moment before the explosion, but his passengers told him he spotted the improvised explosive device and tried to swerve.

The driver's-side front wheel took the brunt of the blast. The other soldiers walked away, one with a broken leg. Kevin's right wrist and pelvis were shattered. His legs were gone – the right above the knee, the left below it.

His lieutenant had told him he didn't have to go on that mission. He had suffered a bad sunburn the day before. But his unit had taken fire two weeks earlier returning from the same village, and Kevin couldn't let his guys go without him.

He spent the next 12 weeks in an induced coma at Brooke Army Medical Center in San Antonio, waking only briefly. He remembers only enough to know how horrible it was.

His sister, Michelle McCloskey-Alicea, dealt with her grief through poetry. Seeing Kevin in the ICU the first time, she wrote:

His eyes slowly opened with an intense gaze,
Searching for clarity in this tragic haze.
And when his eyes stared up at me,
We both began weeping at reality.
I took his hand in mine
Longing for words to ease his mind.
Yet there were no words, only cries,
For bitter anguish has no disguise.

Kevin had 12 surgeries, and spent 16 months in Texas healing, getting therapy.

His mother moved in with him at first.

Two of his best friends from home – Chucky Dugan and Alex Ryzinski, who will be attendants in his wedding – flew down to visit.

"They bitched me up," Kevin says. "'Dude, stop being a baby. Get up. There's guys who got it worse.'"

Early in his recovery, Kevin was in the hospital elevator one day in his wheelchair, without legs.

A burn patient – ears, nose, lips disfigured, his face scarred – looked at Kevin and said, "Oh, man, it feels good to walk around today."

Kevin fired back: "Oh, I had a great shave today" – something the burn victim obviously couldn't do.

The burn victim loved it. He'd been busting on people hoping somebody would bust on him right back. The two visited often in the hospital.

Kevin flew home for the first time on Halloween, 2008. Police escorted him up I-95 from the airport. A flag the size of a small state flew from a fire truck outside his house.

"Every person I knew my whole life was standing there with a flag in their hand," he said. "Friends were clapping and crying. I didn't know what to do at first.

"That's where reality hit me in the face. That's when I knew I can't ignore it. I got to do this for them. It's not just for me anymore. I got to get back to who I am. I got to get off these crutches for them."

* * *

That first Christmas, home for a visit, he was just beginning to put full weight on his prosthetic legs. He was at a bar and had to urinate. His friends threw his crutches across the room. Kevin yelled for 20 minutes, then finally got up and took a step, and another, shocking himself and everyone else that he could walk.

He emerged from the bathroom and found his buddies in a puddle of tears.

One night, in the fall of 2009, 15 months after his injury, he posted on Facebook: "Another lonely weekend in Texas. I can't wait to come home."

Ryan Sullivan, a Marine veteran from Mayfair who had been injured himself, now a city cop, saw Kevin's post. He was at home, waiting to hit a bar in Northern Liberties. Sullivan had waited months to come home after his own rehabilitation.

He got home from the bar at 3 a.m., went online and booked a 7 a.m. flight to San Antonio. He called a sober friend to drive him to the airport.

Sullivan arrived in San Antonio about 9 a.m.

He called Kevin.

"What's your address?"

"What are you sending me?" Kevin asked.

"Dude, I'm here. At the airport."

"The %$#@ you are!"

They got a case of beer. Then went to a dueling-piano bar. They woke up the next morning with matching tattoos, from Elvis, "TCB" – taking care of business. TCB meant Elvis could count on you. TCB now meant these two could count on each other.

Sullivan said, "Let's go to Vegas."

They flew there. The weekend cost $7,000, Sullivan said. Worth every penny. To this day, when Kevin McCloskey needs to talk military, to vent, Sullivan is his man. Sullivan will be in his wedding.

* * *

At no charge, contractors rebuilt the McCloskeys' basement, where Kevin lived for nearly three years.

"He was struggling," said his mother, Joann. "Just to reestablish himself in the community and the world. He wasn't bad. He just wasn't ready to get out there."

Kevin rarely left in daytime. "It was like I was trying to cover up for myself," he says. "Make it seem like it wasn't what it was."

Joann McCloskey said Kevin always had tenacity.

"You have to have that in you to get out of such a deep, dark spot when you realize your life is totally horrible," she said. "How do you dig that deep?"

Despite his pain, emotional and physical, he avoided addiction. "From day one," said his mother, "once he was able to make his own choices, he chose the minimal amount of medication he could take."

In time, he emerged from the basement.

"The last two years," his mother said, "have been more about him becoming independent and rejoining the world."

Bridget had a lot to do with that. And golf.

* * *

When she heard about his injury, Bridget wrote on his Facebook page, "Thinking of you.'

He started calling from Texas. She had a boyfriend but she'd always take Kevin's calls. The boyfriend didn't like it and didn't last.

When Kevin came home for a visit, she'd see him. Their friendship just grew.

Love hit her like a lightning bolt.

"I never had feelings for Kevin in that way," she said. "I loved him as a friend and would do anything for him. It was really out of nowhere. I realized one day, he's really good-looking. That was it for me. I just knew."

"I feel like I am pretty good at figuring out his mood now," she says. "If he's feeling depressed, I know it has nothing to do with me. I got really good at separating that. He knows I'm there if he needs to talk. If he needs space, I'll give him a day."

"I feel like in the last couple years, he's really become way more comfortable with the situation," she says. "He's able to wear shorts now. Two years ago he wasn't able to do that. He's finally embracing 'This is who I am now.' "

Kevin says he has accepted his injuries. "It's almost like a different life now," he says.

Putting on prosthetic legs, most days, is "like tying my shoes."

But not every day.

"If I go golfing and then have to bartend," he says, "next day I'm going to be sore. I'd say once a month, I have that day where I say, 'WTF, I really don't feel like putting my legs on....' That's when I tell myself, 'You're feeling bad for yourself.'...And I move on."

* * *

Kevin is close to Tim Rayer at Prosthetic Innovations, who helped design and fit Kevin with his legs. Rayer played a big role in getting Kevin into golf, taking him on outings, improving his swing.

"I can't say enough good things about Tim," said Bridget. "It takes a special person to give this much."

Many times Kevin has fallen swinging a golf club. He still falls on occasion. But he keeps getting up.

"Golf changed his life, no doubt," said Kevin's older brother, Mike, a glazier. "He can do stuff outside, which is huge. He can compete and talk trash and all that stuff."

Kevin says he'd like to get a job at a golf club. He also has been speaking in schools, and would like to do more. But he has no urgent need to work. For his sacrifice, the United States gives him $5,000 a month. Mayfair hosted a fund-raiser soon after his injury, and that money helped him buy the house. Bridget also works as a waitress at Parx casino.

Kevin is proud of his service, a big supporter of the U.S. military. He usually keeps his opinions to himself, but as he wheeled his trash to the curb the other night, he had this to say about the escalation of fighting now in Iraq:

"I kind of feel like we should stay out of it. We lost all these people. Now this stuff is going on again. Are we going to go back again and lose some more? For something we can't fix right now? We can't fix it."

Kevin did his duty, paid his price, and has done his best to move on. If life is an attitude, perhaps this is a good example of where Kevin McCloskey is:

After golf the other night, he and two friends stopped at a bar and played Quizzo. They lost, but won a round of drinks because Kevin came up with the best team name – "3 players 4 legs!"

POSTSCRIPT

I was working Memorial Day – at *The Inquirer* we never escaped holidays and weekend rotations – and I was assigned to cover the reopening and rededication of a refurbished Vietnam Veterans Memorial at Penn's Landing. It was a beautiful day, and I left early and walked over.

On my way to at the Vietnam Veterans Memorial, I walked past the nearby Korean War Memorial, with its own Memorial Day services underway, and I saw Kevin introduced and speaking. I'd been writing – the whole world had been writing – about all the veterans who struggle with PTSD and addictions, and as I stood there listening, watching, it occurred to me it was equally fascinating and important to tell the story of somebody who lost both legs but adjusted well.

I'm still not sure I completely explained why Kevin succeeded when so many else have struggled. I'm pretty sure it was his friends, his community and his true love that kept him moving forward and gave him incentive to rebuild his life.

I didn't have room for the following anecdote in the original story, and so I tell it here:

In February 2014, Kevin and Bridget went to North Wildwood, at the Jersey Shore, for Leprechaun Leap, a dash into the sea. They weren't going to jump into the ocean; they weren't that crazy. But for reasons Bridget couldn't understand, Kevin insisted she get all dressed up.

"We were walking down the boardwalk," she recalled. "It was raining and cold. I'm so mad. 'Why are we doing this?' We get to Ed's Funcade, and he says, 'Let's go under the boardwalk.' "

She began to comprehend.

This was the spot they first kissed in 5th grade.

He got down on one knee, a gesture he'd been practicing for months. Suddenly, friends, family and a photographer appeared.

He promises that her life will be full of surprises.

Bridget and Kevin as children

Photo by TOM GRALISH

Luis Rodriguez comforts, and is comforted by, his wife Danielle

16

HIS LAST WISH

A dying man makes a final journey
So he could see his family settle into a new home

July 1, 2014

Luis Rodriguez knew it was the house for him and his family when he saw the rhododendron on the side, the size of a tree. He is a landscaper.

His wife, Danielle, loved the size of the lot, a corner, and the five bedrooms. She was excited about all the work her husband could do! This was in Williamstown, a place to raise their family.

Luis never finished high school in Camden. He worked, often seven days a week, to provide for his family. His wife worked full-time, too, first for Comcast, then for Penn Medicine scheduling appointments.

He painted and drywalled and planted, and his favorite memory in 13 years in that house was bringing his baby girl, Katie, now 8, home from the hospital.

Luis left that house on Tuesday.

His last walk out of the family room, through the dining room and kitchen, and out the door into the RV was a parade. His wife led, carrying his morphine and other medicines. He shuffled behind her, unsteady, heavily medicated to ease his pain.

Behind Luis, pushing his oxygen machine, was his best friend since fifth grade, Raul Paneto. Both had risen from the streets, owning their own homes, fathers to their children.

Next came Raul's wife, Clara, carrying a baggie of Q-tips and Chap Stick and the KY jelly that had been, even on such a tragic afternoon, the subject of many a joke. Luis needed it now to lubricate the inside of his nose, dried out from his oxygen and tubing.

Luis, 37, has a few weeks to live. That's what doctors told him. He never would have wanted to leave that house. But when he got sick last summer with acute myeloid leukemia, he couldn't work. He got disability from his employer, but it ran out, and he had to wait three months for federal disability.

Danielle cut back to part time to care for him and their three children, 17, 14, and 8. The bills mounted, she couldn't pay the mortgage, and the bank wouldn't modify the payments. One minute their family income is $80,000 and their daughter is going to dances; the next they file for Chapter 7 bankruptcy and surrender the house to the bank.

"They're such a lovely family," said Mindi Roeser, a palliative-care doctor at Pennsylvania Hospital. "It is a sad example of how even patients who are both employed and insured can still be financially ruined by illness."

Luis had a dying wish. His sister and her family live in Jacksonville, Florida. Danielle's mother, from Swedesboro, had recently moved to Jacksonville. Luis wanted Danielle and the children to relocate there. He knew they would be taken care of by family there – that they could start over, free of debt, of worry.

Luis wanted to see where they would live, see the backyard where his children could play, see that they made it safely. Then he could die, in peace, in Jacksonville.

"I knew my wife could not take care of all these bills and this house," he said Tuesday afternoon, sitting on the couch, hoarse, speaking very slowly, eyes drifting shut.

"It's been extremely hard," he said, "especially as a male provider who has done the best he could. I need to know they will be OK."

His wife was squirting morphine on his tongue with a syringe every three hours, and giving him nebulizer treatments to help him breathe. He struggled to stay awake, focused, alert.

Danielle looked for financial help where she could, when she could. "How many hats do I have to wear?" she asked. "How many hours are there in a day to care for your husband, try to stay sane for your children, be on the phone, get insurance, call disability? Thank God my family flew in. Thank God for friends, and my sister-in-law and brother-in-law have stepped up to the plate drastically. But I am only one. And I know it hurts Luis to see me ripping and running, and trying to care for him.

"There was just no help out there within a time frame or within reach willing to help us."

The family had planned to drive to Jacksonville in July. But Luis couldn't wait that long. Months to live became weeks.

He was in Pennsylvania Hospital from Father's Day till June 20. Doctors huddled for days, but couldn't find a way for him to travel safely to Florida. They thought it too risky.

On June 20, finding her voice, realizing she must call the shots, Danielle took her husband home, in time to see daughter Noemi, 14, before she went to the eighth-grade dance. Luis danced with her, in socks, in the living room, 30 seconds of bliss, before reaching for his oxygen.

Danielle and Luis were so discouraged. It seemed he wouldn't get his last wish to see the family relocate. But Roeser, the palliative-care doctor, suggested Vitas Hospice, a national provider that has offices here and in Florida.

Danielle made her pitch, and Monday morning, a miracle to her, Vitas consented.

Hospice would provide the oxygen and equipment for her to make the journey, and have staff waiting in Jacksonville.

On Monday afternoon, Danielle and her mother and sister-in-law and niece worked the phones and computers for three hours. They rented an RV in Marlton. They booked plane tickets for Grandma and the kids. Raul, Luis' best friend, would rent a truck and bring the furniture Friday night. Clara, his wife, would follow in Danielle's minivan with the dog.

Hospice explained that the worst that could happen was that Luis could die en route. "We're prepared to take that risk," Danielle said.

Danielle's mother, Marge Grasso, 59, had moved from South Philly to Swedesboro to be near her daughter and grandchildren. She moved to Jacksonville three months ago, got a job in a hospital, and rented a four-bedroom house. The family will live with her.

"I would go to Tibet if they went," Grasso said. "They're my whole world."

The children flew with her Tuesday afternoon.

The oldest child, Antonio, will miss his senior year in Williamstown. "Going to be hard, being the man, stepping up and handling a family at 17," he said.

"Not fair," said Noemi, her beautiful face a portrait of sadness. "Him getting sick and the move. I love him so much."

Katie, 8, cute, sweet, was smothered by aunts and cousins.

This is a classic love story. Danielle's best friend was Clara. Clara was married to Raul. Raul's best friend was Luis. Danielle went to visit Clara one day, and there was Luis lying on the couch. "Love at first sight can happen," said Danielle. "You just have to be lucky enough."

"These are really two good people," said Clara. "They turned their lives around. Made their dreams come true. They were so happy when they bought their first home here. They thought they were going to be here forever."

Now husband Raul is talking about selling his business, their home in Pennsauken with the backyard pool, moving to Jacksonville next year, so he can keep his promise to his best friend, and look after his family.

About 7 p.m. Tuesday, Luis was helped into the back of the RV, sitting on the double bed, Danielle by his side. She pulled blankets off all the kids' beds so Luis could feel surrounded by something familiar. The oxygen machine was hooked to a generator. Luis' brother, Frank, 42, would drive. Luis' sister, Kathy Ortiz, 39, would ride shotgun.

Raul couldn't watch the RV pull away. He went over behind that big rhododendron and wept.

The trip took nearly 20 hours. With the oxygen, they had to bypass tunnels. There was traffic. The driver had to nap.

Luis drifted in and out of a morphine haze most of the way. They arrived at their new home about 3 p.m. Wednesday. A hospice nurse met them.

"Things were hectic with him getting into the home," Danielle texted. "He was so thankful for all the support and this actually happening. He was happy to see the kids, mainly."

Barely 48 hours after arriving in Florida, after his dying wish came true, Luis passed away – around 9 p.m. Friday.

"It was peaceful," said Danielle. "I was holding his hand."

She believes he knew his family would be safe, and surrendered to the cancer.

POSTSCRIPT

An editor asked me to check out this story. I had no idea how powerful it would be. So glad I did it. I wanted to go in the van, but there wasn't room.

Fifty-year customer Sue Gagliardi waits for her hair to dry under one of Lucy Giambuzzi's old Turbinators.

Photo by RON TARVER

One of Lucy's customers, Sue Gagliardi, waits for her hair to dry
under one of Lucy's old Turbinators, better known as a bubble dryer

17

LUCY THE HAIRDRESSER

After 48 years, she's still primping
Lucy lifts her clients' spirits – and their 'dos

March 1, 1998

Lucy the Hairdresser 's first customer Saturday morning is always her older sister, Margaret, who has lived across the street for 60 years. Margaret hobbles over to have her own hair done and then helps her sister.

Lucy the Hairdresser, 87, has been cutting hair in her South Philadelphia rowhouse for 48 years. She is Lucy Giambuzzi by marriage, but she introduces herself simply as Lucy the Hairdresser. She cuts and sets the hair while Margaret Crisci, 92 next week, washes it, colors it and collects the money.

The basement salon has the same three art deco chairs and bubble dryers that Lucy the Hairdresser bought when she opened in 1950.

She has 14 customers left, and nobody comes without a cane.

Lucy works only Saturday mornings now, and she walks with a cane too. Yesterday, as usual, she climbed down the stairs backwards, holding on to the rail with both hands.

"We're not teenagers," she said.

Sue Gagliardi, 87, a regular for half a century, arrived about 9:30.

Sue kissed Lucy on the cheek.

"I live three blocks away," said Sue. "It takes me half an hour to get here."

Sue hung up her cane on the coat hook and sat down by the sink so Margaret could wash her hair.

"You know how many hairdressers she passes to come here?" asked Lucy. "About four. And the snow can be that high! [She held her hand above her waist.] She never misses."

Lucy married Rudy Giambuzzi when she was 28, raised a son, went to beauty school and graduated in 1950. The original state license and the first dollar bill she ever earned hang on the wall above the same vanity she used in beauty school and bought for $15 when she started her business.

"I always wanted to do hair," she said. "It was in me."

Margaret washed Sue's hair and then Lucy rolled it, put a hair net on her, and helped her over to the bubble dryer – the Turbinator. All three dryers work.

"I could get a lot of money for these," said Lucy.

"They belong in a museum," said Margaret.

The three women sat and gabbed for 20 minutes waiting for Sue's hair to dry, and waiting for Lucy's next two appointments to arrive, two sisters from Reed Street, Gertrude and Marie.

"Ahhhh, they feel a little rain, they don't come," said Lucy. "We're all old and sick. What do you expect?"

Lucy's remaining 14 customers are between 65 and 92. The others died or are too frail to come. One recently fell and broke her hand. Another has blood clots in her legs. Many need walkers and can't get down the steps anymore.

Sue's hair was soon dry, and Lucy removed the rollers.

Lucy also delivered some bad news.

"I'm gonna retire in May," she said.

"You're gonna retire in May? " Sue repeated in shock. "Ohhhhh…. What am I gonna do?…You better not. If you retire…forget it. You better work."

"Suz, you got to find another hairdresser, that's all."

"You better not."

All of Lucy the Hairdresser's customers have reacted the same way.

"They kiss my hand, my cheek," she said. "They plead with me. They visit the doctor, they come home down. They come to me, I lift them up. I make them so beautiful."

But Lucy is quitting. That's final. Don't call her. Don't ask for any appointments.

"I'll be 88 in May," she said. "Forty-eight years in this one room here. I've had it."

Lucy brushed and poofed Sue's white hair. Then Lucy sprayed Sue's hair. And sprayed it. And sprayed it.

"Put it a little higher, Lucy," asked Sue. She wanted her heavily sprayed hair to stand even taller.

"It's high enough," snapped Lucy.

"I like it high," insisted Sue. "I'm short."

"It's high enough," Lucy said with finality.

Lucy got out the scissors and trimmed the hairs on Sue's neck. Then she buzzed the neck with the electric clippers.

"See the nice neckline she's got," said Lucy. "Some of them got these chicken necks. Not her. Great neckline."

A little more poofing and Sue was done.

"That's it. You're beautiful."

The charge was $8.

Then Lucy sat and Sue sat and Margaret sat and they all rested.

Then Lucy swept the floor.

"Gert and Marie aren't coming," concluded Margaret.

"When they're sick they don't come," said Lucy. "They're old, they're old, they're old."

Margaret got up to go home. "I got to keep moving," she said.

Margaret is a widow for nearly 30 years. Lucy's husband, Rudy, is nearly 92. They just celebrated their 60th anniversary.

Margaret usually cooks dinner and brings it over for Lucy and Rudy. Lucy's granddaughter Stacy, who lives in South Jersey and whom Lucy and Margaret adore, was coming over yesterday afternoon to get her hair done and take them to the grocery store. Stacy is getting married in May, and Lucy of course plans to do her hair for the wedding.

"She's so beautiful," said Lucy. "When we go to the Shop-Rite, or any place, the men always stare. I fight with them. I say, 'What's the matter? You never seen a girl!' "

Margaret grabbed her cane and headed home to cook.

Lucy and Sue sat and talked and waited.

Just in case any customers showed up.

POSTSCRIPT

After I did this story, it sort of blew up. The talk shows in New York called, and wanted her on, but she wouldn't go to New York. So they sent big satellite trucks, which clogged up her small South Philly street, causing all kinds of commotion. She did get an invitation to the Trump Taj Mahal, which she accepted, and brought everyone. Lucy did retire, and a few years later, she died, and so did her sister. I felt so privileged to have shared a slice of that classic South Philadelphia life.

Photo by Bonnie Weller

Agnes Butler coaches one of her foster
children on his reading assignment

18

THE FOSTER MOTHER

Shaping young lives six at a time

In North Philly, Agnes Butler raises boys – 35 in 20 years

December 2, 2001

Agnes Butler was in the kitchen at 7 a.m., frying the sausage and stirring the grits. Two of her younger boys were setting the table. Another, Chip, was showering in the only bathroom. Hakeem was waiting to go next. Charles was still in bed.

Shawn, her sixth boy, sat in the living room, filling out a permission form for a field trip. Shawn, 17, has been with Agnes the longest; he moved in at 9.

"Basically, I think she's a person from God," Shawn said. "My mom couldn't take care of me because she's on drugs. He sent me here. She replaced my mother to give me love and care. I love her. We all do."

Agnes Butler, 47, cares for only six boys at a time, but on any given day you might find a few more.

On Thursday morning, James Hayes, 27, was making the toast. He lived with Agnes from age 16 to 20 and still comes round every morning with his son and fiancee to help. "She is my mom," James said. "She raised me. I come here so my son can see his grandma."

Shandell Moore, 22, home from Penn State University, walked into the kitchen, wiping sleep from his eyes. He moved in at 13, abused, unwanted and illiterate, and in his heart will never leave. He was here for Thanksgiving and he'll be here on Christmas morning, too.

"This is my home," Shandell said. "She is my mom. And all these boys are my brothers. They're the best place they can be – with her."

In all, Agnes Butler has raised 35 boys. Technically they are foster children, but not in her mind and certainly not in theirs. For 20 years, she has given them love and discipline and stability, not to mention hot meals, clean clothes, books to read, hugs. She has taught them to read, fish, cook, fold laundry, manage a weekly allowance, clear their plates, and, yes, make their beds every morning.

"It's almost like ministry to me," Agnes said after the boys had been ushered off to school. "I dig down and pull out – something. I would say it's an inner feeling. I feel that I have to help these kids be successful."

She walked to the bureau and picked up Hakeem's eighth-grade report card: A's in English and computer lab, a B in science, and C's in math and social studies.

"I can't ask for more than this," she said. "I'm going to try my best to give him a good Christmas present."

* * *

Agnes never expected to be a foster mother. She grew up in Philadelphia, graduated from Gratz High School, and earned an associate degree in child-care administration from Temple University. She never married or had her own children but has always loved kids. Her first job was in a school for emotionally disturbed children. A teacher suggested that she become a foster parent.

Her first placement, a teenage girl, was a disaster. "She thought she was my equal," Agnes said. Ever since, her children have been boys. The first, nicknamed Tag, now lives in Coatesville with his wife and four children, and works in a quarry. He often drops by, she said, putting money in her wallet or taking her to dinner. She has 13 grandchildren.

When Agnes' parents died, her father left her this three-story rowhouse two blocks west of Temple. Four boys sleep in one bedroom, on double bunk beds; the two oldest boys share another bedroom. She has her own bedroom, and there's a spare off the living room for alumni who show up.

There's one more bedroom, for Keith Martin, 36, who has been a brother to Agnes for more than 30 years. Keith's mother helped raise Agnes. Keith goes camping and fishing with Agnes and the boys, to Wildwood and to Busch Gardens.

He's there late at night in case she needs a midnight grocery run to the 24-hour Pathmark, or to chase after boys – like the one who sometimes sneaked out and played video games in an all-night arcade.

In the basement, Agnes has framed a second bathroom but doesn't have the money to finish it. She keeps a bucket of spackle around because somebody's always punching or kicking a hole in a wall. "I make them fix it."

She has attended three of her boys' weddings and one funeral. Two of her boys are homeless. "But they'll come by," she said. "I'll feed them. Always give them a meal." Two others are in prison. One boy stole Keith's gold watch and pawned it. Keith was hot, but he understands these boys are here for a reason.

One time, a boy stole Agnes' van and crashed it. She's on her fifth van in 20 years, a 1999 Voyager with 67,000 miles. Probably the worst thing that ever happened was the fire. Nine years ago, two boys were upstairs in a bedroom throwing lit matches. A third boy didn't like the smell and sprayed air freshener into the flame. Whoosh. Soon the house was on fire.

Agnes got everybody out safely and sat, her head in her hands, on the curb across the street as the house burned. She and her boys spent that night in her van. "I didn't want to leave the house until insurance adjusters nailed it up," she said.

The boys begged her not to let them be relocated into other foster homes. She took all her savings, money her father had left her, and rented rooms for $990 a month in the Korman Suites near Philadelphia International Airport for a year, until her home was rebuilt, "to keep the boys together."

For raising the boys, Agnes receives between $2,000 and $3,000 a month from the state of Pennsylvania. With it, she does the best she can. She's become expert at searching the discount racks at Macy's. And when her boys finally move out, she sends them off in style. "My boys always arrive with trash bags," she boasts, "but they leave with luggage!"

* * *

On Thursday, Agnes drove to the General John F. Reynolds School, where Charles is in sixth grade. She's always stopping in at schools, checking on her boys. She has no favorites, but Charles is special. He came to her at age 6, her youngest ever.

He knew his letters but couldn't sound out a word. She taught him to read.

She started with Arthur books. He got so good at reading that he wouldn't stop. More than once she has had to unscrew the bulb in the lamp by his bed to get him to go to sleep.

Agnes learned to teach Charles to read through a city schools program called the 100 Book Challenge. In fact, last week she won a community service award – and $11,000 for the 100 Book Challenge – from the Eagles.

She sat by Charles as he read.

"Primates are an intelligent animal," he read, "and they have a large brain." He stumbled on capuchins, the name of a species of small monkeys.

"Sound it out," Agnes said, and he did. "A primate's body is suited to its habitat," he continued, but Agnes interrupted him.

"What is habitat?" she asked.

"Home," he said.

"Very good," said Agnes, nodding. "Where you live."

Home is something Charles knows about. All of Agnes' boys do.

POSTSCRIPT

I received an avalanche of response from readers to this story, even though it didn't run on the front page. So many wanted to help her. Many donated money to finish that basement bathroom.

I had a really simple agenda with this story: Just give readers a flavor for life inside her home and give voices to some of the boys she has helped over the years. I thought it was important to say some are in jail and that two of them burned the house down. Those imperfections in the narrative only magnify the degree of her devotion and accomplishments.

I have long admired individuals who dedicate themselves to something with all their being and who seek no attention or reward. I know Agnes would tell you that for all she's given, she received so much more in return.

Ronald L. Speer

MY JOURNEY AS A STORYTELLER

On my first job, learning a priceless lesson

After graduation from college, I took a job with the after-noon paper in Norfolk, *The Ledger-Star*. I was assigned to the news bureau in Portsmouth, a poor little city across the har-bor from Norfolk. My beat was covering Portsmouth police and courts.

I was just 22, fresh out of college. I had never hung out in hous-ing projects, or written about murders. And here in Portsmouth I learned perhaps my most valuable writing lesson of all.

My editor was Ronald L. Speer, who had – in addition to a booming voice better suited for radio – a tabloid heart. He loved the big story, the colorful story, the human story. Ron was a chain-smoking, overweight, mustard-on-his-shirt classic print journalist, a real pro, a defender of the underdog, a man who loved the written word as much as he loved the good it could do.

We were an afternoon paper, and our deadlines were something like 11:45 a.m. for that afternoon's paper. I'd be out all morning, find what I considered an amazing story about life in this new world, and hurry back to the office. I'd walk in and Ron would greet me with that deep gravel voice, "Whattayagot?"

And I'd burst with enthusiasm. "You wouldn't believe what I found!" And I'd tell him all about the story I was going to write. I'd get so excited. He'd get so excited. He'd tell me, "Make it sing!" And as I headed to my IBM Selectric II typewriter with scanner paper (this was the old days), he'd get right on the phone to the front page editors in Norfolk. "Vitez has a great one coming," and really build it up.

I'd sit down and write. And I'd turn my story in maybe an hour later. He'd read it and his face would turn to mayonnaise. "What's this?" he would ask, so much disappointment in his voice he was barely audible. "This isn't nearly as good as the story you told me about an hour ago."

This happened, two times, three, five, maybe even 10 times. Same drill. I'd come in so excited, he'd get excited, then be crushed with disappointment.

So one day I came in, and said, "Ron, you won't believe what I've got!"

And he said, "Shut up!"

He pointed to my keyboard and commanded: "Write!"

And that is one of the greatest lessons I ever learned: *Tell it to your keyboard first.*

And he was right. The stories I began to write were so much better, because all that enthusiasm and excitement was coming out for the first time in written words. When you are telling a story, or describing a scene, *the first time you tell it is the most passionate, the most enthusiastic, with the most power.* And I learned from Ron and from those experiences the equally important corollary: *The first time someone hears the story is the time it resonates the most.*

By telling it to my keyboard first, the passion and enthusiasm is captured there forever, not lost in an oral recounting between reporter and editor. I will often, nearly always, go back and improve the story, refine it, trim it, do many things to it, double-check spellings and quotes. But the basic enthusiasm and emotion and excitement of the moment are locked in that first prose.

This lesson has always served me so well. And when I won the Pulitzer Prize nearly 20 years later, the first letter of thanks I wrote was to Ronald L. Speer, who taught me so much and who believed in me.

Bernice Gordon builds a crossword puzzle

19

THE CROSSWORD QUEEN

Keeping an active mind at age 100

Bernice Gordon is still on her game – creating puzzles

February 18, 2014

Eternal rest can't be too far off – Bernice Gordon is 100 – but for two nights recently, she didn't sleep. Didn't even get into bed.

The primary reason was a crossword puzzle she was constructing for the *Los Angeles Times*.

And there was the Australian Open tennis tournament as well.

Bernice, who lives at Atria Center City, an assisted living community, in an apartment overlooking Logan Square, has been creating crossword puzzles since she was a young widow, home evenings with two small sons and needing something to engage her mind.

She was rejected repeatedly at first. "My child," her mother scolded, "if you would spend as much time on cookbooks instead of crosswords, your family would be happier."

Luckily, she didn't listen.

Since her first puzzle was published in *The New York Times* in 1952, crosswords have given Bernice a lifetime of happiness, friendships, even love.

As she has grown very old, limited by walker and wheelchair, puzzles have become a refuge, where her world remains vast and challenging and rewarding. She corresponds with the nation's leading puzzle editors, who regard her as a regal figure.

"I just revere Bernice," said Will Shortz, the *New York Times* puzzle editor, who came to Philadelphia on January 12 for her 100th birthday party. Three days later, Bernice became the first 100-year-old ever to have a puzzle in the Times – 62 years after her first.

Bernice is one of 62,000 Americans 100 or older, though relatively few remain as sharp as she. It may be that her mind is so healthy because she works it out so rigorously. Research shows that those with an active mind in old age tend to have better acuity and less dementia.

* * *

Bernice still has a goal: create one puzzle a day.

But some take her as long as a week, and the *L.A. Times* puzzle presented a special challenge. (Spoiler alert for anyone in Los Angeles.)

She had FANNYPACK and FENNELTEA and FONDUEPOT and FUNNYBONE as the theme, but coming up with a FIN entry – and then fitting all five in alphabetical order – was bedeviling.

On top of all this, if she is not the most passionate fan of the world's top-ranked tennis player, Rafael Nadal, she may be the oldest. She watched all of the Spaniard's matches live – in the middle of the night in Philadelphia.

At 3 a.m. she e-mailed John Samson, puzzle editor for book publisher Simon & Schuster, and also a lover of Nadal and Spain:

"Juan, I am positively worn out. That was some close game!"

After a 5 a.m. bath, Bernice was restored – and completed her puzzle. She leaves her apartment only with a wheelchair. At home, she uses a walker for every step. Yet she can still climb over the lip of her tub – an Olympic-caliber feat for a centenarian.

Surgeon Richard Rothman has replaced each of her hips twice – the first replacements wore out. She also has arthritic knees. A hot soak is her sanctuary.

"Oh, it was so hard," she said the next morning of the *L.A. Times* puzzle. "I never went to bed." She did take afternoon naps. "The answers had to be in order, A E I O U. I couldn't get a grid. It was fierce. To get it symmetrical was bad, bad, bad, bad."

Her final theme words were FINKOUT. She admired the puzzle on her screen.

"Isn't it gorgeous?"

* * *

Bernice Biberman was raised in Germantown. Her father was a Russian Jew whose family fled the pogroms. He arrived in Philadelphia illiterate at age 8, and sold pencils on the street. He rose to vice president of L'Aiglan, a dressmaker at 15th and Mount Vernon Streets.

"I was brought up in the lap of luxury," Bernice said. "I never made a bed. I never washed a dish."

Her two older sisters attended college at the Sorbonne.

"When my year came," she said, "Mr. Roosevelt closed the banks, so I had to settle for Penn."

She graduated in 1935 with a degree in fine arts.

After college, she married Benjamin Lanard, 20 years older, cofounder of the commercial real estate firm Lanard & Axilbund.

They shared a beautiful life, traveled the world. He died at 52. She was 32.

She started making puzzles, married Allen Gordon.

"He died at the age of 52, like my first husband," she said. "Died in the same hospital as my first husband. Died with the same doctor and the same disease and the same nurses, 20 years later. A repeat performance from top to bottom. Cancer of the liver, both of them."

She raised two sons from her first marriage, a daughter from the second.

Twice a widow, she moved into a high-rise on Rittenhouse Square in 1967 and lived there 38 years. Her sister, Geraldine, lived in the same building. They spoke six times a day. Her death years ago was another blow.

Bernice had surgery for a brain tumor at 90, in 2004. Her younger son, Jim Lanard, a retired pathologist, thought she should move to assisted living in case the tumor grew back.

She was supposed to get annual brain scans, but stopped. "Even if it did grow back," she said, "it's too late for another operation. Enough already."

* * *

"Bernice's themes and puzzles are almost always straightforward, not at all gimmicky or tricky," said Rich Norris, puzzle editor at the *Los Angeles Times*. "Yet there's an elegance in her simplicity. She finds relationships among words that are so obvious when you first see them that you wonder why you've never seen this before.

"One of my favorites," he said, "was a puzzle in 2011 where the four theme clues were Obie, Odie, Opie, and Okie. The answers were all 15 letters...THEATRICALAWARD GARFIELDSFRIEND CHILDINMAYBERRY MANFROMMUSKOGEE...which is no minor achievement. Molding an answer to a certain length and keeping it smooth is a talent in itself."

Shortz has favorites, too, such as this name-puns theme from 1994:

ROSEGARDEN (Place for Pete?)
POWERHOUSE (Place for Tyrone?)
CROSSPATCH (Place for Ben?)
FOSTERHOME (Place for Jodie?)

Samson added: "The first Bernice Gordon puzzle I had the pleasure of editing was called 'Place the Names.' The theme was considered a tricky one at the time, involving names of famous people merging into cities and countries.

"For example, one clue was 'Soul singer seen in subcontinent?' and the answer was FRANKLINDIA (Aretha's surname merging into India)."

Typically, Bernice will propose a theme, and if editors approve, she will complete the grid and write the clues. A grid must look the same when rotated 180 degrees, a design challenge. Bernice for decades created grids with pencil and graph paper, but a granddaughter put puzzle software on her computer 12 years ago, so she now modifies her grids with a mouse click.

The New York Times' Shortz loved the theme for the puzzle that ran after her 100th birthday.

Bernice had proposed:

CARIBBEANC BLACKEYEDP
AFTERNOONT GEOGRAPHYB.

Shortz wanted her to work in two more phrases: ONLYU and WELLC.

She continually revises her clues, trying to improve them. Editors have the prerogative to change them. Her clue for GEOGRAPHYB initially was "Annual contest sponsored by a D.C. society." It appeared as "It's all about location, location, location."

* * *

Beginning in the early 1970s, the nation's leading puzzle constructors would meet monthly in New York City for an elegant lunch.

"We would have wonderful meetings," Bernice said. "Discuss new words. It was a closed affair and an honor to be there."

Norman Wizer of Malvern was 14 years younger than Bernice, but started sitting next to her at the luncheons, then driving her to New York and back. Soon they were a pair.

Bernice created an anagram of their first names, and they published puzzles together as Monica Brenner.

Every Sunday for years she took a train from 30th Street Station, and they would build puzzles at his home. Bernice loved a wooden carousel horse from Mexico, a work of art, at the top of his stairs.

When she could no longer take the train, he would come to her apartment.

They traveled to Europe together. She loved him.

"I was much better at words," she said. "But his [clues] were so hard that I didn't understand the finished puzzle. We were a wonderful team."

When Wizer went into a nursing home, Bernice called morning and night.

He died in May.

"In the end, he had another girlfriend," Bernice said. "She lived near him, and she could drive. I hated her. But she was a great help."

Wizer helped Bernice plan her centennial celebration at the Four Seasons. She wanted an accordion player, but he said classical guitar would be better. He told his niece if he died before the party, see that Bernice got the carousel horse. It arrived on her birthday.

She wept.

* * *

For seven years, Bernice has eaten lunch and dinner with the same women: Sophy Cohen, 99, who moved in the same year as Bernice and is like a sister; Evelyn Levitsky, 92; and Jacqueline Cotter, 92.

The four meet at noon at one table, and again at 4:45 p.m. across the Atria dining room, at another. Two come by wheelchair, two by walker.

At lunch the other day, the quartet sat mostly in silence, spooning lentil soup, sipping cranberry juice through a straw.

"After 10 years, there's not much conversation," Sophy said. "We know all the stories inside and out. So we just sit and relax."

Evelyn recalled the first time she entered the dining room. "I stood and looked and didn't know where to sit. Bernice approached and asked me to eat with her. She sort of saved me. We've been together ever since."

Sophy added, "It's very awkward when you come into a place where you don't know one person. You feel like a lost soul."

Sophy, Evelyn and Jacqueline deeply admire Bernice. "She's brave and strong," Sophy said. "She accepts things. She lost a son just a week before her party. She decided she's not going to cancel. She's just going to continue with her plans. That's the most amazing thing."

Bernice's older son, Benjamin Lanard, who lived in Spain, died at 76 after an illness. Sophy, Evelyn and Jacqueline cried with Bernice in her apartment.

Bernice teaches a crossword class to residents on Wednesday afternoons. She creates an easy puzzle and helps them solve it.

They sit in the Newport Lounge, at a long table.

"One across is part of a college campus in four letters, starting with Q," Bernice began the other day.

Silence.

"Quad," she said, spelling it out: "Q U A D."

And so it went.

They do best with questions from their youth.

When Bernice asked on 51 across, "Bojangles, what kind of dance did he do?" Julie Patillo got that right away. "Tap."

When Bernice said on 59 across, "Comical Allen," Ann Frank knew immediately. "Fred," she said.

The chef walked by and greeted Bernice like a VIP.

"This is the man who keeps me thin," she said.

He laughed. "I try not to give her too much tiramisu."

After the puzzle was complete and class ended, Bernice pushed her walker toward the elevator and said, "I am very patient, but I find it so frustrating. They can't get the simplest clues. It's very hard on my nerves."

Why do it?

"They have learned so much, and they thank me."

* * *

The Census Bureau estimates 442,000 centenarians by 2050. James Vaupel, a Duke University demographer and head of Germany's Max Plank Institute for Demographic Research, thinks that is too conservative, and estimates one million American centenarians by 2050.

"Most babies born in the U.S. since 2000 will...celebrate 100th birthdays," he said, but still relatively few will be as sharp as Bernice.

Yaakov Stern, a neuropsychologist at Columbia University, said that 15 years ago, researchers in aging thought that exercise and mental stimulation just kept the brain fit, improving neural networks that already existed.

But new research involving imaging, he said, shows that these activities actually reshape the brain, helping grow new neurons.

Stern said he's pathetic at crosswords, and one need not be Bernice Gordon. Gardening or even socializing can constitute a rich brain activity.

* * *

Bernice had much fun at her party. A great-nephew flew in from Seattle, a granddaughter from California. Her surviving son came from Arizona; her daughter and granddaughter from Chester County. A godson in Florida sent 100 roses. Samson, of Simon & Schuster, sent orchids.

The sheet cake depicted a crossword puzzle.

Her son said he saw two lessons in his mother's longevity: "You got to be tough to get through life, and you're never too old to be creative, to work, to enjoy what you're doing."

Shortz said he's hoping to publish a puzzle of Bernice's when she's 101.

But Bernice won't be disappointed if she doesn't reach that milestone.

A few days after her party, asked her feelings about death, she said: "It's not far away, and I'm quite ready. I'm in pain constantly, and it's not easy. It's not a happy existence. I'm content here because I love my apartment and I have the things around me that I love, and of course doing crossword puzzles is wonderful. It makes me think, takes me into another world."

Then she began to explain her latest idea for a theme, recasting a popular quote.

Instead of, "Where there's a will, there's a way," she was noodling with, "Where there's a will, I want to be in it."

She'd be up late working on it.

POSTSCRIPT

The day after the story appeared, I received a note from Bernice:

My dear friend Sophy died yesterday after a brief illness, and I am so depressed. In six months I have lost Norman, then Benjie, and now my closest friend. Your write-up gave me a lift and helped ease my depression. Thank you so much, dear Michael, for the thrill of seeing a worn and weary face on the front page.

Bernice herself died a year later, doing puzzles until the end.

To me, the beauty of this story is *showing* how her mind works. Readers truly want to understand how things work. The challenge is being able to explain it to them clearly, in the context of a story. No subject is too off-putting when handled well.

I hesitated a bit when I wrote the first sentence: *Eternal rest can't be too far off – Bernice Gordon is 100 – but for two nights recently, she didn't sleep.* I didn't want to put readers off with a sentence that some might consider to be in bad taste. But I decided it wasn't bad taste, it was true; Bernice would be the first to acknowledge it, and I loved the contrast with how she had stayed up for two nights, bedeviled by a crossword puzzle she was still trying to create. I thought it worked. But you the reader are the ultimate judge.

Dawn Staley grew up playing with the guys
at 25th and Diamond in Philly

20

HOME-COURT ADVANTAGE

Dawn Staley owes her success...
To what she learned on the asphalt of North Philadelphia

November 24, 1991

You can tell by the hightops that this crowd is serious. As they stride onto the smooth, swept pavement, the trademarks flash like dogtags: Nike, Reebok, Adidas, Converse, Fila. As more and more players arrive, rap spills from a living-room speaker set next to an '80 Riviera parked courtside, announcing that the evening's action is about to commence. Sides are chosen, and soon the basketball is in play.

The Moylan Recreation Center at 25th and Diamond is a proving ground, one of several playgrounds where Philadelphia's best players have always come to learn the game, to test themselves, to put their skills on display. Man and boy, they all played, or are playing, at Gratz or Dobbins or Franklin or Strawberry Mansion or a dozen other high schools. Many of them live on the streets around the playground, or in the Raymond Rosen housing project a block away. Some – such as the late Hank Gathers – have found renown. Night after summer night, their hopes – for respect, for fame, for the exhilaration of athletic dominance – flow along with their sweat.

And on this August night, one player stands out amid the giants – a diminutive figure, slight, maybe 5-5, wearing baggy shorts, a St. Joe's T-shirt, and low-cut Cons. The shoes and the height make no difference; neither does the fact that she is indisputably female. Once she takes the court, she is a player, driving to the basket, dishing off passes, swishing distant jumpers. When a pass flies down court, she pulls it in like a wide receiver, drives for the hoop and hits a teammate with a pass behind her back. The defense is surprised, the teammate is not; he lays the ball in, detonating a round of cheers on the sidelines. "That's it, Dawn!" "Count it!"

For another 20 minutes the game goes on, full-court, five-on-five, with all the shoving and shouting and pounding playground rules demand. When it's over, her team is on the wrong end of a 52-42 score, but for once that's not so important. Dawn Staley – Dobbins Tech '88, University of Virginia '92, likely Olympian, and current consensus as the best player on any college women's team in the nation—is home.

* * *

The Raymond Rosen project is an imposing sight. Eight towers rise out of the concrete around 23d and Diamond. Three are empty and condemned. The others all have their share of boarded-up windows. Dumpsters in the street are the first thing you see driving in, plus shards of glass in the street and, depending on the season, shirtless children in old shorts. An outsider might think it's a sinister and depressing place, but an outsider might be in some ways mistaken.

Behind the towers, across a few acres of asphalt, are blocks of rowhouses, six on each side, plus another row in back of those. Little gardens with sunflowers and pink flamingos lie out front, forming a central courtyard. Colored pennants flap in the wind as they crisscross above the courtyard. Little girls ride tricycles, men linger on porches.

This is home to Dawn Staley, the place that made her what she is – respected not only for her skills, but also for her character. It is also a place she'll most likely return to Saturday, when the University of Virginia women will play Temple at McGonigle Hall in a game arranged entirely to let her play once again before a Philadelphia crowd.

Clarence and Estelle Staley both moved to the city from South Carolina as teenagers with their families in 1956 and '57, respectively. They met and married young and, in 1967, moved into one of those rowhouses, which they now rent for $400 a month. Clarence worked 22 years for PennDot, jackhammering pavement. A heavy smoker, he had a heart attack two years ago, at just 47, and now is on disability. When he stopped working, Estelle started, taking over homemaking duties for elderly people in apartments on the Ben Franklin Parkway.

Together, they raised five children, and what they couldn't give with money they made up for with their attention. In an era when gang warfare claimed young lives the way the drug trade does today, the Staley parents simply laid down the law: "There were just some corners you weren't allowed to go," says Dawn's sister, Tracey, who's now 26. "My parents said don't go there, and you didn't go. Not unless you wanted a whupping."

Dawn's brother Pete, who's now 28, once had the misfortune to get caught clowning around on a street corner, making the sign of the Diamond Street gang with his fingers. "My dad grabbed me by the collar and shook me so hard," he recalls, "I never had nothing to do with gangs again."

Dawn, for her part, says, "Growing up around here, that's all you hear – the drugs and the crime. But I was more afraid of what would happen when I got home." She may be the family's only celebrity, but when she comes home she still washes dishes.

Estelle recalls teaching her children "that anything is possible as long as you work for it," and by the time she and Clarence were through, all five of their kids had graduated from high school and into working lives or college. Putting the Raymond Rosen project out of mind, however, was never much of a priority with them. Pete recalls his father periodically piling them all in the car and driving out to the suburbs. "These are the houses you want when you grow up," he would say. One time, Pete remembers, his father hit the number and asked the family if they wanted to move. "We all said no."

* * *

Now – particularly now – suburban upbringing is exactly what Dawn Staley doesn't miss. Although her family remembers the youngest Staley crying over something virtually every day until she was 10 or 11 years old, she was also a tomboy. "She climbed fences, climbed trees. Never played jacks or jumped rope," says Pete. "She never liked doll babies," says her mother. Dawn, now 21, will say only that "I was never the prissy type." And she could be hard. Once after a fight with Pete – he can't remember what it was about – she grabbed the only trophy he ever won and threw it on the railroad tracks that run behind their house.

Dawn was about 10 when her athletic gifts – and her love of sports – began to draw her outside, and there, they became apparent to the neighborhood kids. Soon enough, the friends of her three brothers would come around and ask not for Lawrence, Pete or Eric, but for Dawn. (Which, according to Tracey, "drove my brothers crazy. ")

She would play tackle football with the boys, always at quarterback, scarring her knees with the rest of them. She would play baseball with the boys, too. But mostly she played basketball, out on the expanse of asphalt separating the Raymond Rosen towers from the rowhouses. The kids called it "The Big Field," and by the time she was in her early teens, Dawn would play there till 2 a.m. Her mom never worried or objected; she figured Dawn couldn't get into any trouble playing ball.

And Dawn played constantly. She remembers her teenage summers this way: "Go out in the morning, play a few hours, come in and take a bath and go back out and play all night. There's not a whole lot else you can do, especially when you don't have a car. I wasn't much for parties. That's all I lived for, sports.

"What if I had grown up in the suburbs? I think about that all the time. There's access to recreation centers, but I don't think it's the same mentality. Here, sports is something like a job. It's something you do every day for hours; there's a game going on all the time. At noon. At midnight. In the burbs, people might be on vacation [summers]. But here, we don't have that luxury.... Living somewhere else, I probably wouldn't have played as much, or worked as hard."

Until she joined her high school teams, she always played against the boys. "Playing that young with guys, you kind of maintain the mentality of guys – you get aggressive," she says. "And they don't care who you are. They treat you as any other guy."

Reared on that kind of competition, Dawn excelled against other girls. She wasn't merely outstanding; she was in another league. Her high school coach, Anthony Coma, who also coached Earl Monroe, says she even played better in high school than the former New York Knicks star. "You knew what Earl was going to do on every play," he says. "You never knew what Dawn was going to do."

Partly, that was because she didn't either. What Dawn loves best about basketball is the spontaneity, the speed at which things happen (and at which she can make things happen). She was such a force in the Philadelphia Public League that she led Dobbins Tech to 60 straight victories and three city championships; as a senior, she was USA Today's scholastic player of the year. Before one game, the coach at William Penn High School had her players literally handcuff Dawn when they came out to shake hands before the opening tip.

In all her high school years, she gave the Dobbins coaching staff only one problem: getting to home games on time. Because the games started immediately after school, players were excused early from their last class of the day so they could dress. Dawn, however, had a computer class in her last period, and she refused to leave; she'd wear her uniform to class and sprint for the gym afterward. "I'd try like hell to keep those games from getting started until she got there," recalls Coma. "Books were more important. She was a rare breed."

By the time she graduated, she was rarer still: In an age notorious for pouty overachievers, Dawn was humble, modest and appreciative; she expected nothing. Almost everyone she knew – not just her friends and coaches, but her teachers, neighbors, even her opponents – rejoiced in her success.

Which is why it was a surprise when she floundered in her freshman year at college. She'd had scores of scholarship offers, but she chose Virginia in part because of its academic rigor – and almost immediately found herself put on "academic warning."

Classes at a historically Southern-aristocrat university were a big change from a city high school. "I wasn't used to taking notes," she said. "I had never taken notes before." At first, she was too scared to talk to professors, to ask for help, to admit that she was lost. But she took advantage of tutors, and of the university's writing center, and learned how to study, how to write a composition. "Once she knew she could do it," says her adviser, Stephanie McElhone, "it might take her twice as long, but she got it done."

Every summer, including this past one, she has taken courses to keep up. In three years, she has failed only one class, in astronomy, and when she took it again she earned a B minus. As a rhetoric and communications major, she's carrying a 2.2 grade-point average, and needs only 27 credits to graduate. When asked what her most rewarding achievement had been so far, she hesitates a moment and says: "I haven't got it yet. I think it will be when I get my degree."

This is saying something, given that she's already elevated her basketball game to the point where she won player-of-the-year awards last season from virtually everyone: coaches, writers, *Sports Illustrated*. She arrived in Charlottesville a flashy player not enamored of playing defense, but gradually set about rounding out her game (even now, she wears several rubber bands around her wrist, and when she makes a mistake on the court, she snaps them against her skin – just like Maurice Cheeks, her favorite player). Last year, she led her team in rebounding – even though her teammates included 6-foot-5 twins – and her defensive skills are beyond question. She is also acknowledged as a master at getting her teammates into the game.

"She just has an uncanny sense of finding the open man," says Virginia's head coach, Debbie Ryan. "She envisions the play before it develops. It's almost like an existentialist view of the game…. We had one game [against Stephen F. Austin, in the NCAA playoffs], we were losing with only a few seconds left. She spread the floor, drove toward the basket, drew the defense and flipped the ball to Heather Burge for the game-winning layup. She does it all the time."

One of the few times she didn't do it also proved revealing. In last year's NCAA championship game, against Tennessee, Virginia saw a slim lead dwindle to nothing as the clock ran out. With the score tied, Dawn grabbed a rebound, dribbled the length of the court, and put up a layup – which was tipped by a Tennessee defender. In overtime, Virginia lost the game and the title.

In the locker room afterward, Dawn was the one consoling her teammates. Even on the bus ride from the airport back to the Virginia campus, she tried to make a few jokes: Would anyone be waiting? Would they get booed? As they drove up, they saw that the parking lot was full. "Over a thousand folks were waiting to greet us, and we didn't expect anyone to be there," said Ryan. "Dawn just cried and cried; she broke down. I didn't even know if we'd get her into the building."

Now Staley is a celebrity in Virginia. After games, she'll sign autographs for an hour and a half; she frequently makes appearances at public schools, where young children mob her. ("Kids can relate to her," says Ryan, "because she's their size.") "A little kid wrote her a letter one time," recounted assistant coach Shawn Campbell, "and the next thing I know she's spending a day at the mall with the girl." Just last month, she even helped talk a 16-year-old fan out of jumping off a parking garage in Charlottesville.

Sometimes, it amazes her family that this is the little girl who cried when she wouldn't get her way, or the teenager who was so shy her aunt once asked, "What's wrong with Dawn? She never talks."

Her sister, Tracey, was stopping for a traffic light on 16th Street last summer when she pulled up beside a bicyclist wearing a Virginia sweatshirt.

"My sister goes there," Tracey said innocently.

"What's her name?" the cyclist inquired.

When Tracey answered, the cyclist erupted: "Your sister is Dawn Staley! Everybody loves Dawn Staley! She put Charlottesville on the map!"

Tracey drove home thinking, "My sister?"

* * *

Gradually, inevitably, the little sister has grown up. During her years in Virginia, Dawn has learned to move as easily among her friends from the Main Line as her pals from Raymond Rosen. She has grown more comfortable with television cameras and national honors. She may well play in Europe next year for a six-figure salary, but after a few years of that, she wants a job. "I'm torn between teaching and coaching," she says. "I'd probably want to teach elementary school. I think people are just letting kids get by. At elementary levels, people can be taught. They can make something of themselves. I'd like to get them while they're young."

Wherever Dawn Staley ends up, her heart will always be here. "You'll never kick the Philly from her," says her teammate Tammi

Reiss. "When Barkley comes on TV, or Randall Cunningham, she goes crazy, 'Oh they're the best!' If we eat a cheesesteak, she'll complain, 'This is nothing like Philly.' She's got a sense of home, and that is where home is – Philadelphia."

Indeed, as Dawn walked back to her home after playing pick-up basketball that August night, everyone said hello – women hanging their laundry, kids on tricycles, men changing their tires, teenagers behind mirror shades. They all knew her and she knew them.

"I always want to come back," she said. "This is where I live. This is where I come from. This is where it all started. That's the code around here: *Don't forget where you came from.* That's the code."

POSTSCRIPT

Dawn Staley went on to amazing career as a player in college, pro basketball and the Olympics and later as a college coach. She is in the Naismith Memorial Basketball Hall of Fame.

In her four years at Virginia, the team went to the NCAA tournament all four years and to the Final Four three years. She was the national player of the year in 1991 and 1992. She scored 2,135 points in college and set an NCAA record with 454 career steals. Virginia retired her number 24.

Dawn went on to play professional basketball and make the Women's National Basketball Association all-star game six years. As a member of the United States team, she won Olympic gold medals in 1996, 2000 and 2004. In Athens in 2004, she carried the American flag and led the American athletes into the Olympic Stadium.

She has coached with distinction at Temple University and at the University of South Carolina, where her team won the Southeast Conference championships in 2015 and 2016, going 37-1 against conference teams.

The Raymond Rosen projects where she grew up have long been torn down, but Dawn's heart and home will always be in Philadelphia.

Harold Finigan, front, and Frank Shepherdson, partners for over 50 years, row together for the first time in nine months, following a near-fatal injury to Finigan. This is a photograph of the original newspaper photo on a microfilm machine.

21

THE LURE OF THE SCHUYLKILL

A life on the river, harshly interrupted

Traffic accident threatens to end a rower's celebrated career

August 21, 1993

The log book tells the story. Harold Finigan signs in at the century-old Malta Boat Club simply as "Harold," in an old man's wobbly scrawl.

But the signature is there day after day, along with the number of miles he rows: six miles Aug. 14, and six more on the 15th. And six again on the 16th, 17th, 18th and 19th. In all, he has 572 miles for the year.

Everyone else signs in with a last name, but not Harold Finigan, a legend and an institution on Boat House Row. He has rowed more miles on the Schuylkill than any person living or dead – between 500 and 1,000 miles a year for 64 straight years. A former national champion, masters champion and Olympic finalist, Finigan, 83, has sculled up and down the river since 1929. He knows every bend, every foot of river bank.

"For Harold, the river is a sanctuary," said Joseph F. Majdan, his rowing partner. "Rowing is Harold's life. He's the spirit of the Schuylkill."

There will be no log entry, however, for Aug. 20. Or 21st. Or perhaps ever again.

On Thursday night, after finishing his row, Harold Finigan was hit by a car as he was getting into his own car on Kelly Drive. Rowers have long complained about the heavy traffic, the speeding cars and the danger of parking on Kelly Drive or trying to cross it. Thursday night those fears were borne out.

Hahnemann University Hospital emergency room doctors saved Finigan's life, and, they hope, his right leg.

Surgeons kept Finigan in the operating room for five hours, until after 3 a.m. yesterday. He was still in intensive care last night.

"He was almost killed from this thing," said Arnold T. Berman, chairman of the department of orthopedic surgery at Hahnemann. "If he were a typical elderly patient, we probably would have just done an amputation. We're treating him more like he's a young man.

"It could be six months of healing, and six months of rehabilitation," Berman added, "but we hope he can go back into the boat."

Of this, his friends and family have no doubt.

"If he's got a pulse," said Frank Shepherdson, 75, a fellow oarsman for 50 years, "he'll be back up rowing."

Finigan, a lifelong Darby resident, is by many accounts a remarkable and wonderful man. Even at his age, friends said, he is a strapping 6-foot-4, 200 pounds, with hands as strong as eagle talons and a heart as large and durable as a catcher's mitt.

"He has a pulse [rate] a man half his age would envy," said Majdan, a cardiologist. It is, astonishingly, in the high 40s or low 50s, he said.

In the last few months, Finigan has suffered from a foot infection, which slowed but could not stop him. "He has trouble walking," said fellow Malta club member Bill Fahy, "but when he's in the boat he flies."

Earlier in life, according to friends, Finigan was a baker, but for most of his years he has run a furniture store on Main Street in Darby. His business card, according to Fahy, says merely:

HAROLD FINIGAN
FURNITURE & ROWING

A widower, Finigan has drawn sustenance from the Schuylkill, friends said. He won the national rowing championship in 1949 in the double shell with Shepherdson. They were Olympic finalists in 1952, when Finigan was already 42. Shepherdson and Finigan won the European masters title in the double in 1980 and 1984.

Even in his 80s, Finigan is a relentless competitor, "challenging every other boat on the river to a race," Shepherdson said.

For the last few years, since Shepherdson suffered a serious car accident himself, Finigan has rowed mostly with Majdan, 42.

"We raced in a Fourth of July regatta," Majdan said. "We met the Ukrainian national team, and as we rowed by someone yelled out, 'Finigan,' and it was the coach. He screamed out, 'Finigan, I remember you. How old are you now?' Harold answered him, and then the coach said something in Ukrainian to his [crew of] eight, and they started applauding."

Majdan was the last man to speak with Finigan before Thursday night's accident.

They put their wooden shell into the water around 7:30 p.m. "It was a beautiful, still night," Majdan said. "The only thing you heard was the oars hitting the waves."

Finigan's oars are old, covered with years of grease from the oarlocks. The shell is light, just 30 pounds, and slices through the water like a splinter into skin.

The pair headed upriver.

"As we were rowing, even at the high strokes, he was telling me how the river changed, about the people he had rowed with," Majdan said. "He was very introspective. He was very insightful into what he had done. And as always he was the teacher.

"He looked at the skyline, and was telling me how the skyline had changed. He was remarking how the Strawberry

Mansion bridge was the style of around the Civil War, how he would see the wooden cable cars, and how he missed them going across the bridge. We were passing by the Mann Music Center, and he told me how he would listen to the old concerts as he rowed by."

Finigan even told his partner about an injured baby squirrel a neighbor had brought him just that day, and how he was nursing it back to health. Finigan is famous in Darby for taking in injured strays.

"When we go through the Girard Avenue bridge – Harold always calls it the cave of Aeolus, who is the wind god – we always yell out, 'Hellooooooooo, Aeolus.'" Majdan continued. "And last night we came through there and I saw Harold silhouetted against the sunset, and the river had turned to a maroon ribbon, and it was beautiful. As always, he was in perfect form."

After they had finished rowing, lifted a few weights and showered, Majdan prepared – as he does almost every night – to give Finigan a ride to his car. Majdan usually parks on Kelly Drive, while Finigan usually parks on Lemon Hill. But Thursday night Finigan parked in front of the boathouse.

"We were standing there talking and chatting," Majdan recalled. "He said, 'I'm parked right here. Just go on home.' And that was it."

A moment later, according to police, at 9:45 p.m., a 1976 Triumph driven by Mark Siemon of the 2300 block of Brown Street struck Finigan and his 1978 Buick Sentry as Finigan was unlocking the door. Finigan's right shinbone was shattered and his left ankle was broken. Police said no charges have been filed.

Doctors asked yesterday that Finigan not be disturbed by reporters. They predicted he could leave the hospital within two weeks.

And perhaps by next August be back on his beloved river.

POSTSCRIPT

This was a news story. But I couldn't begin with a straight lede. I loved the log book, and showing how he rowed day after day, a legend. And I loved being able to say there'd be no entry for today's date. It just seemed a more powerful way to bring the reader into the story. Again, this just came to me as I sat down to write.

Eight months later, I wrote a sequel when Harold Finigan returned to the river, rowing in a double shell with his partner of over 50 years, Frank "Shep" Shepherdson. Shep had nearly died himself in a car crash four years earlier, crushing his spine. Harold had visited him in the hospital every day for seven months. Doctors would tell Harold that Shep would never row again. Harold would tell those doctors, "You don't understand. He's an *oarsman*. He's my partner."

I followed the two men down to the river on their first day back in the shell. Harold pushed his walker to the end of the dock. Shep, bent, was steadied by his wife. These men inspired, not so much by the way they rowed – like gods, still – but by the way they crawled into the boat.

Silently they pulled away, their oars in perfect rhythm, slicing through the river.

Their backs were erect. They didn't speak. After 50 years, thousands of miles and countless oar strokes, instinct took over. Harold set the pace, about 28 strokes to the minute.

The farther away they got, the younger they seemed.

Shep's wife, Betty, stood on the dock, watching.

Doesn't she worry?

"Of course I worry," she said. "But I'd worry more if they stopped."

Harold died at age 95, Shep at 88. They rowed until the end.

* * *

Inquirer correspondent Blake Morrison contributed to this article.

Troy Carter with **Lady Gaga**

22

A WEST PHILLY SUCCESS STORY

Managing Lady Gaga's meteoric climb

As he guided her career, Troy Carter also rose to the top

February 25-26, 2013

Scene One: January 1990: *Troy Carter, 17, was so obsessed with music and the record business that he dropped out of West Philadelphia High School. Every day he walked to Delaware Avenue, to the studio of hip-hop icons DJ Jazzy Jeff and the Fresh Prince.*

He went with his rap group, 2 Too Many, a name they chose because there were three of them, but always only bus fare for one, or food money for one, or whatever they needed or wanted, only enough for one. They hoped to find a way inside, a chance to perform.

Scene Two: Jan. 20, 2013. *Troy Carter, now 40, left his marble-fronted office building across from Sony Pictures in Los Angeles and drove his Fisker, an electric car that sells for $100,000, to the Staples Center, where the artist he manages, Lady Gaga, was performing.*

At the end of the concert, Lady Gaga, with 34.2 million Twitter followers, gave a shout-out to just two people – the pair who teamed with her before she was famous, when she was doing three clubs a night and wearing the same outfit for a year.

"I'd like to thank my record producer, Vince Herbert, and my manager, Troy Carter, for believing in me, and taking care of me so I can travel the world for all my beautiful fans, who I love so much."

After the show, at 2 a.m., Carter and Gaga flew by private jet to Washington to perform the next afternoon at an inauguration party for President Barack Obama, for whom Carter and his wife, Rebecca, have helped raise millions of dollars.

* * *

Lady Gaga has sold 24 million albums and 90 million singles, and has won five Grammy Awards. Her rise was so meteoric that the Harvard Business School produced two case studies on her success. Those case studies focus largely on Troy Carter's role as manager.

His success with Gaga has given him means and access to indulge his entrepreneurial flair. In the last few years he has created what *Billboard* magazine calls a "mini-empire," teaming with Silicon Valley techies and investors to back more than 40 high-tech startup companies, from Uber to Spotify.

Carter says the music business is a meritocracy. Nobody cares about his race, education, or background – only his ability to perform. He had the raw materials for success: brains, guts, resilience, determination. Perhaps he made his own luck, but he believes grace kept putting opportunity in his path. He just made the most of it.

He was willing to do whatever it took, from sweeping floors for Jazzy Jeff to getting a date for Puff Daddy.

* * *

Gilda Carter, his mother, worked for 30 years cleaning surgical instruments at Children's Hospital of Philadelphia. Even after he made it big, she kept taking the bus to work until she reached her 30 years, then moved within half a mile of her son in the San Fernando Valley.

Troy's parents divorced when he was 2. When Troy was 7, his father, who had remarried, shot and killed his new wife's brother after an argument. He went to prison for 12 years. "That taught me about consequences at a really, really young age," Carter said. The couple stayed together, his father rebuilt his life, and today Carter calls him "one of my real heroes."

Gilda Carter threatened her three boys that if they spent one minute on a drug corner, she'd be right out there with them, "and you know your friends don't want you on the corners with your mom."

Because his mother worked, Troy spent much of his time around the corner with his grandmother, Dolores Fuller Crawford, now 80. She has lived in the same house 51 years.

"Manners and respect is never going to go out of style," she told all her grandchildren. "They knew I had rules and regulations here."

Down the block lived the family of Lawrence Goodman, who had started a label, Pop Art Records.

"Pop Art signed DJ Jazzy Jeff and the Fresh Prince to their first deal," said Carter, "Salt-N-Pepa to their first deal."

When Goodman would return to 51st and Cedar to see his family, he'd bring Salt-N-Pepa and other acts. Carter would watch from his grandmother's front step. "That was my first real experience of 'Wow, this is really cool what he's doing, whatever he's doing.' "

As a boy, "Troy always had a composition book and pen," said his grandmother, "jotting down what he had in mind to do." And what he had in mind was the music business. One entry, his mother recalls, noted how he was going to be a millionaire by 25 – only off by a decade, and perhaps an order of magnitude.

Carter won't talk about money now. "Just say I'm doing OK."

His grandmother is not surprised by Carter's success, and says his entrepreneurial instincts are in his blood. Her brother, Gilbert Fuller, ran a popular shoeshine shop at 6300 Germantown Avenue. He was always talking business to Carter as a boy. Carter visited his great-uncle on his deathbed in August, and Fuller told him, "Of all of them, you were the only one that listened."

Carter grew up at 52d and Larchwood, in a two-bedroom apartment with kerosene heat and sometimes no running water. His mother proudly says her three boys always had hot meals, love, and high expectations. But Carter recalls the days his mother would scrape together coins for bus fare. "You know, we were broke," he said. "You can, as a kid, kind of recognize the pain in your mother's face."

He went to Huey Elementary and Sayre Middle School. He tested well but "couldn't understand sitting in school," he said. He preferred the nearby public library. "I read every single thing about the music business."

His fifth-grade teacher, Marybelle Moore, is an educator who stood out. "I was always the kid in the front of the line because I was the smallest," Carter recalled, "and she used to call me 'The Big Guy.' Just by the way she would talk to me, she gave me the sense that I could do anything." Last summer he friended her on Facebook and thanked her.

By his senior year, Carter had stopped going to school. He was spending all his time with 2 Too Many and honing his entrepreneurial skills, promoting house parties all over the city, hiring a DJ and charging $1 to $5 a head. His mother, however, insisted he get a diploma or the equivalent, and enrolled him in Job Corps, a federal education and training program, at a rural Maryland high school.

Carter learned he could master any subject if he applied himself. He soon earned a GED and returned home.

And with 2 Too Many, he resumed his pilgrimages to Delaware Avenue.

* * *

One January day in 1990, Biz and Izod, a rap group, were re-cording at Jazzy Jeff's studio. Biz had gone to high school with 2 Too Many. He let them in.

Sitting in a lounge were DJ Jazzy Jeff and the Fresh Prince – Jeff Townes and Will Smith. They had in 1989 won the first-ever Grammy Award for best rap performance. Smith was just start-ing his hit television show "The Fresh Prince of Bel-Air."

Also in the lounge was James Lassiter, Smith's business part-ner then and now, who has produced many of Smith's movies, including "Hitch" and "Ali." "We literally just walked into the room and said we want to play some music for you," Carter re-called. "Will told us to go ahead and pop the tape in."

The lounge was too small for 2 Too Many's full routine, Carter said, "so everyone went outside and we danced in the snow."

"Basically," said Carter, "they just fell in love with us. We pret-ty much sucked as a group. They loved us and our tenacity more than anything else."

Recalled Lassiter: "Every night someone was down there try-ing to get put on. It was something about these three kids and their personality and sense of humor that we responded to. I don't remember if we thought they were talented or not. They just didn't give up."

"We would just laugh at them," Lassiter added. "I remem-ber plenty of times driving them home. I would say, 'How are you getting home?' They hadn't thought it through. They didn't have gloves. They didn't have a Plan B."

Lassiter and Smith gave 2 Too Many a record deal on their WilJam label.

They even took the group on tour to Chicago. Armique Wyche, a member of 2 Too Many who lives in L.A. now and works for Carter, remembers Will Smith teaching them a new word each day. "I think he was trying to get us ready for interviews," Wyche said. "I still remember *recapitulate.*"

After a year, 2 Too Many lost its contract.

But Carter went to work for Jazzy Jeff in the studio and for Lassiter as an assistant. He swept floors, emptied trash, carried records, even helped Lassiter's kids with science homework.

"There was always something about Troy," Lassiter recalled. "Aside from being bright, he had just a special quality about him. You knew he would be successful in life - if he could avoid the pitfalls that existed in Philly."

* * *

Carter soaked it all in.

"I remember when Will was getting ready to do the movie 'Six Degrees of Separation' [1993], and I was down at Jeff's place, and I remember Jeff putting it on speaker phone because Will was on the line, and Will asked everybody what did they think about this scene he was going to do when he was going to have to kiss this guy.

"And we all thought he was nuts. Nuts. We thought it was going to ruin his career for 'Fresh Prince' or whatever. That one move is what really made him a movie star and got him respect in Hollywood. He's always pushed the limit. He just has this maniacal drive that the only person who even comes close to it in my mind is Gaga. No pun intended, he wills things."

At the same time, Carter had graduated from throwing house parties to scraping together money to promote rap concerts.

In 1995, when Carter was 23, he was promoting a Notorious B.I.G. show in Philadelphia, and Biggie Smalls, a superstar gunned down two years later, was a no-show.

"I got into a huge fight on the phone," Carter recalled. "He was shooting a video in New York when he was supposed to be on stage here. But they ended up coming down that night anyway, and we went to Club Fever, where I was throwing an after-party."

B.I.G. had signed with Bad Boy Records, a company started by Sean "Puffy" Combs, who was not yet the world-famous hip-hop artist and entrepreneur he would become.

"We were having a conversation," Carter recalled, "and I said to Puff, 'Well, tell me about what you do.' And he told me, and I said, 'I want to come work with you.' 'Well, your first job is to get me that girl behind the bar.' And I went and got him that girl from behind the bar, introduced him. So I started interning for Bad Boy."

Carter spent a year and a half with Puff Daddy. He took the Greyhound bus to New York three days a week. What he gained most was confidence that a young black man with no formal education could make it on the business side of the music business.

Not that he was ready.

After Bad Boy, Carter rejoined Lassiter in Los Angeles but began to feel entitled, spoiled, even though he hadn't accomplished much himself. For example, he dated a girl in Long Beach, and ordered car service every night – at Lassiter's expense - to see her.

"James fired me and sent me back to Philly," Carter said. "That was one of the darkest times. My tail was between my legs."

Lassiter recalls administering the tough love: "Troy was responsible. People relied on him. In his nature that's who he was. There was also a hustle aspect to Troy. Usually that's good. The negative part of it he couldn't shake. To me it was a life lesson for him. If you really want it, you want to be successful, you have to leave the irresponsibility behind.

"I would constantly talk to him about it, about work ethic and starting at the bottom and working his way up. When he rejected it, I told him to go back to West Philly. He had to go back and experience this for himself, and come out on the other side."

* * *

Carter didn't speak to Lassiter for a year. He was indignant, proud – immature. He now realizes what a favor Lassiter did for him. In 1999, back in Philadelphia, Carter started over. He knew an emerging young rap artist from Germantown, Eve Jeffers, who asked him to help her find a manager because he knew so many people. After meeting seven or eight candidates, Eve asked Carter to be her manager. That was his start.

He also teamed with Jay Erving, the son of basketball legend Julius Erving, whose surname gave them added credibility. They started a talent management company, Erving Wonder, that flourished. Carter managed solid rap acts like Floetry and Nelly.

Carter had learned much from Smith and Lassiter. In 2003, he helped Eve Jeffers get her own TV show on the UPN network.

"She was part of the Ruff Ryders, a tougher kind of clique," said Keith Leaphart, a local physician entrepreneur, and member of the Lenfest Foundation Board who is a friend of Carter's. "He softened the edges of her and made her more commercial."

Carter moved back to L.A., went to Eve's set every day, learned TV.

In 2004, Carter and Erving sold their company to a British-based firm, Sanctuary. They threw a big celebration at a cigar bar in Philly, and bought 250 copies of *Cigar Aficionado* magazine and put a picture of themselves on the cover. (Carter now is legitimately on real magazine covers, such as *Wired UK*.)

Over the next two years, the Sanctuary deal fell apart, and Carter was out as vice president of the merged company. The cultures of the two firms were just too different, an invaluable lesson for Carter. And a costly one.

He had taken risks with his payday from the sale. "As an entrepreneur you take big swings of the bat," he said. "I struck out."

So he was broke. And then, after eight years, Eve fired him.

He had transformed himself, he had grown, and yet it all had unraveled.

Carter recalled: "Eve's booted me, house is foreclosed, cars being repossessed. Pretty much eviction notice at my office."

* * *

Then, as he sat in his office, in walked two people who would change his life.

First came Vince Herbert, a record producer, who had asked Carter to manage this new talent he had just found, a singer named Lady Gaga, who was right behind him.

"Vince is a big guy," Carter recalled, "and I see him walking through the reception area. And behind him, I see this girl with these big shoes, and big black eyeglasses, and fishnet stockings, and no pants, just a leotard."

It was 2007. Herbert, with a gift for spotting talent, had heard one song by Gaga and had flown her out to Los Angeles the next day. She was making a buzz in New York's gay clubs but otherwise was unknown.

"We hit it off right away," Carter recalled. "Everything she is today, she was when she walked through the door....The music was there. You don't meet a lot of artists with vision, not early artists, not at the beginning."

Herbert knew Carter was down on his luck. But he also knew his friend was deeply loyal, smart, a hard worker who would make the most of an opportunity.

"People still to this day, they don't understand, and try to figure it out," Herbert says. "We still live in this world where there's black people and white people, and people say: 'Vince, you guys are two black guys. Why did you let this black guy be the manager of this white girl?' Because in music no one looks at color. They just look at each other's heart. And when you look at that, it has every color in the book.

"He was going to lose his house. He had no Christmas gifts for his kids. But at the end of the day, if you're a good person like Troy is, good things will come to you."

* * *

Carter's take? "Sometimes you can't beat grace."

The three set out.

Gaga had just been dropped by Def Jam Records. Carter had just been fired by Eve Jeffers, his biggest client. And Herbert had just left his label at Universal to start over fresh.

"So everybody had something to prove," said Carter, "and nothing to lose.

"We went from club to club," he recalled. "She was in the front seat of our friend's truck. Going to four clubs a night, playing for a couple hundred people, between L.A. and San Francisco. She pretty much wore the same outfit for one year."

Herbert adds: "We didn't have money for the ideas we wanted. We didn't have people paying attention to us. We had none of that support. But what we had was each other. We had heart."

Gaga recalled her vision (obscenities deleted) at a recent show in Los Angeles: "I had a dream that I could take the underground New York scene and I could do it worldwide."

Stefani Germanotta had left New York University at age 19 in 2005 and adopted the stage name Lady Gaga. She had a killer voice, loved the pulsing beat of electronic dance music, dressed outrageously.

She was always in costume, always in character. She saw herself as performance artist as well as outsider. Wearing a suit of raw meat or a trash-can lid was a way to make the world accept her on her terms.

As she told fans in Los Angeles: "Whether you are gay, straight, bisexual, transgender, transsexual, you are black, you are white, you are Islam, Muslim, whatever the [expletive] you are, you don't know how free you will feel, how you will fly so [expletive] far above the rest once you stop caring what people think about you."

Carter's job, he said, "was to translate this vision": "It was something no one had seen before. Top 40 radio was telling us we had to get on dance stations, and it was gay music, not what they played."

Carter called club promoters, designers, DJs, media. "This was hand-to-hand combat," he said.

In early 2008, they released her first single, "Just Dance." "It took a year to get the first top 40 station in America to play it," Carter said, "and that was only because she was getting big in Canada. A top 40 station in Buffalo started playing it. That's when it started spreading." It eventually went to *Billboard's* No. 1.

* * *

Gaga was among the first to embrace Twitter, in early 2008, interacting with fans directly. She had started to become known by mid-2009. Harvard Business School did its case studies in 2011 and 2012.

In September 2009, just as Gaga won her first MTV Music Video Award for best new artist, and ended her television performance dangling from the ceiling, covered in fake blood, she was about to begin a big arena tour with hip-hop star Kanye West.

But that same night, before a worldwide audience, West grabbed the microphone from Taylor Swift and trashed her, saying Beyoncé deserved Swift's award. West became toxic and withdrew from the tour.

Carter and Gaga's inner circle had to decide, almost overnight, if she should tour by herself, cancel, or reschedule into smaller venues. He had to consider costs, contracts, partners, fans, staging.

He chose smaller venues. Better to have sellouts every night and demand that can't be met than to have half-empty arenas that take a month to sell out. Sacrifice short-term revenue for long-term benefit.

The tour was a huge success, and her popularity soared.

Then, in 2010, Carter realized her appeal was global, and he wanted a worldwide tour. He told the *Harvard Business Review*: "I asked myself: 'Who is the best in the business?' I need to know how to launch a global tour, and how to protect Gaga financially." He made a deal with the entertainment juggernaut Live Nation to launch a 120-concert tour. It grossed nearly $200 million.

"Troy is an extremely well-respected manager," said Anita Elberse, the professor who coauthored the Harvard studies. "He's really the man behind the scenes – behind Lady Gaga's success. Her rise has been phenomenally fast, and to manage such a quick climb to the top is incredibly difficult. It requires making a wide range of decisions, on touring, on the release of her albums, on forming partnerships with the right people and companies, each of which comes with significant risk."

Carter visited Elberse's class twice. "If he calls me tomorrow and says I want to teach at the Harvard Business School," she said, "I'm going to fight for it. I think he'd be fantastic."

Marc Geiger, head of music for William Morris Endeavor, Lady Gaga's agency, said, "I think Troy works quietly and without a lot of ego, which is for me personally wonderfully refreshing. He more or less is very understanding of how to shepherd the creative He's not forceful. He's a gentle supporter of risk-taking creative, and he nurtures it.

"Troy is like a great coach, like Phil Jackson when he had Michael Jordan or Kobe Bryant. First it takes having Michael Jordan, and then it takes nurturing and protecting."

* * *

The wealth and access that come with managing Gaga has allowed Carter to hone his entrepreneurial instincts in dramatic ways.

He recently founded an angel fund that has invested in 40 high-tech start-ups. He is often in the Silicon Valley.

Besides Carter's music connections, Geiger said, "he went and added a whole new cadre of equally powerful relationships in the new world of distribution and technology."

After Gaga saw the Facebook movie, "The Social Network," she called Carter and asked him if they could have their own social network just for her fans. In response, Carter started talking with people in Silicon Valley and they created another startup, The Backplane, which can provide a platform for a company or artist to build its own "authentic community," what he calls a micro-network.

Last year, Gaga launched www.LittleMonsters.com just for her fans, called little monsters. Carter says 1.3 million fans have registered. They can go to the free site and buy music or concert tickets, chat with other fans around the world, see videos or whatever content Gaga and her fans provide.

A recent discovery: Fans were uploading their artwork onto the LittleMonsters website, and Gaga fell in love with it. It was her idea, Carter said, to start putting their art on T-shirts. Concert merchandise sales increased 30 percent.

Gaga may have 55 million Facebook Likes and 34 million Twitter followers, but those are often passive fans. Carter says that in the future it will be better to have one million or two million die-hard ones.

He said Gaga's artistic vision will always drive her business, but sites like LittleMonsters can provide invaluable data.

"Pretty much no artist up to this point," he said, "has really known who their fan base is – their fans specifically by name, age, where they live, what they do, what they like, who their friends are, which concerts they attended, which music they listen to, which songs they skip, where they skip them, just really understanding, having real data.

"And having that data helps you make better decisions as it relates to the music you release, where you tour, how big the venues are, who you invite, the price of the ticket, how much merch to carry with you. Everything. And these are all going to be data-driven decisions that we're going to be making. It won't be through Twitter. It won't be through Facebook. It will be through your own sites that you build, your own communities that you build.

"This is going to be a very transparent thing that you have with your fans, and information that your fans are going to volunteer," he said, "because they want a better experience."

Gaga's next album, this summer, will be an app. "It will still come out as a CD and a digital file," Carter said, "but the real experience will be built in the app. This is her spending time with app developers, data scientists..." Artists can include videos, whatever experiences they want to provide with the app. "That's going to be the future of album," Carter said.

Was releasing the album as an app his idea or hers?

He laughs. "You know," he says, "we geek out."

* * *

In his own way, Carter feels he is every bit as much a performer as Gaga – managing her and other clients. Working as entrepreneur "is my performance," he said.

He also believes he owes his success in large part to mentors. "What I've been blessed with is opportunity," he told a group of high schoolers in Los Angeles whose circumstances were not much different from his at their age. When he felt unable to see beyond his own environment, "some people were able to give me vision...to pull me up when I was down."

Carter also knows his success could all disappear as fast as you can spell *d-i-v-a*. True artists, he says, lay it all on the line. They don't play it safe. And that's not in his nature, either.

Carter is gambling on a new beverage, Pop Water, a bridge between vitamin water and soda, which his company, Atom Factory, has developed and will roll out in Los Angeles soon.

"He is a person who looks for all the reasons to say yes to an idea," said Banch Abegaze, the chief operating officer at Atom Factory. "That's probably what Lady Gaga appreciates most about him. As a person who is continually being creative, coming up with amazing ideas, to have a manager who says, 'I'm going to find all the reasons why we can do this,' is probably an amazing experience for her."

Gaga now recovering

Carter says that for him, a Lady Gaga tour is like Groundhog Day. Same thing every day – unless something goes wrong.

Two weeks ago, it did.

Gaga was due in Philadelphia for two shows last week, but had to cancel. After a year on tour, a hundred concerts running and dancing and climbing ladders backstage in monster platform shoes, she suffered a hip tear.

"She's pretty tough," said Carter, "so when you get that call from Gaga, you know it's serious."

Gaga canceled the final six weeks of her tour. She had surgery Wednesday in New York. "Talking to the surgeon yesterday," Carter said on Friday, "it was much more serious than what we thought."

"It's been a bit of a busy week unwinding the tour," he added. "Personnel, vendors, insurance companies, etc."

The focus now, he said, is for Gaga to "take the time to rehabilitate."

Gaga pushed herself, and paid for it, something Carter understands and doesn't want to change.

"The most fun for me," he said, "is watching an artist experience new things for the first time. And if you're pushing it, you never run out of firsts, because you're always trying something new."

He could be speaking about himself.

POSTSCRIPT

Troy Carter was in New York, and he bumped into his good friend, Cory Booker, the New Jersey senator. Booker was with Lewis Katz, the billionaire owner of *The Philadelphia Inquirer*, who has since died in the crash of his private jet. They got into a friendly argument – who, Carter or Katz, was more Philly?

The newspaper owner returned to Philadelphia and suggested that the editors assign a story on Troy Carter, who until then, despite his huge success, had barely been mentioned in the paper. The assignment fell to me.

I, of course, wanted to see him in action. He consented to the story, and gave me access to his mother and grandmother and Vince Carter and others – but not to Gaga. I believed she would have loved to talk to me about him, but he told me he wouldn't ask her. So the closest I got was watching her in concert, hearing her praise him from the stage.

My favorite aspect of the story was interviewing his grandmother, with Troy present. He was like any other grandson. It wasn't an act.

Troy is no longer Lady Gaga's manager. A year after I saw her thank him in that concert in Los Angeles, she fired him. He has not shared specifics, though he has admitted he was angry and hurt at first. He understands the music business, and says the separation was, in the end, liberating. He has moved on to more entrepreneurial endeavors, and his company still manages other artists, including Meghan Trainor, famous for the pop hit "All About That Bass."

Ordinarily, I prefer to write about everyday people, *not* stars and celebrities. With everyday people I get more access, and the stories are unfiltered, unrehearsed, more authentic, more inspiring. But Troy Carter was a worthy exception. He has a remarkable story, the salmon that made it upstream, a great example of the American Dream.

Troy Carter relaxes in his office at Atom Factory in Los Angeles

Carter with his grandmother, Dolores Crawford,
at her home in West Philadelphia

Maggie Lucas and her parents, Betsy and Al, before a game

23

ROAD TRIP RITUALS

Basketball parents with a game plan
When Maggie Lucas plays, Mom and Dad do their part

February 7, 2012

As Al and Betsy Lucas pulled out of Narberth on Thursday afternoon, on their way to State College, Al was wearing a Penn State jersey – Lady Lions, 33 – the number of his daughter, Maggie. But wife Betsy wore no Penn State gear. She just couldn't.

After the loss to Michigan State at home last month, Betsy decided she needed to wear "the opposite" – a plain sweater. Maybe the loss wasn't her fault. She is only the mother of the shooting guard. But the Lucases, like sports parents everywhere, love to see their daughter play and thrive, and they have to do their part.

They were leaving around 1 p.m., in time to arrive comfortably before the 7 p.m. tipoff. They always go to a bar for one beer before the game. This is a ritual they don't dare break.

Maggie is a sophomore on the Penn State basketball team, and all last season and this season, until the Michigan State loss, her parents went to an Irish bar. But they now have switched to a Mexican bar. Betsy realizes that if Penn State loses at home again, "we might have to go to the opposite of the opposite" – maybe back to the Irish bar, and even put a Penn State sweatshirt on.

But not yet.

Maggie is a star, a former *Inquirer* player of the year, a McDonald's all-American in high school. Last season, as a freshman, she broke the three-point scoring record for the Big Ten Conference. But she went 1 for 11 in the second-round game of the NCAA tournament, a loss, and vowed to shoot 100,000 shots over the summer. And she did.

That's 100,000 makes. Misses didn't count. One thousand shots a day for 100 days. She kept a spreadsheet.

Even her parents, who have grown accustomed to Maggie's basketball intensity, and are in part responsible for it, couldn't believe her pledge.

"Are you crazy?" her mother asked – and this is a mother who would sit in the car in her pajamas and shine the high beams on the Narberth basketball court late at night just so middle-school Maggie could shoot and shoot.

By the way, Maggie wouldn't wear long pants, truly nothing but basketball shorts, through seventh grade – not to school in winter (the teachers would call home), not even to church on Easter.

As Maggie explained, "I had to be ready if there was an opportunity to shoot."

Maggie did finally wear her first pair of jeans after her AAU team, consisting of girls a year older who had started to wear make-up and act like teenagers, performed what Betsy called "an intervention," and took Maggie to T.J. Maxx and made her buy jeans.

* * *

Maggie chose Penn State for two reasons. One is that college had to be near enough so her parents could go to every home game. And they do.

The second reason was that in August 2008, before Maggie even began her junior year of high school at Germantown Academy, she was already being recruited by many colleges and went back to Penn State for a third visit.

She had already met the college president. This time, the basketball coaches took Maggie and her parents to the football stadium, and walked them down onto the field ("The grass itself felt like Augusta," recalled Al) and Maggie met linebacker Sean Lee, who now plays for the Dallas Cowboys but who was then a star at Penn State. He was handsome and charming and modest and exactly the kind of boy parents like Al and Betsy would love for their daughter to meet at Penn State.

But then, of course, who should walk up to them in the end zone but Joe Paterno. The coach had been prepped and he had come to meet Maggie Lucas and close the deal.

JoePa asked Al and Betsy if they'd mind if he and Maggie took a walk. The Legend put his arm around Maggie and took a stroll toward the 50-yard line, and Joe told her, "I'm going to come see you play. Any of the other football coaches tell you that? We'll have you over for dinner. Sue makes a great plate of pasta…." He whispered in her ear, according to her parents, "Come on, Maggie. Come to Penn State!"

And she was blushing and her parents swore she grew taller that very day.

Two days later Maggie, just 16, committed in words and in her heart to play for Penn State.

* * *

As Al and Betsy approached State College Thursday afternoon, the light on the gas gauge in their SUV came on.

"I should put gas in," Al said.

"That's not our normal routine, Honey," Betsy replied.

"I know," he said.

Their normal routine is always to stop at the Exxon and Dunkin' Donuts as they leave town after the game, to fill up on fuel and coffee for Al. Even though they still had miles to go, they decided to risk driving with the warning light. Didn't want to jinx Maggie.

At the Mexican bar, they had their beer, and were joined by Betsy's parents, Margaret and Carl Milleker, both 79, who had driven up from Baltimore. Then they went to the Bryce Jordan Center for the game.

Betsy carried in four tins of cookies and brownies. She has become known for her baking, a tradition she started when Maggie was in AAU ball.

In fact, after a high school tournament in Brooklyn one summer, the *New York Post* began a story like this: The only thing better than Betsy Lucas's chocolate chip cookies last night was the three-point shooting of her daughter, Maggie....

Betsy had a ritual, of course. When she arrived, she had to give five cookies to the guy at the Will Call window, where she picked up their tickets, and one each to two people working at the souvenir stand right inside the arena. She then brought cookies to Paul Warnick, 99, in the front row, and Lorraine Roller, 75, a stroke victim, next to him.

"We usually win because of these cookies," Roller said.

Al went down to courtside, where he always goes, so Maggie would see him when Penn State came in for warmups.

Maggie is pretty much always smiling, except when Penn State is losing, but she smiled even more broadly when she saw her father Thursday. She nodded to him, and held up three fingers – he says it's because she's a three-point shooter – and then he went off to his seat.

Al sat in Section 107, Row CC, Seat 14. Betsy sat in Section 107 – but Row AA, seat 1. Two rows and 13 seats away.

They haven't sat together at games in a decade.

Betsy started to move away from Al because he just watched the game differently. Al played high school ball in Baltimore (Al and Betsy, 52 and 53, met at Towson University) and he coached their older sons and Maggie in youth leagues, and he sees the game on a different plane. Al knows every play and can see what doesn't happen. He will scream, "She missed a pick!"

This is not Betsy. She's concerned much less with actual basketball than with the emotional well-being and happiness of her daughter. In fact, sons Peter and Ben played on the Lower Merion High School state championship team in 2006, and Betsy says of herself, with both pride and embarrassment, "No one has seen more basketball and knows less about the game."

What really drove Betsy farther away from her husband was when he started yelling at referees by first names, because, of course, going to so many games for so many years he knew them all. She tried shushing him but then people would shush her for shushing him, and she didn't like that.

She says, with both truth and humor, "A lot of parents don't sit together. We're all still married. It was those parents that were sitting together that aren't."

After the national anthem, Al folded his hands, closed his eyes and bowed his head. As the ref was about to toss up the ball, Al said, "Come on, baby girl, do work now."

She did. Within a minute or two, she took her first three-point shot. The ball left her hands. "Boom," her father yelled. And then as if after a delay, the ball floated through the net.

* * *

Maggie was first dragged to gyms when she was 2, and her brothers were 4 and 6, and she was the kind of kid who always had a ball and begged her father to teach her how to shoot. He taught her mechanics, squaring the legs, being on the balls of her feet. And he can tell now by her form, and by her release, whether a shot is going to fall.

He also taught Maggie to release the ball quickly, because Betsy Lucas is only 5-foot-2, and Al himself only 6 feet on a good day, and Al figured if Maggie wanted to play on the college level she had better learn to shoot quickly before somebody taller could come over and block it.

Maggie, amazingly, grew to "an honest 5-9," said her mother, who insists Maggie simply "willed it."

Helped by Maggie's quick scoring, Penn State jumped out to a big lead and Maggie led all scorers with 24 points and Penn State won by 32, and it was a fun and stress-free night for both parents. All the pre-game rituals had worked.

After the game, they waited for Maggie to come out after her shower. Maggie walked up, was about to hug her grandmother when she noticed the new sneakers and stopped short: "MomMom. Nike Frees. Oh, my gosh, I'm so proud of you right now."

The family posed on the floor for some pictures, and when PopPop missed a few shots at the basket, Maggie was very forgiving. But when her father tried and missed, she was less so.

"Oh, my God – that's so bad," she said.

He missed another. Clang.

"You're a disgrace."

(Give the guy a break. He works six days a week as director of operations for Stephen Starr's restaurants. He's out of practice.)

But a voice came down from on high, from the upper level, perhaps from God or a custodian: "If you wear number 33, you can't be missing." Al set up for one more shot. "Can't quit on a miss, right?" he said to Maggie. Swish. "I'm done," he said.

Maggie was off to a late dinner with her grandparents, who were staying in a motel. Al and Betsy hugged everyone, said their goodbyes. Al did the one thing that all fathers of college daughters do before leaving, and got out his wallet. "Let me give you some money," he said.

Al and Betsy stopped for gas and coffee, per ritual.

It was 1:05 a.m when they pulled up to their home, and both would be working in the morning. Betsy is administrator for

Nalls Architecture in Narberth. Al, with complete honesty, said, "I can't wait to do this again."

POSTSCRIPT

My favorite moment is when Maggie emerges from the locker room and notices her grandmother's sneakers and says: "MomMom. Nike Frees. Oh, my gosh, I'm so proud of you right now."

It is a very small, simple exchange, but so effective. One moment Maggie is the superstar hoops player and literally the next she is a loving and playful granddaughter. She is as proud of her grandmother as her grandmother is of her!

This is a classic example of a telling detail or quote that works on multiple levels, conveying more than the literal information.

The observation by Maggie wouldn't be as powerful – it wouldn't succeed – if it lacked context. But because the reader has gotten to know Maggie and her family through the course of the story, this small moment can be understated and slipped comfortably into the narrative flow.

Another valuable moment is the voice from the rafters – the voice of God – telling Al Lucas when he wears number 33 he had better not miss. Even the custodian loves Maggie and feels close enough to her that he can joke with her father. At the same time, the custodian is telling us just how much Maggie is adored at Penn State and just how exceptional the masses perceive her talent to be. All this information is conveyed in one little exchange.

I love these jewels, and I feel confident the reader does as well.

I was a little nervous asking Maggie why she only wore shorts through seventh grade. I didn't want to embarrass or annoy her. But her answer was genius – proof again that a reporter should never to be afraid to ask a question.

Maggie finished a great career at Penn State and plays professionally in the United States. During her off-season, she helps out at Germantown Academy.

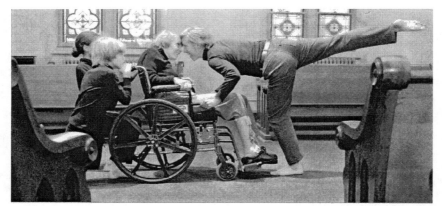

Lisa Lovelace in her dance at church with Nellie Greene

24

THE AMAZING NELLIE GREENE

She had it all – then tragedy struck
But she found a calling that led to a personal resurrection

April 8, 2007

The Rev. Elinor R. Greene – Nellie to all who know her – was hard at work in February on a Lenten sermon for Chestnut Hill United Methodist Church, where she is an ordained deacon.

She propped her broken body against the left armrest of her wheelchair, and, with her right hand, she typed.

Her fist was clenched, with just her pointer finger sticking out. Sometimes her fist opened, like a bird spreading its wings, as she moved to reach a distant key on her computer keyboard, then it clenched again.

Nellie's finger shakes, and often hits the wrong key – two, three, four times. She must then drag her finger all the way across the keyboard to hit backspace, and try again.

For instance, writing the simple word *to* that morning, she hit the *5* key, then backspace, then *5* again, then backspace, then *e*, then backspace, and finally got the *t*. The *o* came on the first strike.

In the end, she would write 2,170 words and strike 9,246 characters in her Lenten sermon – a dead sprint for five weeks.

Because of an accident at age 18, which robbed Nellie of her every dream, she cannot talk, walk, or even feed herself, and sees so poorly the letters on her keyboard are blurry. At 54, she is a prisoner in what one friend calls her "physical cage."

Nellie's primary means of escape is through her sermons – allowing her clever mind and soaring spirit to connect with the outside world.

As a teenager, Nellie lived a modern version of *The Philadelphia Story*. One of four daughters of Cookie and George Greene, an investment counselor, she lived in a house with 11 bedrooms and four gardens on Elbow Lane in Mount Airy.

Nellie's world was literate, loving, full of promise and possibility—dancing classes at the Philadelphia Cricket Club, summers in the Hamptons, boarding school at Chatham Hall in Virginia.

"She had the lead in every play, was on every team, she had endless boyfriends," said her mother.

As a young girl, Nellie brimmed with such energy and effervescence her father would pay her a nickel at dinner just to stop talking!

Everything came easily to her, especially friends. "She loved being loved," said her sister Lilah, "and always had an entourage of admirers."

* * *

Lisa Lovelace, a member of Chestnut Hill United Methodist, for years had little contact with Nellie.

"She's very easy to ignore because of her situation," said Lovelace. "She can't stop you. She can never initiate. She is, like, representing what we would all fear most in our lives. And she's so easy to walk by and not deal with that."

At a church auction three years ago, Lovelace, a dancer, bought the privilege to commission a poem by Nellie. Lovelace didn't want just any poem, and she asked Nellie to write about herself. Lovelace hoped to interpret the poem in a dance and perform it in church.

Nellie wrote the poem, "I Am." It begins:

What determines being human?
Is it thinking?
I think therefore I am.
These words pose a dilemma for me because I have extensive
brain damage as a result of an automobile accident.
Fortunately, my mind wasn't harmed...but what is the mind
without the body?

The poem goes into verse:

Woman with partial sight and whole vision
in my little craft caught in a storm
pitching and weaving on Baptismal water
holding fast to my rudder, which appears to be God.

When Lovelace read the poem, she realized she wanted Nellie in the dance with her.

"I started to get to know her by email, which is the only way to do it," Lovelace said. "I realized she had a sense of humor, she was feisty, and smart, and she was confident.

"Lots of things I never would have suspected from somebody in her situation. And she was so positive. When I see her, I try to keep those thoughts alive, because she can't convey those things when you're with her in person."

They would perform their dance on March 4 before Nellie's sermon.

* * *

Back from a one-year sabbatical, Nellie had just five weeks to write her Lenten sermon.

She would base it on the assigned reading from Luke, in which Jesus urges his followers to enter heaven through "the narrow door."

For Nellie, the narrow door represents the struggle to live by the teachings of Jesus.

While the physical challenges of writing, for Nellie, are almost incomprehensible, she suffers more universally over content and style, her every word and letter.

She will not settle for a comma when she wants an apostrophe, for a small *p* in *Paradise* when a capital *P* is called for. That means hit shift-lock, hit *P*, and then release shift-lock. Extra steps. So be it.

In early February, Nellie was working on a section about how difficult it was for Jews in the time of Jesus to accept him as the messiah because he was nothing like what they had expected.

She had written: "He was not the conquering king of many of the Psalms and some of the prophets, but the suffering servant of Isaiah."

Slowly, she added: "He must have been a party animal, too, because he was accused of being a drunkard and a glutton. His friends were the wrong kind of people, too. They were prostitutes and sinners, and all sorts of riffraff."

That paragraph took an hour.

Nellie writes and rewrites up to the day she rehearses her sermon with the church volunteer who will deliver it. Because of lung damage from the accident, Nellie doesn't have the wind to blow out a candle, much less speak.

"I do my best writing in the morning," Nellie emailed later, "but work at all hours up until 9:30 - 10 PM when I have to go to bed, because of my nurse's schedule. This is one of the difficult frustrating things about living in a nursing home. If the muse strikes after I'm in bed, I stew all night, until I can get to my PC the next morning."

For many years, Nellie lived on her own, in an apartment, with hired aides coming in to help. But when aides didn't show, "she was sunk," said a friend from Wednesday night Bible study, Sherry Olson.

Two years ago, growing ever more dependent, Nellie moved into Cathedral Village, a retirement community in Roxborough, where her mother also lives. Nellie is grateful to be in the nursing wing, with excellent care – an answer to her prayers. But she is not without issues, which she tied into her Lenten sermon.

She was writing about how one responds to God's grace – "We move from doing the right things out of duty to doing the right things out of love" – and how this is a challenge for her:

"For example, practical implications for me come when I choose to be kind and tactful to some of my nurses, when they persist in doing things which really annoy me, like leave my bathroom light on unnecessarily."

(Nellie is a fierce environmentalist.)

"I also choose to be pleasant when an elderly man or woman, who might be lost, strays into my room, uninvited."

* * *

On Sept. 13, 1970, Nellie set off to begin her freshman year at Hampshire College in Amherst, Massachusetts. She had studied Mandarin, and her dream was to learn all she could about China.

"We were going about 60 MPH on route 84, just outside Danbury, CT," Nellie wrote years ago. "Mum started to pull into the left lane to pass the car ahead of us, and changed her mind when she saw another car speeding up behind us. When she pulled back in to her own lane, something happened to our car!

"Our car turned over three times, and I flew out the door as I wasn't wearing a seatbelt. Both of my lungs ruptured and my right arm and clavicle were severely broken.... I bruised a kidney, was instantly blinded, and had a lot of internal bleeding. I suffered two heart arrests on the operating table and this along with other factors resulted in my suffering severe and extensive brain damage."

Her mother was not badly hurt.

Nellie's sister Lilah, then 15, grew close to Nellie during the endless rehabilitation.

"We were in a way two lost souls making the best of a rotten situation," Lilah later wrote. "Nellie had been abandoned by all the glamorous friends who continued their perfect lives without her. I had been abandoned by my parents whose sole focus in life was Nellie's condition."

As Nellie struggled through 30 months of surgeries and therapies, her parents reminded her of a story that would become family lore. When Nellie was 4, her mother awakened from a nightmare: Nellie had been gravely injured in an accident. Cookie Greene roused her husband, who hurried into Nellie's room and scooped the sleeping girl in his arms.

"Remember, Nellie," he urged her, "if you are ever in trouble, never, ever give up!" He made her promise.

In February 1973, Nellie and her mother finished that drive to college.

Compared with today, Nellie had somewhat more function. She could walk with the help of friends. She could type with 10 fingers. But life, even putting coins into the dorm washer, was a constant struggle. Her mother read her textbooks onto cassette tapes and mailed them to Nellie.

Nellie remembers "doggedly pursuing my interest in China and Chinese studies." But when she came home for spring break her junior year, "my parents asked me, quite sensibly, what I could do with such a major, and I didn't have an answer.

"I returned to college in near-despair and, during a sleepless night, received my call to pursue the ordained ministry.

"I can't really describe how it happened. All I know is that one minute, I was crying as if my heart would break, and in the next, my soul was completely at peace and the decision was made."

* * *

Nellie was ordained as an Episcopal deacon in 1993 and has served at Chestnut Hill United Methodist since then.

She gives five or six sermons a year. Her parishioners love it when she interprets scripture through her own experience. It gives them new perspective on their own trials.

"My world is bigger because of Nellie," said parishioner Joy Bergey.

One example: In 1996, Nellie gave a sermon based on a reading in Matthew in which a Canaanite woman persisted until Jesus healed her daughter.

"This woman had a dream, and she wouldn't let God off the hook until she had achieved it," Nellie preached.

Nellie focused the rest of the sermon on "another woman I know," who also had a dream, "and wouldn't let God off the hook until she had achieved it."

"Her dream was...to get her degree and graduate in the usual four years. Only trouble was, this woman could barely walk or talk, couldn't write, and she was too blind to read.

"Like the Canaanite woman, hers was a lonely mission. She had to get up at 5 every morning, because it took her three to four hours to shower and dress for her morning classes.

"She was too proud to use a wheelchair...so when she stumbled on the ice on her way to the dining commons or to class, she got on her knees and crawled....

"This woman didn't feel any great encouragement from God. Instead, she felt God challenging her....

"Most of the time, she was simply too exhausted to give God much thought, and when she did pray, it was to beg God to get her through another day.

"In reflecting about this college experience," Nellie continued, "I realize that Jesus was with her every step of the way. Even when she didn't feel his presence, he was there. He came to her in the person of wonderful professors, who bent over backwards to help her achieve...many friends who read to her, studied with her, ate with her, and just plain laughed and had fun with her.

"Another critical lesson we can learn from this text is that God hears us when we cry out. Even when we think God is ignoring us, God is really there....

"The thought I will close with is no matter how much we might feel like outsiders, this passage demonstrates that all of us belong. Never forget this!"

* * *

Nellie herself forgot this in 1982.

She had just graduated from Yale Divinity School, leaving behind her friends and intellectual life, and had moved into Inglis House in Philadelphia to live among the disabled, to explore her commitment to ministry.

Within three weeks, she was hospitalized in a straitjacket, sedated on Thorazine. She refused to eat, and begged her parents to help her die.

Physicians put a tube in her nose, forcing in nutrition.

After weeks in the hospital, she closeted herself in her bedroom at her parents' house.

"I read and reread all the writings of St. Paul as well as Peter Brown's biography of St. Augustine." She listened to a recording of *Paradise Lost*.

"I didn't care if I lived or died," she wrote. "Life had lost its meaning, and I felt trapped in a body which I hated." What caused the breakdown 12 years after the accident? "I think fear. Fear of everything," said her mother. "Suddenly she was out in the open world."

Nellie's family and many friends going back to boarding school have remained devoted to her. They "dragged me back into life," Nellie emailed recently. "Everyone rallied around me."

Not a day goes by when Nellie doesn't think about all she's lost. She blames only herself – she wasn't wearing a seat belt.

"Thirty-seven years have gone by, and I still can't forgive myself," she emailed. "Nor can I blame God. Shit happens."

Years ago, her mother read her *Man's Search for Meaning*, a book by Viktor E. Frankl, a survivor of Nazi death camps.

"It made a big impression on me," she emailed. "One thing I learned is that all of us have the freedom to choose the attitude toward the circumstance in which we find ourselves.

"We can wallow in misery, or make the best of it, and try to move on. I've chosen the latter. Here is where my faith has helped me. I believe that God is there with everyone, and eager to help us get through any ordeal. All we have to do is ask."

* * *

When Leslie Rector arrived in Nellie's room to rehearse the Lenten sermon, this message was on Nellie's computer screen:

"Welcome Leslie and thank you SO much for coming, and agreeing to do this! Please pull up a chair and relax....

"The way we rehearse is for you to read it to yourself first, then back to me aloud. Then I'd like you to go in my bathroom, leave the door slightly ajar, pretend you're in church, and read it again. My mother has to hear you. She's hard of hearing."

Rector, a church member, hugged Nellie and then read the sermon once to herself, slowly.

"It's wonderful, absolutely wonderful," Rector said.

Nellie glowed.

Then Rector read Nellie's sermon aloud.

Nellie listened intently for 17 minutes. Afterward, she powered her wheelchair up to the keyboard and began to type.

Rector fretted, "Now I feel like the kid who screwed up."

"*S...p...l...d...*"Nellie's hand traveled across the keyboard to the backspace key and deleted the *d*. She typed the *d* again, and once more deleted it. (The computer speaks each letter as she types it.) Finally she typed an *e*, and continued: "*...n...d...i...d!*"

"Splendid!"

"Oh, yeah," Rector gushed.

Nellie kept typing: "Now go into the bathroom and shout!"

"OK," said Rector. "I'm going into the bathroom. But I hope nobody comes and carts me off as a crazy person."

Halfway through the reading, Nellie typed stop. Rector had read, "In the name of our God," and Nellie corrected her by typing, "In the name of God."

Rector concluded, projecting clearly from the bathroom.

Nellie typed: "Thank you. You will be as Tony the Tiger would say, Grrrrreat!"

And then she added, "Please practice at home."

Rector promised she would, and put on her coat.

Nellie typed one more thing.

"May I give you a hug?"

"You never have to ask," said Rector.

She moved in and gave Nellie a long, nourishing hug. For the first time that day, Nellie made a sound. She purred.

Nellie turned to the keyboard and keyed in a symbol, a red heart. And enlarged it to fill the screen.

* * *

Many say the essence of her ministry is that Nellie radiates such faith and love in the face of tragedy.

"I have gone to see her feeling burdened by life – due to personal challenges, personal loss, or just chronic busyness," said her boarding school friend Helen Mirkil. "I always leave unburdened.

"She has let the love of Jesus fill her dark places," Mirkil added, "giving others in abundance what the Lord has given her."

The Rev. Hal Taussig, pastor of Chestnut Hill United Methodist, summed up Nellie's gift this way:

"We all get hurt and make the choice whether to feel the hurt and live through it, or go numb and deny the painful experiences. Part of the territory she carves out, that so many of us don't know about, is the willingness to stay present emotionally to pain rather than go numb."

Bishop Charles E. Bennison Jr. of the Episcopal Diocese of Pennsylvania said that whenever he saw Nellie, he thought of the sonnet "On His Blindness" by the English poet John Milton.

Going blind, Milton wondered how he could still serve God. In the famous last line, Milton wrote:

They also serve who only stand and wait.

* * *

Nellie arrived at Chestnut Hill United Methodist Church on March 4 as she always does – by paratransit.

She was there by 8:30 a.m. and sat alone in the sanctuary, where the driver left her, until another church member happened along to take off her coat.

Nellie can wait an hour or more. She is used to it. She meditates and prays.

"I pray a *lot*," she explained, "and I'm still not completely sure God hears me, but I hope God does. When I'm deep in prayer, something inside me shifts, and God becomes real."

Sitting in her wheelchair, Nellie seemed so broken, so fragile. The dance transformed her.

As Lisa Lovelace recited Nellie's poem, becoming her voice, she climbed on Nellie and on her wheelchair, at one point standing tall on the armrests as two children (including Lovelace's 10-year-old son) pushed them through the sanctuary.

I am the tightrope walker, balancing between two worlds;
I am the prisoner rudely captured,
The anxious rider on an unpredictable horse.

Lovelace, dressed like Nellie in jeans and turtleneck, pulled Nellie out of the chair and walked with her. Lovelace dipped Nellie left and right as in a ballroom dance.

There were delays as Lovelace got Nellie in and out of the chair.

"That's Nellie's life: silence and waiting," Lovelace said later. "I let them feel that."

Lovelace lay across Nellie's lap, pushing the wheel with one hand, making a circle, as she recited the verse:

...in my little craft, caught in a storm...

Lovelace crumbled bread onto the floor, as did Nellie , who can't control her fists, and can't help but crush bread.

Staring at her hands, Lovelace recited:

They make me feel unreal, as if I were half a person.
Am I myself or a monster?

Lovelace ran around the church, leaping and exulting in physical glory.

I was an athlete, a singer, an actor, a leader in school...

And she came to a halt, kneeling, nose to nose with Nellie, and whispered:

I had it all!

Many in the church wept.

* * *

After the dance, a vestment was hung over Nellie's shoulders. Then Leslie Rector stood beside her and read Nellie's words:

"The choice is to accept grace, love and guidance and God's transformative power because of the work Jesus did here, or we can say no. It is a choice and it is a pilgrimage....I struggle with this a lot because sometimes my faith in God feels so weak as to be nonexistent....

"But, even when I know I am falling short, and the way ahead is not clear, I still do my best to go through the narrow door. I think that is the best any of us can do."

POSTSCRIPT

I met Nellie when I spent a year at the steps of the Philadelphia Museum of Art for my book *Rocky Stories*. The book was about people who come from all over the world to run the steps like Rocky Balboa, to celebrate their own dreams, accomplishments and triumphs. Nellie had come to pose for her annual Christmas card photo. "Rocky wishes he could have the strength, the inner strength, of Nellie Greene," her friend Charlotte Caldwell told me. I was so smitten with Nellie and her story that I went back and did this piece for the newspaper. What a brave and remarkable woman. Her sermons were assembled into a book.

After this story appeared, I received an avalanche of responses from readers. Here are a few I saved:

"Your story on Nellie Green was perfect. The fact that it ran on Easter made it even better."

"I just wanted to thank you for the wonderfully written and inspiring article about Rev. Greene. ...I always wonder what to say to people who see their situation as hopeless -- Wow! Your article will be required reading for them. She is my new hero! Thanks for telling her story."

"I must admit I am not very familiar with your writing until this article. I will pay attention more because of this excellent piece. You write with dignity and clarity and respect. You are not maudlin or going for a punch in the gut. Solid writing, telling a wonderful, human story. Please continue with your wonderful work."

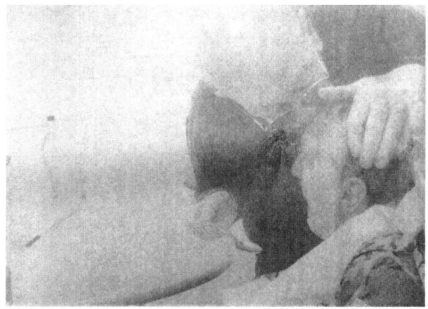

Jim Way kisses his wife, Wynne, as he spoon
feeds her lunch in the nursing home

25

IN SICKNESS AND IN HEALTH

True love is a compassionate love

Jim Way's devotion to his wife, stricken by Alzheimer's

February 13, 1998

Fifty-five years ago, Jim Way went to the library to borrow a book on telescopes.

"I borrowed the librarian instead," he says.

It was London. The war was on. Things happened fast. A few weeks later, she wrote him a note and signed it: "Yours as long as you wish, Wynne."

"It was the wish that endured," he says.

Tomorrow, as he has done nearly every day for nine years now, Jim Way will drive the five miles to a nursing home to spoon-feed lunch – pureed chicken, spinach and apple sauce – to his beloved librarian, his valentine, a woman who hasn't recognized him, and has barely uttered a word, in six years.

His wife is one of two million Americans with Alzheimer's disease.

Jim, 81, cared for Wynne, 79, for eight years in their Drexel Hill home before moving her to Saunders House, a long-term-care facility next to Lankenau Hospital in Wynnewood.

He relented only when he could no longer lift her out of bed himself, when she'd wander outside in her pajamas the moment he went to the bathroom.

"It was impossible," he said. "I had to wash her. I even had to wipe her bottom. I'd put her to bed. Before I was out of the room, she was out of bed, falling over."

He arrives every morning at 11:30. Coming to see his wife is anything but a burden. As he walked in on Wednesday, carrying old, beautiful pictures of Wynne, he explained:

"I enjoy coming. I look forward to seeing her." He spread the photographs out on a table in the lobby. "I'm still crazy about her even though she—"

His voice trailed off.

For the first four years, Jim never took a day off. He'd come seven days a week, feeding her lunch and dinner. "We had a really tough time getting him to do anything but this," said his son, Geoffrey, who visits with his father here on Monday nights.

Now Jim will take two weeks off a year, one to return to London, one to visit a warm beach in winter for a few days with his sister and cousin. He also faithfully rides his exercise bike, walks the malls in winter and reads voraciously. And every Thursday now, he spends the day at the Philadelphia Art Museum attending lectures (yesterday's was on Van Eyck) and then lunching with his old colleagues from Wanamakers, where he rose from floor sweeper to merchandise manager, traveling the world buying merchandise, and always taking along his wife.

On Wednesdays, Wynne gets her hair done in the beauty salon at Saunders House. At noon, Jim greeted his bride. His voice was sweet, soft.

"Hello, Dear...Wynnie...Wynnie..."

He pulled her chair into the elevator.

"Come on, Sweetie," he said. He gently touched her cheeks, then lifted her jaw, trying to get her attention, to let her know he was here.

This woman whose children insist she could once spell anything and who was so robust she could out-wrestle her oldest son – now a black belt in karate – until he was 15, a woman who always had perfect hair and perfect nails, sat in a geriatric recliner, beneath an afghan blanket, pink slippers on her feet, her blue eyes still soft and clear. Her mouth hung open. Her face was red with a rash, a reaction to a medicine. She looked at her husband, but her expression was as blank as the elevator wall. She was silent.

The doors opened on the second floor and down the long hall he pushed her, greeting all the nurses and staff, of whom he is so fond.

"Every lunch, every dinner, you can kind of set your watch by him," said Pam Kamariotis, the registered nurse on the floor. "He's so dedicated. He will sneak kisses. What he does is incredibly uncommon. Just a really nice thing to see."

Jim pushed the recliner past his wife's room, which he fills with stuffed animals and flowers and photographs of their three children and seven grandchildren, just in case, somewhere inside her diseased brain, she recollects these things that were once so dear and familiar.

He pushed on to the solarium at the end of the hall to feed her lunch.

"This thing gets heavier and heavier," he says.

Jim is a small man, 138 pounds, who suffers from osteoporosis and only this winter – after a bout of shingles impaired his vision – gave up night driving and his dinnertime visits this time of year.

A tray of food is waiting. He puts a long paper bib over her head that covers her chest and lap. He grabs a handful of napkins. He stands beside her and begins to spoon-feed her at 10 minutes after noon, mixing the chicken with the applesauce and putting a little lemon water ice on the tip of the spoon.

"The lemon makes her pucker and helps her swallow," he says.

He spoons it back in as it keeps falling out of her mouth, down her chin, over and over. He spoons it in, scraping it back up her chin, or off her bib, back into her mouth. So gentle and faithful.

"Come on, Sweetie."

He kisses her and cuddles her, even when she's covered with glop. He is happy to kiss her. Delighted to have the chance.

"Maybe I didn't do enough of it when she was home," he says.

He carries two poems in his wallet, poems about the endurance of love. The final line of the second poem reads: "Over time and grief prevail recollections – all she is."

She starts to choke. He gingerly wipes her mouth. They keep a suction pump in her room now for emergencies, a recent development.

"They say the smile is the last thing to go," he says. "We've already decided – no tubes."

After the pureed solids, he cleans her up, carries away the dishes and dirty napkins, and turns to glasses of apple juice and iced tea. He puts on a new bib and, spoon by spoon, feeds her the liquids, both the consistency of honey. Anything thinner or thicker and she will choke.

At 1:13 he puts down the spoon. One hour and three minutes. He cleans her up again. Kisses and cuddles her.

Then he sits beside her, quietly, and holds her hand.

After a few more minutes, he wheels her back to her room, where he leaves her in the recliner. A nursing assistant will change her and put her to bed. He puts on his cap and zips his jacket and heads home to Drexel Hill.

POSTSCRIPT

"I am a teacher who is forever searching for present day 'heroes' for my students to learn about," Chris Detwiler, a fifth-grade teacher, wrote after this story appeared. She talked to her pupils about loyalty, love, and the effects of Alzheimer's disease, then 13 fifth-grade students at Walton Farm Elementary School wrote to Jim Way. He responded with thank-you notes to each, leading to a yearlong exchange of letters.

Wynne Way passed away in the spring of 1999, and Jim, who had been healthy, died two months later. That prompted me to research and write another story about the very real phenomenon of dying of a broken heart.

Army Times
Navy Times
Air Force Times
Family Magazine
Military Market
Federal Times

Air Force Times

ARMY TIMES PUBLISHING COMPANY
475 School St., S.W., Washington, D.C. 20024 • (202) 554-7113

U.S. OFFICES: Chicago•Detroit•Los Angeles•Miami•New York•Philadelphia•San Francisco•Washington•OVERSEAS OFFICES: Frankfurt•London•Paris•Tokyo

Oct. 29, 1976

Dear Mr. Vitez,

I'm sorry but we do not have a summer internship program.
Our work is too specialized to make much part-time employment
practical.

I would like to give you a couple of suggestions, however,
which may help if you intend to pursue other newspaper jobs.

One is to write individual letters, not duplicated ones, to
each prospective employer. The impression given by a
"canned" letter is that you are not really interested in a
specific paper, just blanketing the field.

The second suggestion is that you copy-read your basic letter
closely. When you apply for a writing job, your letter of
application necessarily becomes a sample of your wares. Frankly,
the syntax in your second paragraph is a disaster.

The above is meant to be helpful, not discouraging. Good
luck with your future plans. I hope they include a major in
journalism if reporting is your goal. Let me know when you
complete your schooling and are looking for full time work. No
promises but, if you're interested, we can talk about it.

Sincerely,

MY JOURNEY AS
A STORYTELLER

The best rejection of my life

In my second year at the University of Virginia, as a busy staff writer at *The Cavalier Daily*, I was full of hubris. I was writing front-page stories for the college newspaper and I was breathing rarified air and ready for the big time.

I wanted an internship at a major newspaper or news organization that summer and believed who could be a better candidate than me? So I wrote a cover letter, copied several of my favorite clips, included a resume, and dropped packages at 60 offices in the National Press Building in Washington, D.C, where so many of the nation's biggest newspapers and newspaper chains had offices. Truly, I just went door to door on every floor.

Then I went back to Charlottesville so satisfied and waited for the offers to roll in.

I received one reply.

A rejection.

It was from a newspaper I had never heard of and didn't even realize I had applied to: The *Air Force Times*.

"Dear Mr. Vitez," the letter began, "I'm sorry but we do not have a summer internship program. Our work is too specialized to make such part-time work practical.

(I should have stopped reading there.)

"I would like to give you a couple of suggestions, however, if you intend to pursue other newspaper jobs."

(Not good.)

"One is to write individual letters, not duplicated ones, to each prospective employer. The impression given by a `canned' letter is that you are not really interested in a specific paper, just blanketing the field."

(Gets worse, much worse.)

"The second suggestion is that you copy-read your basic letter closely. When you apply for a writing job, your letter of application necessarily becomes a sample of your wares. Frankly, the syntax in your second paragraph is a disaster."

There was one more paragraph, but I couldn't bring myself to read it. Honestly, I was too humiliated and angry and embarrassed. The man was so right. It was the most painful medicine, but so necessary and, looking back now, so kindly dispensed.

I vowed then and there that I would show this man, and really myself.

The letter was dated Oct. 29, 1976. Roll the clock forward about 11 years. I was at *The Philadelphia Inquirer,* a feature writer, and I won my first-ever journalism award – third place for feature writing in the New Jersey chapter of Sigma Delta Chi, the Society of Professional Journalists.

The award-winning story was about people who fall in love in the toll plazas on the Atlantic City Expressway. This was long before EZ Pass. The traffic to the Jersey Shore would back up for miles on summer weekends as drivers lined up to pay the tolls. I wanted to hang out there for a weekend. What I discovered, what interested me, had nothing to do with traffic but with *love.*

Love stories abounded. Toll takers would strike up relationships with casino bus drivers and limo drivers who came through daily, even several times a day. There would be these quick exchanges, conversations, flirtations, enough to spark a romance. One toll taker had accepted a marriage proposal right in the booth, got into the limo, and waved goodbye as she pulled away – presumably to live happily ever after.

(I realize now, rereading that story from 1987, what should have been the first paragraph, what we call the lede, was my fourth paragraph: "Even though 37 million vehicles cruise this highway annually – traffic zooms through this plaza at the rate of a car every three seconds – there is still time to fall in love.)

After I won my award, I decided it was time to contact Mr. Bruce D. Callander, the man who had so helpfully written me that letter years earlier. I wanted him to know I was a successful journalist now, doing good work.

I called the *Air Force Times* and learned that he had retired to Mullet Lake in Michigan. They gave me an address. I made a copy of the letter he had sent me – coffee stained now, a worn and invaluable part of my daily life – and wrote him a letter.

I wrote something like this: "Dear Mr. Callander, I'm sure you don't remember me or the enclosed letter you wrote me years ago. But I wanted to thank you. As upsetting as it was to me at the time, the letter had a huge impact. It motivated me and made me better...I'm so grateful you took the time and I want you to know I'm at *The Philadelphia Inquirer*, doing fine, and just won my first award..."

At light speed, a letter came back. I am quoting from memory here: "Dear Mr. Vitez, Thank you, thank you, for contacting me. You have no idea how badly I felt after sending you that letter so long ago...." He went on to say that from the moment he mailed it, he regretted having written it. He feared he had taken an ambitious, talented, enthusiastic young journalist and turned him off to the business forever. He was relieved to know I had made a career in journalism.

Another decade rolls by, and in 1997 I win the Pulitzer Prize.

Again I wrote to Mr. Bruce D. Callander in Mullet Lake, Michigan. As I remember it, my letter began, "Dear Mr. Callander, You're never going to believe this...." I enclosed the prize-winning series and thanked him again for his influence on my career.

Again, a letter came zooming back. He congratulated me. And he told me that when I am his age, what will resonate and what I will cherish is not the recognition I won but the work I did.

The rejection from Bruce D. Callander, and the motivation it provided, is an example in my own life of a good thing that followed a bad thing.

I hope the stories in this book will affirm that I've come a long way since the arrogant college student with bad syntax. The preceding 25 stories have focused primarily on resilience, on people who overcame difficulties and tragedies and losses. The next five are a bonus. I'm not sure these fit any particular category, other than stories that celebrate the human spirit.

Photo by ERIC MENCHER

Michael Erdos kisses Diane Anhalt, his bride-to-be

26

GIVE ME A RING SOMETIME

A musical backdrop for 'marry me'

He was wooing her softly with his very own song

October 7, 2001

Michael Erdos wore a rumpled gray suit. His identification – as a prosecutor in the Philadelphia District Attorney's Office – hung around his neck. But this wasn't exactly official business.

He was on a mission of love.

He walked into the West Philadelphia office of radio station WXPN-FM. He didn't call ahead. How could he explain over the telephone? These stations would give him one chance, maybe. Better take it in person.

He sat in the lobby 15 minutes.

Station manager Vince Curren came out to see him.

Michael, 36, took a deep breath, and made his pitch: He was in love. He'd written a song, had it professionally produced. It was a pop love song. In the lyrics of the song, he was proposing to his true love, Diana Anhalt, 33, another prosecutor. Now all he needed was a radio station to play it – on Friday night, her birthday.

"It's a little bit of a long shot," Curren replied. "We haven't done anything like this before. We have lunatics – and you're obviously not one – and somewhat-less-than-lunatics coming in here all the time."

"Are you sure Lynne Abraham would be OK with this?" Curren asked, referring to the district attorney, Michael's boss.

"Oh yeah," Erdos said. "She's into love."

Michael Erdos made cold calls to eight radio stations a couple of weeks ago. Several receptionists asked whether he could leave a copy of the song. He couldn't. He had just one copy, in his suit pocket, still in need of mixing and mastering. If he could just play it for somebody...

In the waiting room of WIOQ-FM in Bala Cynwyd he told himself he really wasn't asking for a lot: "The earth has been around five billion years, so five minutes of radio time can't be that much."

At another station, he told his story to a receptionist, who was smitten by his idea. "Do you think my girlfriend will say yes?" he asked. "If she doesn't," the woman said, "she's an idiot."

* * *

Michael, of course, was the idiot.

Four years ago, Michael and Diana started the same day as rookie prosecutors in the District Attorney's Office. Their desks were next to each other. They were thrown into court from the first day. And almost from the first day they became best friends. By three months, they were dating. They dated for more than two years.

Michael couldn't commit. Diana broke it off.

"Go out on your own," she told him, "and figure out what you want." She hoped he would work it out, and told him to stay in touch. Her parting words: "Give me a ring sometime."

Roll ahead eight months to New Year's Eve. Michael was at a party – without Diana.

"I became palpably aware of this pervasive empty feeling," he said. "A tremendous lightbulb went on in my head and I said to myself, 'What the hell am I doing? She's the greatest thing. She really was the one for me. She's my best friend. We have everything in common.' "

He left a message on her machine saying he missed her. Back at work, after the holiday, he begged for a second chance. She gave him one.

He knew right away he wanted to marry her. One Saturday in January, at Tower Records, he had an epiphany: He would propose to her in a song – a pop love song. He adores pop love songs: "Mandy," "My Best Friend," "Still the One," "Our House"…

Michael solicited the help of his brother-in-law, a professional musician in Boston who has played backup for the Dixie Chicks.

He hired professional musicians to sing his song, play it. He rented studio time to produce it. All told, he spent – well, more money than he'd like to see printed and more hours than he can count – and he told Diana more lies than he can remember about where he was going. But he got it done.

The song is called, "Give Me a Ring Sometime." The title, of course, has a double meaning. It plays off her comment to him and his proposal to her. The song is 4 minutes and 13 seconds, with swelling violins and sweet lyrics:

Down on my knees,
Will you marry me
Pretty please
I know we are meant to be
Let me have and hold you eternally.

Several radio stations expressed interest. Michael chose B-101, WBEB-FM, and its show "Nightmoods."

"In my 12 years of doing a love-song show, I've never once had this happen," said Mary Marlowe, the DJ who dubs herself Philadelphia's "First Lady of Love." Shane Dixon, producer of the show, liked the song so much he told Michael, "If she says no, I'll say yes."

Michael had the big day all planned. He was going to meet her with flowers as she walked to work. He had decoy earrings to give her before dinner at Le Bec-Fin to throw her off any notion of a marriage proposal.

He told her his birthday present would be a journey back through time. After dinner, sitting in his BMW outside his home in Society Hill, he would give her a series of gifts: an antique watch from the '20s; tickets to "The Producers," a Broadway show that takes place in the '40s; a paisley blouse from the '60s; a Larry Bowa warmup jersey from the '80s; and for the present...

Everything was set.

* * *

On Friday night, at 9:05, Michael and Diana got into his car. She had changed from her little black dress into Yale gym shorts and T-shirt. She had no clue.

He ran through the gifts. She put on the Bowa jersey.

For his final gift, Michael told Diana, he was taking her someplace but needed to call ahead. He slipped out of the car and called the station on his cell phone to say he was ready.

He got back in the car.

He turned up the radio.

At 9:35, Mary, the DJ, told her listeners that Michael Erdos had written a special song for Diana Anhalt.

Diana started crying that instant. Then she realized it was a love song for her. She cried even more.

The first time she heard, "Will you marry me?" she leaned over and hugged and kissed him.

"Yes!" she cried. "Yes!"

The song wasn't even half over.

In the middle of the song, a car pulled up beside them. The driver rolled down his window, asked whether they were leaving. Parking on a Friday night in Society Hill is murder. Tears rolling down her cheeks, Diana waved off the driver with a quick, fierce gesture that left no doubt: "Not now!" The puzzled driver moved on.

As the song ended, Michael got out of the car, came around, dropped to his knees on the cobblestones of Delancey Street, dug the diamond ring out of his pocket, and proposed again, this time with his own voice.

He slid the ring on her finger.

POSTSCRIPT

This story was suggested to me by Jayson Stark, the great baseball writer now with ESPN, who is a cousin of Michael Erdos. I was there in the park, watching, when the driver pulled up at the very worst moment and wanted the parking space. Life is beautiful in the big city.

I was interested in doing this story only if I could accompany Michael on his quest to find a radio station, and I needed to be there for the big moment. The photographer, Eric Mencher, and I were far enough away that we were unnoticed and didn't interfere with the drama.

Michael has gone on to become a Philadelphia judge.

Jackie is welcomed home by Jovie as Lisa Lithgow enjoys the moment

27

PEACEMAKER'S ORDEAL

A price for trying to break up a fight

After 9 months in the hospital, home for Thanksgiving

November 28, 2014

After 275 days and nights in a hospital, Jackie Lithgow went home.

The parade of goodbyes lasted all morning. The chef baked a farewell strawberry shortcake. Housekeepers, kitchen staff, therapists, doctors, nurses all stopped in Room 442 at Magee Rehab for clenching hugs and tearful farewells.

Erin Trudell, his physical therapist, made Jackie stand up to hug her goodbye.

"I'm so proud of you," she said.

Dan Ryan, a physician, came in with two last words, "Cole Haan," which Jackie repeated, their little bond. When Jackie walks again, the doctor wants him wearing stylish shoes.

"Jackie, I am honored to have been the one to hear your first words," speech therapist Aimee Aranguren wrote on a goodbye blanket hanging on his wall, the last thing to come down. "You are a rock star."

Jackie's mother, Lisa Lithgow, also hadn't been back to their home in Carlisle in 275 days. Jim Lithgow, Jackie's father, had been back only three times. Either Lisa or Jim slept in Jackie's room every night since Feb. 23.

Val Palmer, a nursing assistant, came in on her day off. "Just to see the miracle that took place here is a real blessing," she said. "To be able to eat. To be able to speak. Each time they took a tube out was a celebration."

The goal for months was for Jackie, 19, to get home by Thanksgiving, and Tuesday he was discharged. "Goodbye, room," said Lisa, around noon, the last one out. "You've been good to us. We're not going to miss you. Just the people."

His mother, on leave from the Hershey Co., gave away 72 boxes of Pot of Gold chocolates that morning, and bracelets bearing one word: "Believe."

Therapists Paula Bonsall and Erin Trudell, who worked with Jackie from the beginning, before either was convinced his spirit was still alive inside that injured brain, walked with the family as they wheeled Jackie out.

"Enjoy being home," Bonsall told him.

"You can't imagine," Jackie replied.

His father hugged Bonsall one last time. Jim's eyes were rimmed in red from so many tears. "Thanks for everything. You are awesome, an awesome person."

Jackie was strapped in the front seat, window down. With his right hand, his good hand, he gave the V sign for victory as, finally, the family Honda rolled away.

* * *

Jim and Lisa, 54 and 53, fell in love at Bloomsburg University. When their son enrolled last year, he wanted to pledge his dad's fraternity, Zeta Psi.

On February 22, he received an invitation to join, and that night went to a party at a fraternity brother's off-campus apartment.

At 1 a.m. four football players from Kutztown University showed up and tried to force their way inside.

A fight ensued and spilled onto the street, according to police and witnesses. Another freshman and friend of Jackie's, Donald Hoover, was punched in the head by one of the Kutztown players, then kicked repeatedly on the ground.

"During Hoover's assault," the police report states, "Jackie Lithgow was heard by several persons to ask the Kutztown males to stop fighting and leave. At this time, Angel Cruz [a 230-pound Kutztown fullback] was seen by numerous people to punch Lithgow in the head with extreme force causing him to fall backwards and strike his head on the pavement. Lithgow was seen to be bleeding excessively from the back of his head and did not regain consciousness."

When Jim and Lisa, en route from Carlisle, nearly 100 miles south, reached the ER doctor from their car around 3 a.m., his first words were, "How far away are you?"

Physicians at Geisinger Medical Center in Danville had to remove the top of Jackie's skull to make room for his swelling brain. Then he got a blood clot in his jugular vein. After weeks at Geisinger, Jackie came to Magee in Philadelphia – but wasn't there 12 hours before a brewing infection in his brain, the antibiotic-resistant MRSA, sent him to Thomas Jefferson University Hospital for 44 days and removal once again of a piece of his cranium.

He also got meningitis.

"Here's a young man with a future full of promise, and was acting as a peacemaker, and he was struck with a single blow that has completely changed his life," said Columbia County District Attorney Thomas Leipold. "And on the other side of the coin, for the defendant, he struck a single blow, and I'm certain did not foresee or anticipate how bad the result of that could be. And unfortunately, that just goes to show what the intersection of alcohol and ego and attitude can do – it can just produce absolutely tragic results for everyone involved."

On Nov. 10, Cruz pleaded guilty to assault. In custody since his arrest, he has been advised not to comment until his sentencing Dec. 5.

* * *

Jim and Lisa haven't taken a moment yet, truly, to process how much their own lives have changed. They have been consumed with keeping Jackie alive, and helping him get better.

"There's a ton of emotions on hold," said Lisa. "If I would go down the path of *Why? Why my kid?*, Jim would bring me back. 'Lisa, you can't change it. Lisa, that's just a waste of energy.' "

Her outlook now is clear: "Jackie easily could have died," Lisa said. "Instead of damning God, I'm thanking him."

Jackie has no recollection of the accident. One night, Lisa told him what happened. "I don't understand why someone would do this to another person," he told his mother. And cried and cried.

When Jackie started at shooting guard for the Boiling Springs Bubblers his senior year of high school, he was 5-9 and 130 pounds. In the hospital, his weight fell below 100. He couldn't speak, stand, swallow, sit up. Every part of his brain was injured. Brian Kucer, the doctor in charge of brain injury programs at Magee, believes Jackie's brain sustained multiple blows. Lisa wonders if he was kicked on the ground like the other boy.

Everything that once came naturally – balance, movement, speech – must be relearned. "He has to think about everything before he does it," says Bonsall, his occupational therapist.

The left side of his body remains contracted, his left fist clenched. Every few weeks, a neighbor from Carlisle would bring

Jackie's dog, Jovie, an 85-pound golden retriever, for a visit. Jovie would try her best to lick Jackie's hand open.

His therapists say his brain is young and his body is strong, and they think that in five years he will be nothing like he is now. "I still believe Jackie can be able to walk on his own, to take care of most of his basic daily needs," agrees Kucer, his doctor. "But that's a long road, and he's got a long way to go."

Jim and Lisa believe Jackie will return to college, marry, and have a family.

"The dream is not over," Lisa often says to Jackie. "Just delayed."

* * *

Day 262, November 12, was Lisa's night to stay.

Jackie's sister, Lindsay, 25, called from her home in Bethesda, Maryland, as she did every other night.

"Nothing, just chilaxing," he told her.

Lindsay shared a story. "Oh, my god," Jackie said, and started laughing. Even though he has a tube in his stomach, bladder issues, and still can't take a step without support, he laughs all the time.

Jackie sat on the side of his bed in T-shirt and boxers. Tucking his right leg under his left, he lifted both and swung them onto the bed.

"Oh, my god, that was fantastic," said Lisa, who would rise at midnight, 3 a.m., and 6 a.m. to help a nurse turn him.

"OK, buddy," Jim said to Jackie. "I'll be back around 8:15 to start over."

He kissed his wife and left. It was his night at the hotel.

Lisa emerged from the bathroom in sweat clothes, her pajamas.

She leaned over, kissed Jackie's cheek.

"Love you," she whispered.

"Love you, too," he said.

His eyes closed.

Lisa grabbed her Philadelphia Flyers fleece blanket, orange and black with team logo, and curled up beneath it on a little chair that pulls out into a bed, and turned out the light.

* * *

People have been wonderful.

Golf outings, bake sales, and fund-raisers at home and at Bloomsburg have netted more than $50,000 to help with bills. Five kids from the neighborhood sent $15.08 they raised from selling Tang.

Lisa's coworkers at Hershey gave her their vacation days. Jim, a special-education teacher in Boiling Springs, had 180 sick days accrued from 30 years of teaching and used them all. Magee used charity funds to help pay their hotel bill.

Jim and Lisa have no idea how much their medical bills are or how they will pay for Jackie's care going forward. He begins daily rehab in Hershey on Monday. They haven't worried about it. They will find a way. They will sell their house if they must.

In six months at Magee, Jackie left one time for nonmedical reasons – to watch the Philadelphia Flyers practice two weeks ago in Voorhees. Jackie inherited his Flyers obsession from his father, who grew up in Warminster.

The players gave Jackie signed hockey sticks, jerseys, and team sneakers. They invited the whole family into the locker room, praised his progress, and encouraged him to keep battling.

Jackie's therapists say he came back from that day and initiated more, spoke more, smiled more. He believed more in his own possibilities. His progress had already begun to accelerate, and really took off.

Going home by Thanksgiving became a reality.

* * *

The family pulled up to their home in Carlisle on Tuesday afternoon.

Balloons were tied to the porch railing. A sign on the storm door read, "Welcome home, Jackie. Home Sweet Home."

Jackie started to swing his legs out of the car before his parents could get the wheelchair.

Out bounded Jovie – into Jackie's lap, right there in the driveway – smothering the boy's face with kisses.

Jim and Lisa wheeled Jackie inside.

"Thank you," he said to his parents.

"For what?" said Lisa.

"For bringing me home. It's awesome."

They ordered pizza, and he sat at the kitchen table and ate two pieces with his right hand, like any other hungry college kid, although his parents repeatedly pleaded, "Jackie, little bites."

Then he forked down two pieces of strawberry shortcake.

Lisa had opened a kitchen drawer to get that fork.

"Oh, my gosh," she said. "Real silverware." She stood there looking down into the open drawer.

"I can't believe for the last nine months and two days, until now, we were in a hospital."

They slept in their own beds.

Today, for Thanksgiving, they hope to visit Lisa's parents in Hershey. Jackie can't wait for his grandfather's famous mashed potatoes.

"I'm going to pig out," he said.

POSTSCRIPT

I heard about the story from a friend who brings therapy dogs to the hospital. She had visited Jackie, and she told me that his mother or father had been there every single night. I knew I wanted to tell the story. I then heard he was hoping to go home by Thanksgiving, and I thought the day he finally went home would make a great narrative.

The story keeps getting better. Eleven months after he went home, Jackie walked two miles in a charity 5k for the Flyers. In January, almost two years to the day from when he was hurt, Jackie went back to Bloomsburg, living in a dorm, a student again. Jackie took a public speaking class, and titled his first talk, "Growing Up Twice." He described his journey of having to learn how to walk and talk and swallow again. He has a girlfriend and is steadily and surely rebuilding his life. "He is without a doubt a living miracle," his mother said.

Angel Cruz was sentenced to 22 to 36 months in prison. Before his sentencing, he told the judge: "Every day I wish I could take away what happened that night…. I am sorry for Jackie, his mother and father, his sister. Nobody needs to feel sorry for me because I understand what I have lost is nothing compared to what Jackie has lost. I accept what I did was wrong."

Jackie and his girlfriend, Lily, at Christmas
2015, before starting back to college

On a date, Mary and Barney discuss old times

28

HEALING A HEARTACHE

An old love that was never forgotten

Mary and Barney go out on a date 75 years later

November 11, 1998

Mary Silvers had a date Monday night with an old boyfriend, Barney Josephs.

They were going to dinner near his home, in Ventnor.

Mary, who turns 97 next week, was waiting in the lobby of her Center City apartment building at 3 p.m., with her walker and her cane, when her daughter arrived promptly.

"Why don't you put a little lipstick on?" Mary said to her daughter, Reta Eisenberg, who turns 70 next month.

"Mother," protested her daughter, "I just came from work."

Mary's daughter, a widow and grandmother herself, who lives in Gladwyne, often drives her mother down to meet Barney, who just turned 100.

Mary and Barney were in love from 1918 to 1921. Both were from South Philadelphia – she from Fourth and Snyder, he from Fifth and Tasker. How Barney loved Mary in those days! He bought her an imitation silver brush and comb and mirror set. He bought her a beaded handbag. He took her to the shore, to Atlantic City's Steel Pier. They danced and danced.

"I met Barney when I was 17," Mary explained. "I thought I was in love. He was a marvelous dancer. And I loved to dance. And he was a stunning dresser."

Barney wanted to marry her. She was beautiful, always surrounded by men. But how could a man propose marriage without a penny to his name? Mary's parents didn't think he could provide for her.

She listened to her parents and broke his heart.

* * *

Mary married Sam Silvers, a stock market trader, and they had three children. He died young. Mary has been a widow for 50 years.

Barney married a girl from Atlantic City. They had three children and were happy for 60 years.

Barney still walks every day along the boardwalk in Ventnor.

Three years ago, Barney was walking on the boardwalk when he recognized Mary's cousin.

"How's Mary?" he asked. "Is she OK?"

He learned Mary was a widow living in Philadelphia.

He got her phone number.

After his wife died in 1987, Barney had often thought about Mary. He had always carried a flame. But he was reluctant to try to find her. He hadn't seen her since 1921. He assumed she was still married.

"I was afraid," he explained. "I didn't want to hurt her. I didn't want to hurt myself."

Now he knew she was alone.

Barney dialed Mary's number.

"Hello, Mary."

"Who is this?" she asked.

"This is the best man you ever went out with," he said.

"Is that you, Barney?"

Mary recognized his voice right away, 75 years later.

She was so shocked – and flattered – that she called her daughter.

"I don't know I was dreaming," she said to Reta, "but I got this phone call…"

Barney and Mary had their first reunion at a casino in 1995.

"Mary," he told her, "I would recognize you anywhere, because you have the same beautiful brown eyes you had at 17."

They see each other a few times a year now, usually meeting in Atlantic City. And they talk on the phone every week.

"He calls her his girlfriend," said Barney's daughter, Lois Lambrakis. "I think it's his last hurrah."

Monday afternoon, Mary and Reta drove to Barney's house in Ventnor for the first time.

"Oh, I knew there would be steps," Mary lamented, pulling up in the car. "I don't think I can make so many steps."

She climbed slowly, Reta helping.

Barney was waiting at the top, in suit and tie.

"Hello, Barney," said Mary. "How do you walk up these steps, anyway?"

They went inside. "Barney, how do you feel?" she asked him.

"I feel good," he said. "Give me a hug."

He leaned over her walker and hugged her firmly.

"You were my first girlfriend," he said.

"I know," said Mary. "Seventy-five years ago."

They sat in his living room, looking at family pictures. He had a few old pictures of the two of them and their friends.

"Barney, you look marvelous here," she said. "You were a good-looking guy.…And here I am. I don't know how I got so old."

"It's nice we have each other," Barney said. "That that we can understand each other."

Barney wanted to take Mary to the Crab Trap in Somers Point. Reta went along.

So did Barney's daughter, Lois, and her husband, John.

Lois and John rediscovered one another 40 years after dating in high school and married three years ago. "It runs in the family," said Lois, 61.

At the restaurant, Barney pulled out Mary's chair and helped her get seated.

When hot rolls were served, he spent over a minute trying to open a packet of whipped butter for her. Finally, he peeled off the top and handed Mary the soft butter.

The restaurant was crowded and noisy.

"Mary, I'm so glad you came to my 100th birthday party."

"All my doctors know about you, Barney. They're waiting to hear about our evening...."

After a long, pleasant meal of chowder, salad, crab and shrimp, the waitress handed Barney the check.

"Barney," said Mary. "If you need some money, I got some cash."

Barney wouldn't hear of Mary or anyone else paying.

After dinner, they stood in the foyer of the restaurant. Reta and Mary would return to Philadelphia. John and Lois would take Barney back to Ventnor.

"You always wanted to take me to dinner," said Mary. "I enjoyed it."

"I'm glad you had a nice time," said Barney.

He leaned over her walker again and gave her a hug and a kiss.

"Stay well," he said.

Mother and daughter chatted all the way home.

"I enjoyed the evening," Mary said. "I'm glad to see him. He's getting older. He's not going to be here long – not that I'm going to be here long, either. But it was a nice evening.

"He took his old girlfriend out on a dinner date."

POSTSCRIPT

I thought the only way to tell this story was to go on a date with them. I knew the best material would come from being there, from seeing them interact, and following them for an evening would give the story a narrative structure.

I had to wait weeks for the next date – perilous when he is 100 and she is 97 – but worth the risk!

I can't express the joy I felt when I heard Mary reprimand her 69-year-old daughter about not wearing makeup, or when I saw Barney insist on opening the butter packet for his 97-year-old date. To me, these moments are more beautiful than any sunset.

Mary and Barney loved the story, and shared it with all their doctors. Both died not long after the story appeared.

Photo by MICHAEL BRYANT

Tony Ciliberto and his pumpkin made the cover
of *The Inquirer's* Sunday magazine

29

1,000 POUNDS OR PIE

In their quest for a heavyweight champ
Some pumpkin growers will do almost anything

October 29, 1995

Don Black lives in a four-room house in upstate New York, only a few miles from the Canadian border. To say his house is a bachelor pad is to be polite. Don's walls are bare – except for a few world-champion pumpkin plaques. Don used to have many more, but he burned them in outrage last year. Don's laundry is heaped in piles all over the floor. He has two dressers, but all the drawers are filled with 300 babyfood jars containing pumpkin seeds. These drawers are the home of what Don claims is the world's only pumpkin-seed museum. Why doesn't he keep his clothes in the drawers? "Then where would I put my seeds?" he asks.

To earn a living, Don laces bedroom slippers together in a factory about 21 miles away. On a good day, when Led Zeppelin pumps through his headphones, he can lace 108 pairs in eight hours. He gets paid by the piece, and Don says he makes "$16,000 a year if I'm lucky."

Don leaves for work at 5:30 a.m., but before he goes, as well as two or three times every night, he trudges out behind his house to the pumpkin patch – a patch so neat, so loved, it's hard to believe it is tended by the same man. The earth is as dark and moist as devil's food cake. Don comes out to check for intruders – woodchucks, deer, teenagers or, the most insidious, saboteurs.

Don, 38, is not paranoid. He is practical. Could he afford it, he might try what Norm Craven, his nemesis across the Canadian border, has installed in his patch – sensors and infrared cameras.

"People don't want anyone to grow a bigger pumpkin," Craven said. "No matter what."

* * *

Don Black and Norm Craven, along with about 5,000 competitive growers, have been trying to grow what was once considered impossible, unthinkable, the 4-minute mile of pumpkindom: a 1,000-pounder.

It will be "like a moon landing," says Ray Waterman, president of one of three feuding pumpkin organizations. Wrote Tom Norlin in the spring issue of the Midwestern Pumpkin Growers newsletter: "The winner will be remembered and written about for generations."

Last year, Herman Bax of Brockville, Ontario, grew a 990-pound pumpkin, the largest in history. Some credited the seed. Others the weather. Herman praised his septic bed, over which he grew his pumpkin. Herman's neighbor and friend, Barry DeJong, grew the second largest in history – 945.5 pounds. Together they split $28,000 in prize money – not bad for two 30-year-old guys who help make Tide soap in a Procter & Gamble factory.

Herman sold his pumpkin to a restaurant outside San Francisco that hosts an annual pumpkin festival. Two Las Vegas casinos bid for Barry's pumpkin. The winner, the Excalibur, flew Barry, his pumpkin and his wife out to Vegas for a week and greeted Barry and his wife with a stretch limo. The pumpkin went on display in the casino lobby wearing a crown, a security guard by its side round the clock. Two days before Halloween, the pumpkin was trucked to Hollywood, where a professional pumpkin carver waited to sculpt the world's largest jack-o-lantern on *The Tonight Show With Jay Leno*. But at the last moment, Leno was a no-go. "Because the pumpkin had spent 10 days under the spotlight," lamented Barry, "it had started to get soupy inside." Barry's champion pumpkin ended its charmed life in a Hollywood dumpster.

The Scottish philosopher David Hume once wrote that avarice and ambition drive all men. As these twin desires drive the Trumps and Madonnas and Gingriches and Iacoccas, they also motivate the Pumpkin People. On a smaller scale for sure, but with no less ferocity. These men and few women come from all walks of life. They are firefighters and farmers, park rangers and stock brokers, engineers and appliance salesmen. Like all backyard gardeners, they start out growing giant pumpkins for fun. But soon these innocent gardeners quickly submit to the raw power of the pumpkin.

In just 70 days, a championship pumpkin swells from the size of a marble to the size of a kitchen stove, and is about as shapely. But no pumpkin grower cares about looks. "Pounds talk, everything else walks," barks Waterman. "This ain't a damn beauty contest."

During July and August an Atlantic Giant pumpkin can gain 35 pounds a day. "There's nothing that grows faster than a giant pumpkin," says Ron Nelson, a Washington state grower. He should know. His pumpkin was well over 900 pounds last year when it literally exploded just nine days before the international weigh-off. "Its shell simply couldn't stand the stress," said Hugh Wiberg, a New England grower. "God never intended pumpkins to be pushed to such limits." Although Nelson says he handled the tragedy well, other growers say he was bereft. "He didn't sleep for two nights," said Wiberg.

These pumpkins create their own gravity, cast their own spell. Soon the act of growing is no longer enough. "I push and push," says Leonard Stellpflug, a New York state grower. "I go for broke. I either want the world championship or nothing."

Stellpflug walks around with divining rods – coat hangers inside the shells of Bic pens – searching for "water domes" and "energy fields." Wayne Hackney of Connecticut, after seeking advice from photobiologists at a GTE testing laboratory, installed 1,000-watt lights in his patch and shined them all night. "It looked like Yankee Stadium," he said. He stopped after two years, but only because somebody stole them. Joel Holland in Washington state uses solar panels to raise the temperature of his irrigation water from 50 to 80 degrees so his pumpkin plants won't experience shock.

Don Black, founder and curator of the pumpkin-seed museum, ran his well dry this summer watering his pumpkins. So then he ran a hose 300 feet from his brother's well. And he showered at his sister's house.

And Norm Craven? He installed those infrared cameras and sensors last year after his involvement in what many consider the most heinous act in the history of pumpkin growing. He felt such hostility from other growers this year that he concentrated on cabbages instead.

Pumpkin people pine to be the first to break 1,000 pounds, to get their names in the Guinness Book of Records, to strut on *Regis and Kathie Lee*. They are local celebrities, featured in newspapers and on television around the world. Their phones ring with calls from awestruck growers less evolved on the pumpkin chain. They work relentlessly, and while they won't kill their rivals to succeed, some of them will bicker, whine, hate, lie and cheat.

They are as American as, well, pumpkin pie.

* * *

Tony Ciliberto had a special feeling this spring as he prepared his fields outside Wilkes-Barre with 4,000 pounds of manure.

"My personal gut feeling is someone will hit the 1,000-pound mark this year," he predicted back on May 16. And of course Tony hoped he would be the one.

Tony, 41, is a big man at 6-foot-4, 240, a bricklayer, with hands as large and leathery as catcher's mitts. Tony would love to grow pumpkins on a farm in Ontario, with smooth soil and a summer sun that doesn't set until after 10 p.m. But he comes from this corner of Pennsylvania, and so does his wife. This is where his roots are planted. And it is here, in Bear Creek, Pennsylvania, on the side of a rocky Pocono Mountain foothill, that he has carved out his pumpkin patch. Perhaps no grower in America has met with more natural adversity, more bad luck, than Tony Ciliberto.

In those first years, his patch was so steep, pumpkins would snap off the vine overnight and roll down the mountainside. Over the years, Tony has graded the property with uncounted truckloads of dirt and manure, and bordered his patch with railroad ties. He has turned this patch into the puffiest, richest, softest and most productive mountainside of dirt in Pennsylvania. His biggest pumpkin before this summer was 734 pounds, a state record, but nothing compared to what Tony knew he was capable of. Tony knew, always, the secret of a big pumpkin was choosing the right seed and praying for the right weather. What he wanted more than anything was sunlight. Day after day of brilliant sun. July and August are always getting cloudy up his way. A couple of years ago, he chopped down a dozen oak trees to give his pumpkin plants another 30 minutes of daylight. Give me sun, he would say every year. Give me sun.

All winter Tony considered which seeds to plant. This is the biggest decision any grower makes. He settled on a seed from Mark Woodward's 511-pounder, the mother of Herman Bax's 990. He also chose a seed from Norm Craven's 836, and seeds from three Joel Holland pumpkins: the 827, 722 and 792. "I'm not much of a gambler," Tony said. "I'm not trying anything new.

No seeds from last year's pumpkins. I know enough growers and I've traded enough seeds. I have the seeds that produced all of last year's big pumpkins. I'm planting seeds that have already proven themselves."

On April 24, to speed germination, he took his wife's emory board and gently filed the edges off his five chosen seeds, as if he were giving a pedicure to a Hollywood starlet. Pumpkin season had begun.

Tony put his seeds into small pots with soil that had been treated with fungicide and warmed under lights in his den. After three days, the seeds had germinated. Seedlings began to emerge like claws from a crab. On May 7, Tony transplanted five precocious plants – each only six inches tall, but full of promise – into his patch. Immediately Tony covered each plant with homemade greenhouses the size of doghouses. Like any celebrity today, a giant pumpkin is rarely left alone.

Over the next several weeks, Tony fertilized heavily with Miracle-Gro – he buys it in 12 1/2-pound boxes. He sprayed heavy doses of calcium nitrate, in the form of deodorized fish emulsion. "It's really just fermented fish juice," he explained. "It smells just awful, but they say it's good for the plants." He loved to pour on Garden's Alive liquid kelp (seaweed) because "it's loaded with trace elements – copper, zinc, magnesium, all things a growing pumpkin needs." He even fertilized with modest doses of Epsom salts, not for sore feet, but close: for sore bottoms. Later in the summer, a pumpkin can suffer soft spots where it rests on the ground, soft spots that can lead to leaks and certain disqualification, if not death.

Tony was usually out watering before dawn, and back again after work until dark. He waged organic and chemical warfare against cucumber beetles that ate his leaves, squash vine borers that mangled his vines. By late June, Tony sprinkled Snarol – snail- and slug-killer pellets – out in his patch. And on occasion, he has dropped a woodchuck with a rifle, when the varmint tunneled under the windbreak that surrounded his patch. We are talking giant pumpkins. Ciliberto shoots to kill.

* * *

So what is a pumpkin, anyway? A pumpkin is not a cucumber and it's not a melon (although the word pumpkin comes from the Greek *pepon*, meaning "large melon") and it's not a summer squash, although it belongs to the same botanical family. Giant pumpkins, Cucurbita maxima, are in the same genus as winter squash and gourds. Giant pumpkins and squash are essentially the same in size and shape. In fact, you can plant two seeds from the same giant pumpkin, and one might give you a green monster, while the other gives you a pumpkin-color one. Cut them open, and they look identical on the inside. But don't think they are equal. Oh, no, they are not.

The competitive pumpkin world discriminates viciously on the basis of color.

A championship pumpkin is often a warted, lumpy, hunchback of a blob that is absolutely tasteless and useless. But it must be yellow or orange, although now "cream"-colored pumpkins are acceptable at weighoffs. A squash is green or gray. A pumpkin is what turns heads and brings in the most prize money. After all, Linus doesn't hang out on Halloween night waiting for the Great Squash.

Which brings us to a second question. Why do people love pumpkins? Pumpkin stories and lore go back, it seems, to the beginning of time. Cinderella's carriage came from a pumpkin. Peter Peter Pumpkin Eater had a wife and couldn't keep her. Colonial Americans consumed so much pumpkins they made up a rhyme: *We have pumpkins at morning and pumpkins at noon; if it was not for pumpkins, we would be undoon.* And Whittaker Chambers hid his microfilm of documents Alger Hiss gave to the communists inside his pumpkin. Pumpkins have been used in stews and soups and beer and pies, and on every doorstep in America this week sits a jack-o-lantern. Perhaps most astonishing, Alan Hirsh, a maverick scientist in Chicago, recently found that no aroma sexually aroused men more than a combination of lavender and pumpkin pie. Hirsch attributes this to Freud and Oedipus, etc. Howard Dill – whose biography is titled *The Pumpkin King* – has a simpler answer: "There's always something about a giant pumpkin that had the power to make people happy."

* * *

In the summer of 1993, Don Black grew an 884-pound pumpkin, setting a world record. Days before the October 1 weigh-off, Don loaded his pumpkin into his pickup, and then he drove 22 hours straight to Nova Scotia, to be with Howard Dill.

Dill, a dairy farmer in Windsor, Nova Scotia, began growing pumpkins in the late 1950s and spent the better part of 20 years breeding them for size. Ultimately, Dill created a new variety – Dill's Atlantic Giant. The U.S. Department of Agriculture awarded Dill plant variety protection, similar to a patent, and Dill started selling his seeds around the world. Dill won four consecutive world championships, 1979 through 1982, and his seeds or their descendants have been responsible for virtually every world champion in the last 20 years.

Black had promised himself that if he ever grew a contender, "I would take it back to its birthplace." He kept his promise. "When I pulled up his driveway," Black recalled, "and Howard come out and saw my pumpkin, he put his hand on his heart: 'Oh my gosh. I never thought they could get that big.' "

The decision to drive to Nova Scotia for Don Black was an emotional one. But it was also a political one. The pumpkin world was plunging into civil war, and Don Black had to choose sides.

* * *

The fact is, we live in an era of giant veggies, in which contests are held and prizes awarded for the largest carrot, sunflower and watermelon, not to mention the longest zucchini (104 inches!). Ray Waterman, 45, a farmer and restaurant owner in Collins, N.Y., near Buffalo, was the visionary. It was he who first conceived a worldwide weigh-off – giant pumpkins, of course, would be the main event. Waterman called Dill in 1982 after reading about him and presented his grand idea. "I envisioned an Olympics of Gardening," Waterman recalled. "The average grower was sick of growing the same old beans, radishes and cucumbers in his garden. People need a challenge."

So Waterman and Dill created the World Pumpkin Confederation. Dill gave the organization credibility, but Waterman gave it the gas. Over the next several years, the WPC grew and grew, with 12 weigh-off sites, primarily in North America. On the first Saturday in October, growers would bring their giant pumpkins or squash or rutabagas to weigh-offs at WPC sites, and the winners would collect prize money, usually a few hundred dollars. Waterman printed newsletters and sent out hundreds of press releases with Howard Dill's picture, and got tremendous media attention. When another world record was set, Waterman got the grower's name in the Guinness Book of Records.

But even from the beginning, peace did not prevail in pumpkin land. Out on the West Coast, a rival pumpkin organization, the International Pumpkin Association, had taken root. Terry Pimsleur, a publicist who represents a pumpkin festival near San Francisco, was its leader. Pimsleur, Waterman and Dill initially talked about merging. They met at Waterman's restaurant in 1983 and egos collided. Pimsleur said Waterman "tried to keep me out of all the pictures." Waterman says Pimsleur "tried to take over." Neither had a kind word for the other – and still doesn't. "Don't believe anything Waterman tells you," Pimsleur says.

And disenchantment with Waterman began to spread. By 1993, relations were so bad that four of the largest WPC weigh-offs – in Topsfield, Massachusetts; Windsor, Nova Scotia; Anamosa, Iowa; and Nuttree, California – abandoned Waterman and the WPC and created a third international pumpkin organization, the Great Pumpkin Commonwealth. Dill and Wiberg led the revolt. "Boxing has three different champions," said Wiberg. "So do we."

Waterman, sitting in his restaurant recently, eating a slab of pumpkin pie, seethed over the situation. "I made it happen," he said of the success of the pumpkin weigh-off. "I made the damn thing happen." He accused other growers of jealousy, of spreading lies and gossip about him, of using their rival newsletters for "yellow journalism – or, in this case, orange."

"They want to take the credibility of the World Pumpkin Confederation and put it to their own use," he said, then vowed: "I won't let that happen."

In 1994, however, the top 10 pumpkins in the world weighed off at Great Pumpkin Commonwealth sites.

Nothing fueled this exodus from the World Pumpkin Confederation more than what Ray Waterman did to Donald Black and his 884-pound pumpkin in the fall of 1993.

* * *

On July 3, Tony Ciliberto rose at 5 a.m. and started his drip lines, hoses surrounding his five giant pumpkin plants. This was a critical day. This morning he would pollinate his pumpkins.

His plants were now full grown, vines as thick as pipes, leaves larger than toilet seats. The plants were strong and green and healthy and ready to begin the second half of the season, actually growing the pumpkin.

Growers hand-pollinate for one primary reason. They want to mate a Michael Jackson with a Lisa Marie Presley, a male blossom from a Bax 990 with a female from a DeJong 945.5. Such hopeful pollination won't make this year's pumpkin any bigger, but the next generation of seeds could be Herculean. The single best explanation for the dramatic rise in pumpkin size over the last few years is the superior seed. In 1984, a 500-pounder was still a dream. Now experienced growers consider a 500-pounder a failure.

Each pumpkin plant produces male and female flowers. The female flower is fertile for only six hours. If the bees or the growers don't come calling, that flower will produce no pumpkin. Growers like Ciliberto inspect their patches each night beginning in late June, and on into early July, looking for female flowers that seem ready to open the next morning. Then they arrive before dawn, ahead of the bees.

Ciliberto, on his hands and knees, pulled back the giant leaves of the Mark Woodward 511 plant, reached down and gingerly snapped off one male blossom, and then another, like Romeo picking flowers for Juliet. Like most champion growers, Tony never actually sets foot in his patch. He stands or kneels on small pieces of wood, the size of cafeteria trays, to avoid compacting the dirt. To move about, he picks up the board behind him and places it in front of him. Tony steered a path out of the 511 plant and over to the open flower on the Joel Holland 827.

He kneeled again, peeled off the petals of the male – the same way a romantic would play "she loves me, she loves me not" – and held only a long, firm stamen in his hand. Little particles of pollen covered the stamen like a fine yellow dust. Ciliberto reached in and robustly painted the female pistil with the stamen, spreading the pollen all around. This was hardly a delicate gesture. Ciliberto looked like a backyard barbecuer swabbing his chicken with sauce. He repeated the process with another stamen, just for good measure.

Ciliberto pollinated several flowers that morning. And he would again for several mornings to come, pollinating several female flowers on each plant. Then he would watch. Carefully. At the base of every female blossom is a small pumpkin , about the size of a lemon drop. Once the flower has been pollinated, this pumpkin will grow. Swell. In the coming weeks, Tony Ciliberto would coldly, repeatedly, make life-and-death choices – choosing just one pumpkin per plant to grow. The others get aborted with his pocket knife. Cut and heaved into the compost pile. If he wants to win, there's no other way.

* * *

In the fall of 1993, Don Black weighed his championship pumpkin on a tarp. Most weigh-off sites use a tarp. It's a faster and safer way to lift pumpkins on and off the scales. After they weigh the pumpkin, officials weigh the tarp. Don Black's pumpkin weighed 890 with the tarp. The tarp weighed 6 pounds. A weight of 884 was verified by two government agricultural experts who served as judges, and a representative of the Toledo Scale Company, present at the Great Pumpkin Commonwealth weigh-off in Nova Scotia.

Don Black had set the record. Or had he?

Twelve hundred miles away, on the shores of Lake Huron, in Port Elgin, Ontario, on that very same afternoon, Norm Craven's pumpkin was weighed and recorded at 836 pounds, the second largest pumpkin after Don Black's. Port Elgin is a World Pumpkin Confederation site, under the auspices of Ray Waterman. Port Elgin's sponsors offered their winner a new pickup truck, and Craven drove home a happy man. A few days later, Craven would drive that new pickup to New York City and appear on *Regis and Kathie Lee* with his 836-pound pumpkin.

This didn't bother Black. Because he knew in the next edition of the *Guinness Book of Records*, to be published in September 1994, he would be listed as the world record holder. His name would be there, Donald Black, in all 1.3 million copies. But when the book came out, Don Black couldn't believe his eyes. He saw Norm Craven's name instead of his. There was no mention of Don Black or his 884-pounder. Nothing. Not a word. Ray Waterman was responsible for this. Don Black went home and took every WPC plaque he had ever won, threw them all into a metal barrel in his backyard, and burned them.

Waterman simply refused to recognize Black's pumpkin, and he had the ear of the Guinness people. His reason was simple, and he defends it today. WPC rules state clearly that no pumpkin can be weighed with a tarp. Even though this is a common practice around the world, Waterman is absolute. "I'm just out to protect the sport," he contends. He told the Guinness people to ignore Don Black. And they did.

Howard Dill hired a lawyer, who sent a barrage of letters and legal papers to the Guinness folks in England. Dill and his supporters argued that everyone uses a tarp, that a tarp couldn't possibly weigh 48 pounds, the difference between Black's and Craven's pumpkins. But the Guinness people held firm. So then Dill and his people went after Norm Craven and his pumpkin. Craven's pumpkin, they contended, was weighed with a tarp, too. And worse. Much worse.

"Norm Craven was in my workshop the night before he was to leave for Port Elgin," recalled Phil Lillie, a veteran pumpkin grower. "He cried to me it was rotten under the bottom. But he thought they might not inspect it. And he had the stem with silicone in it, because the stem was all split. He was saying, 'Gosh, you know, it's going to be disqualified. But I'll take it. Maybe they'll never notice.' The judges didn't notice because it was so big. They were so overwhelmed by the size."

Harry Willemse, 41, a Canadian and 13-year veteran grower, was also at Port Elgin at the weigh-off. "It's questionable whether Norm's pumpkin should have qualified for the weigh-off," he said. "One of the rules is the pumpkin must be solid, and no soft spots. Basically, it was rotting. You could just see the juice seeping out slowly. Norm's had a very wide split in it and it was seeping out. He must have plugged it up with something, for it to be oozing out like that."

Craven denies all of this. "All made-up stories," he says. Craven claims he always assumed Don Black's pumpkin would be listed as the world record until he was notified by Guinness. "Everybody started coming down on me, as if I'd done something," he said. "And I didn't. I was just sitting on the fence."

His silence has cost him many friends in the pumpkin world.

"Nobody's happy for you," says Craven. "Just the opposite. They're out to get you."

Meanwhile, the poor Guinness people have found themselves in the middle of an awful fight.

Sarah Llewellyn-Jones, the deputy editor who handles vegetable records, was exasperated in a recent telephone interview. "We have more than 10,000 records in the Guinness book," she said. "This has been the most troublesome one ever....You have the truth being perverted time and time again. None of them I can trust anymore."

Guinness is considering dropping pumpkins altogether.

* * *

On Sunday, September 10, Tony Ciliberto built a house. Around his pumpkin. He drove in 8-foot stakes around the plant grown from the seed of Joel Holland's 722-pounder – one plant occupying an area almost the size of a tennis court – and covered the wooden frame with Remay, a fiberglass that traps in heat, but allows water and light to pass through.

On this date, Tony's pumpkin was among the largest in the world – estimated at 903 pounds. It rose high and muscular off the ground, rippling, like the neck of a bull. The color was a tender orange, tending toward cantaloupe.

Every Monday, Tony entered his patch with a tape measure and chronicled the growth, beginning with pollination on July 3. On July 10 he wrote "size of a baseball." July 17: "50 inches in circumference, bigger than basketball." A week later it was 86 inches around, and a week after that 114.

On this Sunday morning, his pumpkin was 164 inches around, or nearly 14 feet. It was 104 inches over the top one way, 99 inches the other, for a total of 361 inches – rather auspicious, given that Herman Bax's 990 was 371 inches. And Tony still had time on his side.

Tony calculated his pumpkin's weight by using Len Stellpflug's chart, a bible among pumpkin growers. Stellpflug, a retired Kodak engineer, had plotted these three measurements taken from scores of pumpkins over the years and used regression analysis to calculate a pumpkin's weight. The chart wasn't a guarantee, but it was a good reference point.

All summer, Tony had gotten the sunshine he wanted. His leaves loved the sun, which threw photosynthesis into high gear and fed his pumpkin well. But on the flipside, he knew that too much direct sun on the pumpkin itself could be fatal, and he kept the pumpkin garaged under plywood during July and August. "The sun actually can cook them," said Tony. "The temperature inside a pumpkin, it can get so high they actually explode."

The summer drought didn't bother his plants, either. Tony just kept his wellwater flowing, telling his wife to hold off on the wash as much as possible. He rerouted his drain pipes and sent water from the household shower and sinks into his patch. But summer was now rapidly turning to autumn. And now he need- ed to keep his pumpkin warm, to keep it growing 3 1/2 more weeks. The temperature in the mountains had dipped to 32 the previous night. His new greenhouse would keep his pumpkin warm, perhaps keep it growing. The weigh-off was October 7.

He had 26 days to gain 97 pounds.

On Thursday, October 5, just two days before the international weigh-off, a dozen men assembled at Tony Ciliberto's house. Hurricane Opal arrived about the same time.

Normally, Tony would have left his pumpkin on the vine one more night. But he had a big decision to make – where to take his pumpkin for weigh-off, a GPC site or a WPC site? It all depended on the weight.

Waterman had announced he would pay $50,000 to any grower who came to a WPC site with a 1,000-pound pumpkin. Many growers were skeptical. "He'll never pay," scoffed Don Black. Tony was planning to go to Ottawa, a GPC site, but the $50,000 was calling him. He had to know.

So Tony and his pals, including his brother Dino, descended into the patch, now a pen of mud. The patch Tony tended so carefully was trampled by men, as Tony ripped vines out of the way so they wouldn't trip. His wife and kids and parents and in-laws all stood in the rain and watched. Tony pulled out his knife and cut the umbilical cord. The pumpkin was free.

The men surrounded the pumpkin. They needed to roll it on one side, and then the other, to slide the tarp beneath it. Tony pushed harder than anyone.

"Arrrgghhhhhh!" He winced like a woman in childbirth.

The men hoisted the pumpkin and placed it gently on its throne: a skid covered with straw resting on a forklift.

Tony Ciliberto, who hadn't smoked a cigarette in more than a year, lit a Newport.

The forklift driver placed the pumpkin carefully on two old scales Tony had placed side-by-side on his driveway.

The rain stopped and the sky cleared, if only for a moment. The crowd gathered around. Tony balanced once scale while

Dino balanced the other. Each man had to place counterweights on his scale and then slide the little weight across to get the arm to balance.

"What are you at, Dino?" Tony asked.

"397," said Dino.

"I'm at 510," said Tony.

A voice in the crowd yelled out, "907!"

There was silence. The skies were gray again. Rain was falling.

"She's not even 900 pounds," Tony said with disbelief. "We've got to subtract for the skid and the tarp. She's about 847."

"Can't be," said his wife.

"No way," said his dad.

Tony just circled his pumpkin. He was devastated, but his expression did not betray him.

He did not mourn the $50,000 he would never see – no, that money never seemed real anyway. Tony felt broken-hearted. Like a seductress, this pumpkin had romanced him, had led him on, only in the end to deceive him.

That night, he called Don Black.

"She's a lightweight, Don," he said with merciless honesty. "She just didn't measure up."

* * *

Tony, Joan and the kids towed the pumpkin to Ottawa, which might as well have been Cooperstown. Herman Bax and Barry DeJong were there. So were Don Black and Len Stellpflug and many other big growers in the pumpkin world. The weigh-off was held at Farmer Gus's pumpkin farm. One rookie grower gazed upon Tony's pumpkin and whistled. "That would make a lot of pies," he said. No doubt. But the next time Joan Ciliberto makes a pumpkin pie, the filling will come from a can. Two years ago, she actually baked pies from a 300-pound pumpkin.

"She was chopping it up with a bowsaw," Tony said. "She spent the whole day in the kitchen, boiling it down."

"Never again," vowed Joan.

All the veterans could tell immediately that Paula Zehr's was the pumpkin to beat. Tony and Don checked it out. Tony knocked on it with his fist.

"No thud there at all," said Tony. "Solid."

"Oh, yeah," agreed Don. "The meat is 10 inches thick, easy."

Tony's pumpkin weighed officially at 845. Paula Zehr's weighed in at 963, the heaviest in the world this year. Her pumpkin had virtually the same dimensions as Tony's on the Stellpflug scale, but carried an extra 118 pounds.

Perhaps the difference was maternal. Twice each day, Zehr hugged her pumpkin. "For about five minutes at a time," she said. Obviously the pumpkin responded.

Tony clapped for Paula, and walked over to congratulate her. But as she stood behind the scale with her champion, posing for the networks, the tears rolling down her cheeks, Tony's eyes seemed watery, too, welling with disappointment.

Tony Ciliberto is accustomed to setback. After all, he is a pumpkin grower. He knew and his wife knew and every grower there knew this sadness would soon pass. The quest for the first 1,000-pound pumpkin would continue.

"We'll be back again," Tony said, gazing off into the middle distance, perhaps already thinking about next year's seeds. "We'll be back again."

POSTSCRIPT
I just simply have to include this letter:

OTTAWA-ST.LAWRENCE GROWERS
c/o FARMER GUS's
7930 Bleeks Rd., RR 2, Ashton, Ontario K0A 1B0
Telephone (613) 838-5435   FAX (613) 838-2088

November 8, 1995

Philadelphia Inquirer Magazine
c/o Philadelphia Newspapers Inc.,
400 N. Broad St.,
P.O. Box 8263
Philadelphia, PA, 19101

Attention: Michael Vitez

Mike:

A great story. Loved every word of it. No one in pumpkins should be displeased with this presentation, unless they are displeased with the truth.

It has been a privilege! All the very best!

Gus Saunders

Gus Saunders
Director,
Ottawa-St. Lawrence Growers

TRANSMITTED BY FAX 1-215-854-5193

Johanna Hantel wanted the bomber to know
what he had taken from her

30

THE BOSTON MARATHONER

The explosion knocked her down
But she tells the bomber she won't stop running

June 26, 2015
BOSTON

Johanna Hantel got up Wednesday morning and went for a half-hour run around Boston Commons. It seemed appropriate. The Malvern woman was in Boston to speak for the runners.

Hantel was 10 feet from the first bomb, closer than almost any other runner, when it exploded April 15, 2013, killing three and injuring 254. A police officer died later in a shootout with the bombers.

One of the proudest days of Hantel's life was the first time she qualified for Boston.

Wednesday was even prouder.

She faced the bomber, Dzhokhar Tsarnaev, and spoke to him before a judge officially sentenced him to death.

She had waited two years for this moment. She had worried she would forget her words, or stumble or freeze, because of how the blast injured her brain.

So she wrote them out.

"I am a runner," she began.

Hantel, a medical researcher who has run 80 marathons, described her injuries, from shrapnel wounds to hearing loss, broken fingers and of course the brain injury. She still wears braces on her teeth, a consequence of her jaw being knocked out of alignment.

Tsarnaev, 21, looked down, fidgeting in his chair like a boy who could not wait for class to be over. Hantel was just starting.

"My brain sometimes does not let my mouth speak the words that I am trying to say," she read slowly from her script. "I am easily confused. I feel tired all of the time and lack energy. I am anxious, have mood changes, crazy sleep patterns, and simple things are now overwhelming. I have a constant headache, dizziness, loss of balance, blurred vision, and ringing in the ears. I am easily startled and jump at everything."

Hantel, 55, recounted all this because she wanted Tsarnaev to understand what he had taken from her.

"I belong to the old school of the Boston Marathon, when the only way to get in was to qualify with a fast time. ... Because of this horrific act, I can no longer qualify."

Of everything she said, this may have been the most striking: "I cannot shake this guilt."

For Hantel, the guilt was over the fact that spectators were so badly injured, and they would not have been there if not to watch runners like her.

Others who spoke Wednesday – Hantel was the 17th – felt the same emotion for different reasons. One first-time runner expressed deep guilt that she had allowed her daughters, who lost limbs in the blast, to wait for her at the finish line. Survivors express guilt that they lived or escaped more severe injury.

"I will say that I have come to peace with Mr. Tsarnaev," Hantel continued, carefully directing her words to the judge, as lawyers had instructed. "And amidst the tragedy of this horrific act, I have seen and felt overwhelming goodness and kindness."

She paused. She fought back tears. She looked right at Tsarnaev. Her back stiffened.

"And if I have to crawl," she continued, "I am going to continue to run Boston each year even if I cannot qualify, because I will not let this sickening act take that away from me, and there will be four angels waiting along Boylston Street for me to finish.

"I'm sorry for you, Mr. Tsarnaev," she continued. "I hope you are able to do some good during your life. Good will always conquer evil."

When she was done, the judge announced it was time for a recess.

Hantel walked into the lobby. She was shaking.

"That is the hardest thing I've ever done."

"He looked at me," she said. "At the end. He was listening."

Denise Richard, whose son Martin died in the bombing, came up and hugged her.

"Can I run for Martin?" asked Hantel, who ran the marathon last year and this, despite her injuries.

"Absolutely," said the mother. She was in tears.

A man came over and hugged her. Hantel didn't know his name, only that he was a Boston firefighter. "Thank you for being brave," he told her. "You're not alone."

After lunch, Tsarnaev spoke for the first time. "I'm sorry for the lives that I've taken, for the suffering that I've caused," he said.

Because of her hearing loss, Hantel couldn't hear a word of his statement to the court. People around her told her that he had apologized.

"I'm glad that he did that," she said.

She said she thought she could move forward now, with Wednesday's task accomplished.

"But it's all very sad," she said. "And now, even though he has to be held accountable, one more person is going to die."

MICHAEL VITEZ

POSTSCRIPT
I met Johanna Hantel through Howard Palamarchuk, a podiatrist at Temple University's School of Podiatric Medicine. I've known Howard for decades, and for years he's taken teams of his students to work the medical tent _ a busy place for foot doctors _ at the Boston Marathon. I wrote a story about him maybe 20 years ago when he took students to work the New York Marathon.

Howard first told me about Johanna, how she was injured in the blast. And when I first wrote about her, she told me how Howard had helped her with foot issues for years, and has been a great source of support to her since the bombing. Howard was working in the tent that day as well, and will forever remember the carnage, and also the great work his students did that day.

When I heard Johanna was going to Boston to testify, to face the bomber, I felt I had to go with her and do a daily story, a short narrative about her experience. I tried to put the reader in the courtroom with her, and be there with her as she came out. I admire her courage and her resilience.

We are all just Americans one day, and when extraordinary circumstances present themselves, we find this well of strength within ourselves. We are capable of things we never imagined. Johanna is a perfect example. I still get chills when I think about her story, her testimony.

Johanna Hantel, shown in the circle, just as the
Marathon bomb explodes to her left. She was knocked
off her feet. "I just remember orange," she said.

MY JOURNEY AS A STORYTELLER

The rules and tools that I live by

I end this book with the rules and tools I have developed over a lifetime. I hope that in many of the stories in this book, you have seen these rules and tools brought to life and put into practice. I present them here in the hope that, if you aspire to be a journalist, they will help you in your own reporting and writing.

1. Have a sense of wonder. In the 1999 movie *The Sixth Sense*, the main character, a 9-year-old boy, says, "I see dead people." Well, I see stories. I see the world in stories. One day, walking down the street on the University of Pennsylvania campus, I saw a busy Chinese food cart. Its sign said, "Le Anh." Then I saw another cart directly across the street, equally busy. Its sign said, "The Real Le Anh." How many journalists had walked down this street, seen these two carts, and kept on walking? But I had this gut feeling – there must be a story here. I had no idea just how good. You must be curious. You must have a sense of wonder. Where others see egg rolls, you must see stories.

2. Do not hesitate when inspiration strikes. Put yourself out there. I was driving down the road in Cherry Hill, New Jersey, one day and saw two women riding by on scooters. They were dressed, identically, in patriotic clothing. They were so out of place among the speeding cars of suburbia. Who were they and where were they going? I knew that if I didn't stop, I'd never see them again. I stopped, and stopped them, and eventually told their wonderful story in *The Inquirer*. They were both disabled, physically and mentally, but in different ways. One was colorblind, so the other picked out identical clothes for them to wear each day. Neither could have ever lived alone. But together, since meeting as teenagers at a school for people with special needs, they had been able to live independently together for decades. They had built an amazing network of support. It was a wonderful story. I'm glad I stopped, and so were readers. This rule applies to all stories, even the biggest and most complex. The world is not static. Things Change. When you have an idea, go for it. Do not fear approaching strangers or asking hard questions, or pursuing a story nobody else may see. It is fine to swing and miss. But you will regret it if you never swing.

3. Be sincere. When I give talks about storytelling, the first question I am usually asked is *how* I get people to talk with me at the most sensitive moments of their lives. How do I get them to trust me and let me in? There are many answers, but the most important is this: be sincere. People trust me to tell their stories and allow me into their lives because I am sincere. This may sound simple, but it is so true. If potential story subjects sense that you have an agenda, or that you are bored, or that this is just a job, they will reject you, especially if you are trying to write about them at a sensitive time. But if they feel your passion and your sincerity, your excitement and genuine interest, they will be more willing to let you into their lives, or at least give you a chance. And over time, as they see you work, their trust in you will only grow.

4. Radiate confidence. To illustrate this point, I use the analogy of the grandmother and the crying baby. New mothers are often inexperienced and nervous. And their babies cry. The moment – and we've all seen this – a baby is handed to a confident, experienced, relaxed grandmother, the baby stops crying. The baby can tell that he or she is in good hands. I feel that when I approach somebody for the first time, asking if I can tell that person's story, I need to be the grandmother: calm, confident, and radiating a good vibe so the person will trust me and accept me. This confidence comes from experience, and from preparation when possible. It also comes from a firm belief that I am going to give readers a gift. If I treat the subject with the highest respect, my trust will be rewarded with a great story.

5. Tell it to keyboard first. As I explained in an earlier chapter of "My Journey as a Storyteller" – with a lesson learned from my editor Ron Speer – the first time you recount a powerful scene or moment is the time you will do so with the most passion and verve. So, instead of talking about the story, sit down and tell it to the keyboard first.

6. Write while it's fresh. Memories and details fade, and as they do, so will the passion. I remember reporting in the intensive-care unit on the first story in my Pulitzer Prize series. What I would see in the hospital rooms was so intense, I would grab blank worksheets from the nurses' station and just sit on the floor by an elevator and write on the back of those sheets. I had to get it down on paper. Nowadays I carry a laptop, but the idea is the same: write while it's fresh.

7. Let quotes and details be the heart of your story. The best material comes from hearing the main character interact with those around him or her, and from details that only come from putting in the time and paying attention. These details and conversations, often subtle and small, make for the richest material in a story. This leads to the next rule...

8. Spend the time. When I taught for a semester at Princeton, I had a hard time convincing students to spend enough time with their subjects. To them, it seemed so inefficient. For example, one story was about the culture in the dormitory laundry room. Students were constantly taking another person's clothes out of a washer or dryer, rudely dumping them, and starting their own wash. It was a ruthless culture. If you were a minute late, your clothes were tossed. Some of my students couldn't grasp that if they wanted the best quotes, the best details, the best scenes – if they wanted to tell the best story – they needed to spend a whole evening or afternoon in the laundry room. My student writers wanted to just interview five students and be done in 15 minutes. It's much better to see the laundry room's culture in action. With patience and diligence one discovers gold.

9. Create an image in the mind's eye. Let the reader see. This is one of the oldest rules in writing, and for good reason. You need to be able to see it in your mind's eye in order for the readers to see it in theirs. Show, don't tell. This is easier if you can follow the next rule...

10. Report in real time. I always prefer to follow a story in real time. *Be there.* The best way to put the reader there, the best way to show, is to be there yourself.

11. Love your story. If you don't love your story, how can you expect the reader to love it? In my stories, the most powerful moments are often small ones, but they are carefully set up to have maximum effect. You must care enough to make your story its best, or the readers will flee – and who could blame them? I like to say writing is 85 percent heart, 15 percent craft. Success so often depends on what you bring to the story. Put your heart into it. Care about it. The rest will come with sweat and discipline.

12. Be ruthless with yourself. Nothing is as short as a reader's attention span. To get attention and keep it, ruthlessly trim your prose. Every word must carry its weight. Michelangelo's David started as a slab of marble; the artist chiseled and chipped and trimmed until all that was left was perfect. Cut. Cut. Cut.

13. Write in blocks. The readers must have their bearings at all times. The readers must always understand where they are in a story, what time it is in the story, and whom they are reading about in the story. Confusion is an invitation to the readers to walk away. I find it helpful to write in blocks. Whether my story is 20 inches or 200, I rarely go 15 or 20 inches without a break in the narrative. Think in sections and scenes, separated by a subheadline or a typographical device like an asterisk. Writing in a block allows me to keep my focus. Each block has a specific purpose. Blocks give me structure and control, and this makes it easier for the readers to follow. The pause between blocks also allows the readers to confirm their bearings and move on in the story.

14. Follow the Star Trek Prime Directive. Every Trekkie knows this rule, and journalists do, too. In *Star Trek*, the Starship Enterprise with Captain Kirk and Mr. Spock travels the universe. The prime directive is that the crew can't interfere with life on other worlds. Their mission is to explore and observe and report back. Their presence must not alter the course of events. As a journalist, neither should mine. I realize this is at heart a conceit. Just by being there, I am altering the natural order. I also have discovered that my being there, asking questions and sharing in the experience, can be rewarding for the people I write about. But I do not ask them to do things they would not ordinarily do, or to do anything differently on my behalf. This is a moral code.

15. Sleep at night. Since I immerse myself in people's lives and write about sensitive moments, my stories are necessarily very personal. I make sure immersion does not become exploitation. The story must be honest and authentic; that is the source of its power. But I protect a person's dignity as well. I often write about people far from headlines, with no experience with the media or any idea of the impact that a front-page story can have on their lives. I practice the Golden Rule, treating them in a story as I would want to be treated. Ultimately, my measure is: Can I sleep at night?

Bonus Rule: Listen, stupid! Interviewing is an art, not a science. For most of my career, I never used a tape recorder. I trained my ear to hear the best quotes and wrote them down. This is tightrope walking without a net. If you don't get it the first time, it is gone. This practice forced me to distill and keep only the best. However, with digital recorders and then iPhones and voice recorders, I began to record much more often because it was so easy. Actually, recording can create more work. I transcribe the quotes and then, in the story, let them run too long. My ear has gotten lazy. And something else I learned: When I would listen to the recorded interview, I was often horrified at myself. How could I be doing interviews for so many years and still do them so badly? For reasons and rules stated above, I am good at getting people to talk to me and open up to me. But what I found too often was that I interrupted them at the absolute worst times. When they were talking about a particularly difficult or painful moment in their lives, when they were getting to the good stuff and would stumble or stutter or slow down or pause, I would interrupt them to try to be nice. I might finish their thought for them. Madness! I have learned to fight that urge. Let them finish. But at the same time, I remind myself that interviewing is an art. I know what information I need and what topics I want them to talk about, and so at times I need to steer the conversation. But not when they are sharing deep thoughts and emotions. So, remember: *Shut up and listen, stupid!*

ACKNOWLEDGMENTS

I thank Gene Foreman, the former *Inquirer* managing editor, for his careful editing, guidance and advice in preparing this book. It was comforting to know it was in the hands of the best.

I also thank my good friend and former colleague Peter Landry for his thoughtful suggestions. I so value his judgment and friendship.

And thanks to Bill Marsh for his brilliant cover and help with page design. His gifts are evident here.

This book wouldn't have been possible if Gerry Lenfest, the former *Inquirer* owner, and Bill Marimow, the *Inquirer* editor, had not granted permission to publish this collection of my stories, along with the photographs and headlines that accompany them. I am grateful, and I hope students of journalism and fans of storytelling will find these pieces valuable and instructive.

I profoundly thank all the photographers whose work is published here. I've long marveled at their skill and valued their friendship. Their work and mine so well complement one another.

I also owe a great debt to all the staff writers, assigning editors, copy editors, news editors, librarians and countless other colleagues at *The Inquirer* over the last three decades. They made my stories better, caught my mistakes, wrote headlines and captions, and designed the pages. Putting out a daily newspaper is a marvelous and amazing accomplishment, requiring teamwork at its best. Sadly, as resources diminish, that task is getting harder all the time.

Maureen Fitzgerald, my wife and colleague, deserves extra special thanks because she's been improving my stories for years, including many in this book. She is thoughtful, deft and decisive, excellent qualities in an editor. I also thank our children, Tim, Sally and Jonathan, for their enthusiasm and support, and Tim, in particular, for suggesting the title.

Finally, I thank all the subjects of my stories over the years who have let me into their lives at the most critical moments and trusted me. They have given me a great gift.

I note there was room for only 30 stories in this book, and I tried to include a variety. Many stories that are dear to me were left out. Maybe one day we can do a volume two.

ABOUT THE AUTHOR

 Michael Vitez won the 1997 Pulitzer Prize for Explanatory Journalism for a series of stories on changes taking place in America at the end of life. He was a staff writer at *The Philadelphia Inquirer* for 30 years, leaving in the fall of 2015. He has taught feature writing at Princeton and the University of Pennsylvania. Today, as the director of narrative medicine at the Lewis Katz School of Medicine at Temple University in Philadelphia, he brings a focus on storytelling and humanism into medical education. He is the author of two previous books, *Rocky Stories: Tales of Love, Hope and Happiness at America's Most Famous Steps (2006)*, and *The Road Back: A Journey of Grace and Grit (2012)*. He is married to Maureen Fitzgerald, the *Inquirer* food editor, and they have three grown children.

CPSIA information can be obtained
at www.ICGtesting.com
Printed in the USA
LVOW10s0532180817

545468LV00008B/41/P